FAST FORWARD

FEATURING

Ken Auletta, author and columnist

George Bell, CEO, Excite@Home

David Bohnett, founder, GeoCities

Mark Cuban, co-founder, broadcast.com

Esther Dyson, chairman, EDventure Holdings; editor, *Release 1.0*

Peter Friedman, president and CEO, Talk City

George Gendron, editor in chief, *Inc.* magazine

Richard A. Grasso, chairman and CEO, New York Stock Exchange

Terrell B. Jones, president and CEO, Travelocity

Dr. C. Everett Koop, former Surgeon General; co-founder and chairman of the board, drkoop.com

George D. Lundberg, M.D., editor in chief, Medscape

Paul Matteucci, president and CEO, HearMe

Halsey Minor, founder, chairman, and CEO, CNET

Kathy Misunas, president, chairman, and CEO, brandwise, LLC

Ellen Pack, founder, senior VP, and general manager, Women.com

Robert W. Pittman, president and COO, America Online

Linda G. Roberts, director, Office of Educational Technology, U.S. Department of Education

Charles R. Schwab, founder, chairman, and co-CEO, The Charles Schwab Corporation

Man Jit Singh, president and CEO, Futurestep

Steven Swartz, president, CEO, and editor in chief, *SmartMoney*

Jeff Taylor, founder and CEO, Monster.com

David Thornburg, Ph.D., director, Thornburg Center

Alvin Toffler, futurist and author of *Future Shock, The Third Wave,* and *Powershift*

Ross Wright, entrepreneur, sales representative, and musician

FAST FORWARD

AMERICA'S LEADING EXPERTS
REVEAL HOW THE INTERNET
IS CHANGING YOUR LIFE

ALFRED C. SIKES with **ELLEN PEARLMAN**

WILLIAM MORROW
An Imprint of HarperCollins*Publishers*

HarperCollins books may be purchased for educational, business, or sales promotional use. For information please write: Special Markets Department, HarperCollins Publishers Inc., 10 East 53rd Street, New York, NY 10022.

FIRST EDITION

Designed by Stanley S. Drate / Folio Graphics Co., Inc.

Printed on acid-free paper

Library of Congress Cataloging-in-Publication Data has been applied for.

ISBN 0-380-97828-8

00 01 02 03 04 RRD 10 9 8 7 6 5 4 3 2 1

To the Student/Sponsor Partnership, which makes it possible for "at risk" teenagers to attend a better school and receive support from a personal mentor. The partnership will share in the royalty proceeds from this book.

CONTENTS

AUTHORS' NOTE

Throughout the book, addresses of recommended Web sites do not include the letters www in front of the address, which earlier generations of Web browsers need to be able to read the pages you are accessing on the World Wide Web. Accessing a Web document requires typing in the URL (Uniform Resource Locator) address of the home page in the location section located near the top of your Web browser (for example, if you wanted to go to amazon.com, the complete address needed would be http://www.amazon.com or simply www.amazon.com). The Web addresses in this book were accurate when the manuscript was completed; however, addresses can change or sites can fold.

The most popular Web sites listed in the chapters were provided by Nielsen//NetRatings. Nielsen//NetRatings obtains its data from over 33,000 Internet users whose surfing activity is directly fed into the NetRatings database. These users are drawn from a random sample of U.S. households via telephone recruiting. The sample is representative of the entire U.S. home Internet user population. The rankings are based on the size of each site's unique audience during January 2000.

The other suggested sites are based on recommendations from the authors, as well as some of the people interviewed for this book. They are not meant to be an all-inclusive list, rather a starting point for your Internet surfing experience or some new places to add to your old favorites' list.

ACKNOWLEDGMENTS

The authors would like to give credit to many people who have been instrumental in making *Fast Forward* a reality. In particular, we'd like to express our heartfelt gratitude to the two dozen distinguished executives who took time out of their extremely busy schedules to share their views of how the Web is reshaping our lives today and in the future. Their impressive credentials can be found in the "Biographies" section. In addition, our thanks to their staffs, who were instrumental in making these interviews possible.

Our appreciation goes to Bill Adler of Adler Books, Inc., for the initial idea for the book and Tom Dupree of HarperCollins for his editorial sharpness, clarity, and good advice. And to Tom's assistant, Kelly Notaras, for coming up with our title.

Several people were instrumental in helping us collect "real" online stories about how the Internet is changing people's lives: Ellen Pack and Colleen Noonan of Women.com; Steven Swartz, Jennie Baird, and Tanya Keller of Smart-Money.com; the Hearst New Media Center; and Tom Dupree of Harper. We'd particularly like to thank the 115 people who shared their stories with us; we wish there was room to include more of them in this book.

We'd also like to acknowledge Jane Koz of Hearst New Media for helping with many administrative details; Steve Korn for his careful reading of the manuscript and helpful suggestions for headlines; and Carole Ludwig for the long hours she put in transcribing the tapes of our interviews with our distinguished subjects. Credit also goes to the team at Nielsen// NetRatings that provided the Web site traffic data that appear throughout this book.

Finally, we'd like to thank Marty Sikes and Jonathan Pearlman for their support, patience, and valuable suggestions during the many months this project was taking much of our attention.

FAST FORWARD

INTRODUCTION

THE POWER OF THE WEB

There's a cyberphobe dying every day and there's a cybernaut being born every day to take his place.

—**Mark Cuban, broadcast.com**

In just four years the Internet industry is almost the size of the auto industry. It's changing everything.

—**Paul Matteucci, HearMe**

My first thirty years were spent living in the UK. My life changed in 1995 when I met a student at Rutgers University online. Six months later I sold everything I had, packed two suitcases, and came to America. Fast forward to now: We have been married nearly three years, own a house in New Jersey, and are expecting our first baby. Moreover, I've been able to use the skills I gained from all of those late-night online hours by becoming creative director of interactive design at iXL. Is this the American Dream or the Digital Dream?

—**Steve Coulson, New Jersey**

It is easily the most analyzed and discussed subject of the last decade. It has led the federal government to order free connections in the nation's schools. It has caused one-third of U.S. households to add another $20 to $100 to their monthly media bill. It has created two- and three-year-old companies with billions of dollars of market capitalization, while putting twentysomethings on the Forbes 400 list of the nation's wealthiest people. It is the single most important development in international relations and economics since the spread of free trade in the second half of the twentieth century. It is the Internet, the electronic interactive community, linking the world's people and businesses.

Didn't the same hoopla occur with the invention of the television or the telephone? What about the automobile? Did the nation go slightly nuts? While history shows these developments were seismic and confronted an awestruck public, it also shows that their effect on our national personality and stock markets were not nearly so pronounced so quickly. The computer (through its ability to shorten product life cycles), receptive capital markets, competitive media reporting, and a select number of universities acting as business incubators have intensified this force. They have accelerated what, on its own, is an extraordinary development.

How many people were connected in 1999? Well, with computers at an all-time low cost (it's possible to buy one with Internet access for as low as $299 or even find offers of free PCs) half of U.S. households had a PC and one-third of all homes in America were online. The growth in home use of technology has been phenomenal: five years ago only 27 percent of U.S. households owned a computer and a mere 6 percent were online. And now a few companies are offering free monthly connections.

It is hard to interpret the Internet's impact, both socially and commercially, in a book. Writers often find themselves writing the last chapter of their book as a new advance in technology or breakthrough Web site arrives on the market. Just as they turn off their word processor, another inventive application is launched. By the time the book gets printed, bound, and distributed it seems hopelessly out of date.

Conversely, newspapers and magazines can keep up with the latest changes, but often are written from a singular perspective, or sometimes no perspective. So, where do we turn to get both current information and informed perspective and perhaps a touch of real vision? Where do we go for help in conceptually calculating what impact this new medium is going to have on our personal life, existing business, or educational assignment? If we want to participate in the extraordinary formation of new businesses and wealth, where can we get some insight before launching a new career or business?

This book is designed to deal with all those issues. We have chosen insights from diverse perspectives. Each person interviewed for this book has talked from his or her unique circumstance and perspective. Two dozen of the most active and prescient minds in the United States, men and women who work with the Internet every day, agreed to talk about the Internet's impact on people's lives today and in the future. All interviews were conducted during the spring and summer of 1999. With so many contributing to this book the views are both fresh and timely. While ours won't be the last book you will want to read about this amazing new medium, it won't be already obsolete or limited to a single perspective.

The book is divided into ten chapters, covering how the Web is having an impact on every aspect of your life: family and relationships; health; money; education and learning; business; career; shopping; privacy and security; entertainment; and finally, some predictions from our gifted thinkers on how the Internet will affect us in the future.

What is the Internet? George Lundberg, editor in chief of Medscape, an online site for comprehensive medical information for both patients and doctors, perhaps said it best:

> The Internet is simply a library, instant access to everything, good and bad. The Internet is the telephone, the Internet is a circle of friends, the Internet is billboards, the Internet is radio, the Internet is television, the Internet is books, the Internet is journals, the Internet is discussion in a bar, the Internet is a church bazaar. The Internet is anything. It's nothing but a medium.

It would be incorrect to either be worried about or pleased with someone going to the Internet any more than going to the library. The Internet is every form of human communication except for smell and touch. So it could be good, it could be bad, it could be indifferent.

Halsey Minor, founder, chairman, and CEO of CNET, a technology news and shopping site, put it into context by explaining that with the Internet, "a parallel economy is being born, so that almost everything that you do in the real world, you'll be able to do in some form in the virtual world." Whether it's staying in better contact with family members, exchanging pictures, shopping or planning for your retirement, nearly all aspects of your life are being translated into the Internet.

The primary benefit, said Minor, is making communication better and easier than ever before, but the Internet also ensures that you're much better informed about everyday decisions, from choosing whether to have surgery for a medical condition to knowing whether you're getting a good deal on the products you buy.

But perhaps the Web's greatest impact will be its ability to bring together people who would otherwise never have met. In June 1999 we posted an invitation on several Web sites for people to tell us how the Internet had affected their lives. You'll read a sampling of these stories in the chapters that follow. But it is noteworthy that of the 115 stories we received, close to half of them came from men and women who felt finding love or friendship had been the greatest benefit they received from going online.

Is it imperative that you get online? Esther Dyson, chairman of EDventure Holdings and author of *Release 2.1: A Design for Living in the Digital Age*, puts it this way: "If you're happy and you're set in your ways and you don't want to go online, don't bother. If you're young and you've got a career in front of you, you probably should figure out how to use this medium, simply to have the choices that are available to everyone else around you. You don't need to learn how it works. Do you know how your TV works? Most people don't, but they still feel completely comfortable with it. If you want to be part of the modern economy and the modern world, you're going to have to get online, but it's not a moral question."

Noted futurist and author Alvin Toffler says, "Your kids will use the Internet and in time you will find it indispensable. If you don't, if you have some principled objection to technology like Mr. Kaczynski [the Unabomber], that's okay. But, in fact, the rest of society will be there."

And what do some of the people say who sent us their personal Internet stories? Chip Izard from Texas exclaims: "The Internet moved me into the twenty-first century! It is amazing when I think that just five years ago I would never have told anybody to 'e-mail me.' I now spend a majority of my time using the Internet to communicate with customers, friends, and family; do research on competitors; and to announce new products and initiatives. I also use the Internet to purchase books, computer equipment; do medical research; book travel; do all types of financial research trading, and all my banking. My whole way of living has changed. I can get connected anywhere with my Hewlett-Packard palmtop or my laptop."

George Kramer from Florida—who turned eighty during 1999 and lives alone—was finding life depressing. His doctor prescribed medication. Then he decided about a year ago to buy a computer. As George tells it, "It saved my life. I started dating through the Internet and met some nice ladies, which enabled me to get dressed up and go out to a fine restaurant. It made me feel human again." Not only that, but George, a casual investor on Wall Street, decided to give online trading a try. "I found a wealth of information and guidance, mostly for free, and have been modestly successful. In almost no time, it paid for my computer, a digital camera, and a two-week trip to Eastern Europe. Talk about changing my life. I haven't felt this good about myself in I don't know how many years."

Hold on for a life-changing ride.

ONE

THE VIRTUAL BACK FENCE

When I was five my oldest brother married and moved away. He and my divorced parents fought over something I have never been allowed to know. Throughout the years my eight brothers and sisters and I have often wondered what became of his life. Last year I bought a computer and immediately connected to the Web. One day my brother was visiting and we were showing each other tricks we knew about the computer. We both said, "Wouldn't it be bizarre if we were able to track down Bob?" In less than an hour we were able to locate the name and address of our long-lost sibling. It has been twenty-five years since I last saw him. We have spent the last nine months conversing. I feel like a part of me was made whole again.

—Kerry McCarthy, New York

I met my husband over an e-mail. I was widowed in 1996 and a single girlfriend talked me into joining a local matchmaker service. There were a lot of losers, but eventually I got a short, interesting e-mail from a fellow in a small town close to Austin. We met for dinner in a catfish restaurant; it was love at first sight! A week later, on my birthday, he proposed. We're both in our forties and this isn't our first rodeo, but it's the best one!!

—Joyce Weaver, Texas

Four years ago few people had even heard the phrase "dot com," which denotes the closing address for a commercial Web site. Today that often-used expression appears everywhere, from T-shirts to newspapers, television, and radio. It's not just affluent men and computer-savvy teenagers who are familiar with Internet lingo; women are using the Web to do research, shop, and communicate with family and friends who are emotionally close but geographically dispersed. According to an Intelliquest research company study of 1,100 households in the first quarter of 1999, women constitute 47 percent of U.S. adults online.

Just a few years ago that was not the case. Ellen Pack, founder, senior vice president, and general manager of Women.com, ventured online in the early 1990s and discovered little to keep her or other women coming back. So she set out to create a welcoming environment for women. Since then the Net has become a lot more hospitable for everyone.

Pack has seen attitudes toward using the Internet change, even within her own family. Every Christmas she and her husband visit his parents, who are retired in Myrtle Beach. In past years she got them connected to the Internet and showed them how to use it. This year she saw a dramatic difference in their awareness and usage. Says Pack, now they are "addicted to the Web."

They are not alone. Regular use of the Internet is having a dramatic effect on families and other interpersonal relationships. Friendships that have dwindled across the miles are being rekindled through the touch of a key. Family members separated by time zones can now connect in virtual time, and people they've never met are offering help, support, and advice about everything from hobbies to life-threatening diseases.

David Bohnett, founder and former CEO and chairman of GeoCities—based on the concept of creating online-themed neighborhoods—explains that his entire family is planning on gathering for his niece's graduation. But instead of discussing travel plans on the phone, his parents, sister, brother, and uncle are reviewing options on e-mail. This is "taking the place of a lot of telephone conversation," said Bohnett.

GeoCities.com is one of the fastest-growing communities of personal Web sites on the Internet (in June 1999 it was merged with Yahoo!). There are over 3.5 million homesteaders, or members, occupying virtual neighborhoods that reflect their interests and expertise.

Why do people want to create their own online communities? Bohnett believes the motivation is to meet people of similar interests and share their experiences with others. "There are folks in this world who seem to be born organizers and networkers," he explains, "and these are the ones who take the initiative to form their own online communities."

Transitions like this have come so rapidly that sometimes we don't appreciate the amazing alterations that have taken place in our lives owing to electronic communication. After all, even the most well-established Web sites have been around for only four to five years. While the Internet was once used primarily by scientists, now consumer interests dominate. Today many people log on in the morning to get weather and news and check in throughout the day for stock market prices, entertainment information, or travel plans.

Teenagers have an easy time embracing the Internet: they're naturally comfortable with technology and they don't have ingrained habits to change. The number one reason for teens going online, according to Yankelovich Partners research with kids nine to seventeen, is for e-mail (67 percent), while half of those surveyed said it was for school or homework. It might interest parents to know that 48 percent said they went online to learn new things, even though playing games was mentioned by 58 percent of respondents. Moreover, research showed that more kids are giving up television to use the Internet (32 percent) than any other activity.

The Internet is also becoming the place to find a date or a mate. Enterprising singles seek one another out in chat rooms, while some entrepreneurs have discovered a way to turn a search for romance into a business. Match.Com, an online dating and matchmaking service launched in 1995, claims that more than 1,400 members have credited the service for their marriages.

Moreover, if you're searching for information on a long-lost relative or just want to create a family tree, the Web has a treasure trove of birth, death, and other records useful for genealogists. The Church of Jesus Christ of Latter-Day Saints, known in genealogy circles for having the world's largest ancestral archives, launched an online searchable database [familysearch.org] in May 1999. On its first day in operation the system temporarily ground to a halt, overwhelmed by 30 million hits on the site.

Of course, with radical change comes concern, and sometimes resistance. How is the Internet changing our definition of community? Is the Internet redefining how people meet? Are women approaching the Web differently from men? What are the new rules for raising kids in the Digital Age? Is family life being altered by the growing presence of connected computers in our homes?

These and other questions are addressed by Pack and Bohnett, with additional insights from America Online president and chief operating officer Bob Pittman; futurist Alvin Toffler; EDventure Holdings chairman and author Esther Dyson; Excite@Home CEO George Bell; and HearMe CEO and president Paul Matteucci. However, if there is one maxim to help guide you and your family through life on the Web, it's this: The same rules that apply to your conduct at home, in the office, or on the street also apply to your behavior online.

The Electronic Grapevine

■ **Bob Pittman** When people go online, they find that it's like stopping at the end of the driveway and checking their mailbox for mail. Every night you sign on religiously; it becomes a habit. You open your mailbox, check, see if anything's there, check other things that are important to you—maybe a stock portfolio, maybe some hobbyist group or some special interest you have—and then you do things that are unique to that day and the activities you need. What you find is you take a chunk of time every day to manage your life off of this box and in return, you save yourself a lot of time.

■ **Ellen Pack** The Internet is revolutionizing the way families communicate, interact, and relate. Important family events like the birth of a baby or a relative's wedding, which were once only enjoyed by family living nearby, can now be shared through the Internet. Geographic barriers are being rendered irrelevant, and family members, regardless of where they live, can now take part in the event, through e-mail, live Web casts, posted photographs, and video and audio clips.

I get many e-mails now from family members I would never have talked to throughout the year, except at holiday gatherings. I've found that through e-mail, we're much more likely to keep in touch and talk about a broader range of topics. I regularly get e-mail from my mother-in-law—not just about the family, but about articles that she thinks are interesting, which she'll pass on to me. Certainly, part of the appeal is the convenience of the communication.

■ **David Bohnett** In the last year and a half, virtually everyone in my family, either through work or through America Online or some other Internet service provider, has gotten connected with e-mail.

My whole family was out visiting me for Christmas and we took a lot of pictures. In less than half an hour, I had created a Web page on GeoCities about our family Christmas using photos I scanned in. I've seen a lot of families post pictures of their kids so that their grandparents and parents can view them from any location.

The Changing Family Structure

■ **Alvin Toffler** My wife and I look at the family in society as a system, a family system. When we were researching *Future Shock* in 1966, we asked all the experts we talked to, "What's going to happen to the nuclear family," and they said, "Nothing." Their view was that this is a fundamental, universal, eternal family structure, and nothing's going to change that.

Looking at the rest of what we were about to write, we said, "Wait a minute, that doesn't make sense. Everything else is going to change in society but the family system is not?"

We argued that we were going to see a demassification or a diversification of the family structure. In *The Third Wave* we went further in that direction, arguing that this fits with the increasing customization of products; that we'd go from mass-produced products to increasingly demassified production; from mass markets to increasingly demassified markets.

In the sixties, people began talking about market segmentation, which was followed by niche markets, boutique markets, micro markets, and now it's particle markets, one-to-one. What you see happening is the production, distribution, and marketing—the whole system—becoming more molecular, more granular, more internally differentiated.

Now the connection between production and distribution or consumption in the United States is the media, demassified media. The entire system is moving in that direction. To me, the changes in the family structure simply parallel these others. The family is not just a passive recipient of changes that come from business, technology, and other things. It has a major effect as well, but its effect doesn't come until twenty years or so later, because the effect is through your kids. We will continue to see a great diversity of family formats, and I hope that we develop a sufficient social tolerance to accept that.

■ **George Bell** We've had a pretty clear disintegration in the family unit caused by the incursion of communication, new forms of media, and the unprecedented pace of our lives, which makes it impossible for any family to sit down to dinner five nights a week without a television turned on and have a family discussion for two hours. I don't know anybody who does that anymore.

This has indirectly created a place for Internet communities to start to fill some of that void. I'm not sure it's the best solution, but it's the best of the choices that have been presented. It's almost a throwback to an agrarian way, where you can talk around the digital fire. I think it's actually bringing back something that's very old-fashioned and quite valuable.

■ **David Bohnett** It's very easy to blame the Internet for lack of communication within a family, but I don't think the Internet has much of an effect compared to the more important issue of how parents are raising their kids. It's the same as watching television or using the telephone; it all has to do with the environment that the parents create.

For example, my brother and his family in New Jersey share Bible study classes on the computer. On GeoCities many schools and teachers have set up Web sites providing information about classroom assignments and school activities, which gets family members involved in using the Internet for a common purpose.

Redefining Community

■ **David Bohnett** The Internet gives you the opportunity to meet other people who are interested in the same things you are, no matter how specialized, no matter how weird, no matter how big or how small. It's one of the reasons online communities are so popular.

There's a never-ending debate over what creates community because everybody has their own definition of it. I believe community is created by the participation and responsibility that each community member brings to his or her neighborhood.

> *"The online environment doesn't replace the experiences you have in the real world."*

We have forty-one different neighborhoods on GeoCities; one of the more popular ones focuses on entertainment and music. We have users who set up their personal home page to talk about their favorite bands and artists. Most of the sites on GeoCities have a mechanism to gather feedback and communication. A person might invite others to send an e-mail to let him know if they liked his page or want to suggest a link to another site. Members use surveys to gauge opinion, or a counter to find out how many people visited their site.

Some people will say all that is just personal publishing. But I go back to my definition of community, which says people gathering together, and having the opportunity and responsibility to participate, creates a feeling of belonging to something. You put your time and effort into building and creating the environment; that's what community is all about.

The important thing to remember is the online environment doesn't replace the experiences you have in the real world. It's simply another set of experiences, some better, some worse. It's just another way of connecting people.

■ **Ellen Pack** People who aren't involved yet in the Internet sometimes have this fear that it will replace talking to their neighbors and seeing people when they communicate with them. Online community is supplemental—it is not going to take the place of face-to-face communication. You still want to be friends with your neighbors, you still want to know the mothers of the kids at your children's school, you still want to be involved directly in your community.

But there are also tons of opportunities to communicate and build community around things that you can't do just next door. For example, we have a very strong small business area on Women.com. Women come to our entrepreneurs club and connect with one another and share advice and experience. Many of these women are working from their homes, so they don't have the office watercooler; their geographic neighbors are not necessarily interested in the same things they are; they don't have an easy way to network with other business owners.

The Internet has the ability to help women who may not have the support they seek directly in their own community.

■ **Paul Matteucci** I've been in chat rooms where I've observed, for the first time in my life, African-Americans and white supremacists talking to each other. I'm not sure that's a good thing or a bad thing, but if you go through the threads of the conversation, by the end you'll find there's less animosity than there was at the beginning. It's not pretty sometimes, there's shouting and obscenities, but these groups of people would never even talk to each other in real life. They would talk through the press at each other or they would talk through hate sites. But here they are online, actually talking to each other. I find that fascinating and uplifting.

Tech-Savvy Kids

■ **Esther Dyson** Two hundred years ago children were part of the adult world. You got born, you probably hung out with the animals and the milk nurse for a while, and then you just were underfoot. Your parents were on the farm, and you were there doing little things, carrying out the lunch pail or what have you. My great aunt went to work in a cotton mill when she was four years old carrying spindles around.

Then we created this separate world for children with nursery schools and governesses and special books and special kinds of clothes and a little fantasy world for children where everything was nice. Not all children were able to enjoy that, but there was a notion of a very separate safe world for children.

In the last thirty to forty years, partly because of mass media and partly because of what parents let kids watch, children have become witnesses to the grown-up world. They watch adult TV, they may even see adult movies. It's all around them. Until recently, when a child was in the adult world he was recognized as a child, but now the child can go online, engage in conversation, and be treated as an adult. A child can start an online business or join a chat group and pretend to be twenty-nine when she is only eleven. It's all very interesting and I don't know what it's going to mean. I do know that families need to do a better job raising kids for this new world and schools also need to change.

■ **Alvin Toffler** If you are a peasant in a medieval village and life goes on the way it has for centuries, you'll always be a peasant; your ancestors were peasants, your descendants will be peasants, nothing changes. Then the most valuable knowledge you can have is knowledge of how it was done in the past, because the past is the same as the present, and the present is the same as what the future will be. Where do you find things out? You talk to the elders.

Now change that around, go to a society in which everything's changing rapidly, and the consequence of that is the kids are saying, "It's going to be different. It's not the same.

What do you know? Your experience is irrelevant. You keep talking about the good old times." The acceleration of change devalues knowledge from the past. Now when you put a layer of technology on top of that, you get a pretty snotty bunch of kids, that's what you get.

Teach Your Children Well

■ **Esther Dyson** The only advice I'd offer parents is to be a good parent. Remember that the best thing you have to give to your kid is time, and that means time doing things together, whether it's going for walks in the country or exploring the Internet or reading bedtime stories. Explain to them what the world is about. You have to treat them as children but also help them to grow up.

Help them to have the understanding and the wisdom to make the choices they're going to have to make. Help them understand the motives of people who are communicating with them online. Is this advertising or is it editorial? Why is this piece of information here? Is someone trying to sell you something? Are they trying to get you to vote for something? Are they trying to persuade you to do something? What's the purpose of this information here? Is it the truth? Why do you believe it?

It's going to be a pretty complex world, and parents need to help their kids understand it. Of course, parents face the challenge of figuring it out for themselves too.

■ **David Bohnett** With the increasing availability of choices and information comes an even greater responsibility for parents, which is something that's worrisome because parents have less and less time as it is.

Any new advancement brings good and bad. The only

way around the bad is to spend time with kids online when they're young until they are old enough to form their own judgments. Teach them how to judge their experiences: where it's appropriate to go; where it's not appropriate to go and

> *"For kids, being online is just part of growing up."*

why. You have to create a sense of responsibility in your child and that can only come from parents spending time with their kids.

I see huge differences between kids' use and adults' use of the Internet. I'm old enough to remember stories about the telephone; how my parents' grandparents would use the phone with trepidation or only would assume it was bad news if somebody called. They wouldn't think of just chatting on the telephone. For kids, being online is just part of growing up. It's something they're comfortable with, something they see as a tool for daily living. Many of the rest of us see it as this really new thing. When today's kids grow up, they won't understand what the world was like without the Internet.

■ **Ellen Pack** We know that some women use the Internet to "keep up" with their kids. There is a common fear among these moms that if they don't keep up with technology, they might eventually lose touch with what their kids care about. The Internet offers some promise, of not only keeping them current, but also keeping them connected.

Another aspect is that moms want to be able to know where to go online and how to help their children find things. A mom may worry about not having the answers that her family needs, and more and more, she is turning to the Internet to find these answers.

■ **Bob Pittman** The online world is a reflection of life off-line—both the good and bad aspects of it. In some cases we're able to control and mitigate some of the bad through technology; parents can set Parental Controls on AOL and decide what they want the service to be for their kids. Unfortunately, we do not have that same sort of capability in our offline life.

Women and the Net

■ **Ellen Pack**   We've done studies where we go in and we talk with women in their homes as they are using the Internet. It might be at ten o'clock at night after they've put the kids to sleep or during the day when they are on a break, but regardless of the time, what we consistently find is that women use the Internet as a productivity tool. They see it as something that's going to help them get things done.

> *"The main difference between how women and men use the Internet is that women are seekers and men are surfers."*

Often women will go online with a written list that they keep by the computer or in their date book, with the idea that they are going to do these ten things. They may not get every one of those things done, but they do get a sense of satisfaction based on how much they have accomplished during their online session.

We know a lot about what frustrates women online as well. They don't have patience for unclear navigation and slow-loading pages, largely because they're focused on utility and saving time.

The main difference between how women and men use the Internet is that women are seekers and men are surfers. Women go online with a very specific purpose in mind whereas men are more likely to cruise around looking for interesting sites. I see this even in my own home. We'll be eating dinner and my husband will tell me about an "interesting" site he has found—the last one was about Russian calculators. For him, randomly discovering bizarre sites is a wonderful use of the Web. My usage, however, is very different. It's primarily utility focused on things like looking up when the movie starts or gathering information about a trip that I'd like to plan by pulling up some hotel reviews for both of us to read and review.

Chat isn't a huge application for women because many just don't have time. There's a segment of the population that loves to chat—they're very active, tend to be people who are young or at home and have more free time. At Women.com, we find that message boards seem to be a stronger way for women to communicate regularly, while also getting access to the peer support and information they seek. Message boards are more efficient (and therefore more popular) because instead of waiting through an irrelevant conversation, women can post a question and come back later at a convenient time to find the answer.

It all gets back to how women make decisions. One way is to look for the authoritative sources of information about an issue. Another way is to look to our peers, other women, or a support group for answers.

A lot of parents come into the message boards, new moms, who'll say, "Okay, Johnny's doing this. What should I do about it?" And you'll hear an outpouring of support saying, "This is normal, don't worry about it."

There is a lot of community advice and support which is very unique and never really existed before. You now have the ability to gain access to the collective wisdom of women who have faced the same or similar situations as you have.

We've done a lot of research about women and the Internet and have found that often the computer is located next to the television—right in the center of the action where they don't have to be disconnected from everybody; they can be with the family while they are online.

Online Dating

■ **Ellen Pack** I know a couple of people who met online and who are now married, so I do believe that it can work. However, you should be just as careful when meeting someone online as you would be when meeting someone offline. You don't know who's on the other side of the computer, just as you don't know who's on the other side of a telephone, or who's on the other side of a personal ad. I would advise that the first time you meet someone, do it in a public place and bring a friend. Use the same kind of common sense you would use in meeting someone you don't know through a dating service.

> "You should be just as careful when meeting someone online as you would be when meeting someone offline."

■ **David Bohnett** People lead busy lives, and they need ways of meeting people more efficiently than they used to, and if there's anything that the online world offers across all segments—whether it's business or consumer—it's efficiency. You can meet a lot more people online and exchange profiles and interests more quickly than you can in the real world.

There's going to be no end to people who criticize, who think it's impersonal, who think it's dangerous, and it's all those things. But for better or for worse, we're in a free market economy, and people vote with their time, with their feet, and with their keyboard. The more interesting thing to think about is, How do you create businesses that facilitate meeting online and tap into that energy and power?

Online Infidelity

■ **Ellen Pack** Infidelity is a hot issue online. We had a poll about this very thing, and the majority of people did not feel that flirting online was infi-delity. Who knows? Of course, I think that it's all about where it leads. Does flirting make you

> *"The majority of people did not feel that flirting online was infidelity."*

want to meet the person? If it's exchanging e-mails online, I don't think it's too dangerous, but it can get there. Again, it just speaks to the situation that the Internet is not just an in-formation vehicle, it's also a communication vehicle and a community vehicle as well.

■ **David Bohnett** You know in your conscience when you are cheating or not, whether you're doing it at the office at the wa-ter cooler, whether you're doing it online, whether you're do-ing it on the telephone. It just depends how good people are at fooling themselves. As I've said before, for better or worse, on-line is just another form of communication.

Making Friends and Keeping Old Ones

■ **Ellen Pack** There is a service called ICQ, which is an instant messaging service that AOL recently acquired. It's interesting because it shows how the Web is truly a global communica-tions tool. You can go online and enter your name, and it will quickly come back with a list of people who share your name. You can instantly send them a message and ask, "Could we be related?" I think being able to talk to people from other coun-tries in our message boards about news, politics, family issues, and life in general is pretty amazing. This type of international idea exchange has incredible potential—to both positively affect world change and to increase understanding of common global issues that are important to everyone.

While our boards are primarily U.S. based, we have members from Canada, the UK, and Australia who come in and talk about various issues. It's fascinating because when would you ever be able to sit down and talk to women from these different countries?

■ **David Bohnett** The buddy list or instant messenger or the Yahoo! pager lets me know, when I'm online in California, that my ten-year-old niece has signed on to her computer in New Jersey. She can say "hi" to me and I can say "hi" to her while I'm doing other things. Tools like this, along with e-mail and family Web pages, are facilitating your ability to stay in touch with people.

My parents are in their mid-seventies, retired, and live in Florida. It would be a challenge for them to set up a PC and learn how to use Microsoft Windows, but they've got no problem with Web TV. In fact, they are on their second version of it. They have a group of friends who have all acquired Web TVs because they've seen my parents use it. That's really the way the Internet works, through word of mouth.

■ **Ellen Pack** When your friends or family members get online for the first time, they send you lots of e-mail, and inevitably they start sending the dreaded e-mails filled with joke lists. Well, one joke is okay once in a while, but when they start forwarding joke lists from thirty of their friends . . . ugh. If you're a person who gets a hundred e-mails a day it's not too much fun.

What I find nice is e-mailing with my husband throughout the day. I travel a lot, so we'll exchange two or three e-mails a day. Tiny, one sentence kinds of things, but it brings a different type of humor and intimacy to a relationship that you don't necessarily get over the phone.

How to Find Your Way Around the Backyard

■ **George Bell** The search box, even three, four years ago, became very well established as the window onto the Web. So, if you didn't know where else to go on the Web, you could type the words into the search box and start with some search results, and at least you could get going. That seems to be a pretty well-understood metaphor.

The search product today offers even more. For example, if you were to type in the name of a public company on Excite [excite.com], above the search results you would get the price at which the company is now trading, links to financial charts and SEC reviews, disclaimers by the management team, and these sorts of things. Then you'd get a section of daily news about that company, including a news release if it has one or more articles written about it.

The Web search results, culled from our index of 250 million URLs, are prioritized to offer the most sought-after content for a public company: a live stock quote. It even gives you the address and the home page of that company.

We call this "channeling search," wherein we create an instant channel of information around the keywords that are typed into the search window. We've done the same thing with sports teams. If you type in "dolphins," we presume that the most common use of the word on the Web is for the sports team the Miami Dolphins, but you'll see that if you want other interpretations of dolphins, you can get that too. You can check bottlenose, for example, and it would be added to the dolphin keyword, and then you can search again. Essentially what you're doing is taking people through an iterative process where they're refining their queries as they go.

If you typed in "Knicks," you actually bring up the team colors, their team page, and their calendar; since it's basketball season now, that information is available. In addition to the Knicks' calendar of games, you've also got a red link that allows you to lift the Knicks information and put it onto the sports section of your personalized Excite start page. In addition to allowing people to create their "newspaper of me" on their start page, we've now made it possible for people, as they move through the site and find things they like, to cut and paste that content onto their newspaper, and it's automatically refreshed.

We are looking for ways to be able to lift chunks of content off other areas of our service and paste them onto your personal page so you can constantly refresh and update that "newspaper of me." About 43 percent of our entire user base has personalized their experience on Excite.

One of my own favorite personalization modules is tides. I like tracking them because my wife and kids are at our summer home in Maine from June 15 through Labor Day. I actually put up the tides for Portland on my front page, so I know not to call during low tide because the kids are always down at the beach.

Getting Personal

■ **George Bell** We've added notification technologies to our service. So, for instance, if you've been active in the tennis community, and there are four people posting new messages to you from that community, we can let you know. Perhaps you've been active in a chat discussion, and there are new threads that have been added to that discussion. Maybe you've asked us to alert you if any of your stocks drop below 5 percent of the industry mean or rise above 5 percent of the mean, we can do that too.

With these notification technologies, personalization becomes not just the content you want, in the quantity that you want, but personalization becomes live, it notifies you of things that you believe are important to you. Notification takes the form of e-mail, voice mail, and so forth.

All of our plans are built on a strategy that says, number one, we will not sell or otherwise traffic in your data—your name, your e-mail, your zip code, things like that. If you build a page at Excite you're asked to register, and we ask you explicitly whether we're able to send you notices from us or from third parties or from anybody, or whether you want to restrict any of that.

Since we don't charge our customer anything for our services, we've got to be especially clear and protective of their rights because the relationship is very fickle. It's not defined by a check that comes every month, and so switching barriers are very low. It's easy to go off to Yahoo! and build a personal page if, somehow, we've angered you.

■ **Ellen Pack** The Internet provides a way for people to express themselves creatively (sometimes more effectively than offline). I've received online résumés from people with links to some personal information, such as a photo of their boyfriend. I'm sure they are thinking that they're using the Web "creatively"—however, for a job application, it borders a bit on oversharing.

I don't think it's going to come down to everybody having a personal expression Web page with their favorite photos and hobbies, but I do think everyone will have Web pages for certain things related to their work, their families, or their school. Web pages that I share with my family are very different from

Web pages I would put out in a job search. As Web page-making tools get easier, and the concept becomes more ingrained in people's lives, home pages will have the potential to become personal calling cards.

Eventually, you're going to be able to go to someone's Web page, click on it, and leave a voice mail. Your Web page is going to be your personal space for communication—a place where you might have a weekly mini–family reunion.

■ **David Bohnett** The last thing some people want to do is create a home page for everyone else to look at. Fine. They can create their own private home page and only share things with their family. But a surprising number of other people love to share everything they know with the rest of the world.

I believe that different levels of privacy and sharing will evolve over time. I see it as a series of concentric circles, where the innermost circle is your own private home page that might include your diary, your stock information, and your checking account information. The next circle out is where you have things that you want to share with your own family. The next circle is less personal and may include information that you'd want to share with a group of friends or business associates. I believe all of us will choose to have one or more of these circles.

Living in the Fast Lane

■ **Bob Pittman** The Internet's not the cause of the fast pace we're living at. It's the other way around. The fast-paced life is the cause of the Internet. It's because people have to do a lot of things, and they have to keep up with a lot—communication, information, et cetera—and the Internet is a solution to that problem. It has allowed us to move very quickly, to get a lot more done, and to make our lives a little richer.

Of course, it's a bit different for me. I'm not the normal human being because I'm working in the industry, and for those of us working in it, it sets a fast and relentless pace. If I were simply a user it would be saving me time, but in my case it eats up my life. But that's really the consequence of being with a very high-growth company, dealing with a very hot product, and understanding that we have to superserve our members, who truly do expect us to work day and night to give them the product they're looking for.

■ **Ellen Pack**   At times it may seem like we're moving toward a speed-hungry, immediate gratification culture and that the nature of technology can make it harder for people to take the time to think and relax. I don't personally relate to that scenario; I tend to be more relaxed the more information I have, but for many this is an issue. The bottom line is that people will always have a choice. However, if you're very career-minded, and you want to stay off the technology wagon, well, that's going to be pretty hard.

The information revolution is happening all around us and it's not just about the Internet. It's about twenty-four-hour news channels, it's about FedEx, it's about cell phones and beepers and information everywhere. I think the Internet has the potential to personalize information and bring in a valuable community element, and I think that that's something that people who don't know it well don't understand.

The important thing to remember is that the Internet helps and enriches lives. I really believe that. You can always turn your cell phone off or not check your e-mail. But if you opt out altogether, you'll be missing out on all the ways that the Internet can positively affect your life.

Woman Talk

Do you consider having online sex or a "hot chat" relationship an affair? (Women.com poll, as of June 1999: 36,035 respondents)

52 percent	No
35 percent	Yes
13 percent	Don't know

Do men and women have different investing styles? (Women.com poll, as of June 1999: 1,138 respondents)

86 percent	Yes
10 percent	Not sure
4 percent	No

Most Popular Web Community Sites

(Source: Nielsen//NetRatings)

about.com	guestworld.com
angelfire.com	gurlpages.com
classmates.com	miningco.com
delphi.com	onelist.com
epinions.com	talkcity.com
fortunecity.com	theglobe.com
freeyellow.com	tripod.com
geocities.com	xoom.com

TWO

TAKE CHARGE OF YOUR HEALTH!

The Internet helped me at a crucial time in my life—my miscarriage. It was hard to let go of the idea of being pregnant. I didn't know who to talk to. Two weeks after my miscarriage I found a Web site on parenting, with a section on miscarriage support. I sat down for two hours, read every message, and cried. I posted a message and asked for support. And did I get it! The women were wonderful. I printed those e-mail messages and put them in a box to reread when the pain comes back.

—Theresa Vaz, Ontario

In 1998 my twenty-two-year-old daughter had excruciating back pain. An MRI showed a rare spinal cord tumor. We went to several neurosurgeons, but they said they didn't know anyone who could remove the tumor without causing serious complications or death. Finally, searching the Internet I came across a doctor across the country, in New York, who specializes in these tumors. He did a wonderful job and she has her life back. I hate to think what would have happened without the Internet.

—Karen Roach, Idaho

Today it is almost impossible to find a doctor who makes house calls. If you are ill you have to drag yourself into your physician's office, no matter if a Nor'easter is threatening to blow you over or if your fever has just spiked to 103 degrees. Your time with your doctor, dictated by managed care, will probably not exceed eleven minutes; hardly enough time for your doctor to examine you, give a diagnosis, and answer your questions.

Do you have an alternative? Absolutely, if you are willing to take the advice of Dr. C. Everett Koop, the outspoken, pioneering pediatrician and U.S. Surgeon General from 1981 to 1989, who urges consumers to "Take charge of your health!" This is essential under managed care, he cautions, since if you don't do it, "no one else will do it for you."

In the pre-Web days it was extremely difficult for patients to be in control of their health destiny. Doctors were thought to have a monopoly on health wisdom and few patients felt they needed to spend hours in the library looking up their illness, diagnosis, or medications. Today that is changing. Managed care has altered the patient/doctor relationship and there is a dizzying array of alternative treatments along with traditional protocols to consider. Moreover, the Internet provides easy access to health information, supplying you with the tools you need to be in charge of your treatment. The doctor still won't come to your door, but you stand a better chance that he or she will communicate with you.

At eighty-two, Dr. Koop, the first surgeon in America to devote his practice to children, is still actively involved in finding new ways to empower people to be wise health consumers, but now he's using the power of the Internet to help get the message across. Koop has been preaching the gospel of preventive care for decades. As Surgeon General he singled out smoking as the single most preventable cause of death, and during his tenure the U.S. Public Health Service required cigarette manufacturers to print health warnings on every package of cigarettes.

Koop is "extraordinarily comfortable" with people using the Internet to learn more about staying healthy. The Internet fosters prevention, he notes, and therefore makes for better patients and less expensive care. Unlike many doctors who refuse to criticize their own, Koop tells it like it is and is openly critical of doctors who don't listen to their patients. However, he is optimistic that doctors can change and that e-mail is a tool they will use to help them communicate with their connected patients.

Dr. George Lundberg, editor in chief of Medscape, formerly the editor of the *Journal of the American Medical Association (JAMA)*, also sees the value of doctors using e-mail, even at times as a replacement for a visit, but warns it should never be used if an in-person relationship hasn't first been established. Lundberg is also comfortable with people using the Internet for health information, but cautions that the Net is "just a medium" and the messages it contains can be incorrect.

Lundberg, like Koop, is no stranger to controversy. Early in 1999 he was fired from *JAMA* after the journal published a survey of college students' sexual attitudes that coincided with the impeachment trial of President Clinton. He was quickly hired by the oldest, established ongoing medical site, Medscape, to oversee its editorial content. He is also an adjunct professor of health policy at Harvard University and a lecturer at Northwestern University. In these pages he speaks out on many issues, such as prescribing drugs online, medical record security, comparison shopping, and alternative medicine.

Search the Web for "health" and you'll get over 18 million selections to choose from. Clearly, it can be confusing for you to know what's available online, what's accurate, where the best information is, and how to use that knowledge for your benefit. In addition, technology is opening up new health care purchasing options, such as shopping for medications online. No one knows how fast or even if filling prescriptions online will catch on, but CVS, the second largest pharmacy chain in the nation, isn't taking any chances. In May 1999 it bought Soma.com, an online drug retailer. The following month, Rite Aid Corp., the nation's third largest drugstore chain, bought a 25 percent stake in drugstore.com.

The online consumer health care market is expected to grow to $1.7 billion by 2003, according to research from Jupiter

Communications, but that's still a fraction of the estimated $205 billion that is expected to be spent for health goods overall in that year. How do you navigate this new health environment? Here's what Dr. Koop and Dr. Lundberg prescribe.

Patients Lose Their Patience

■ **Dr. Koop** Taking charge of your own health is harder than it used to be because when I was young, physicians were held in tremendous awe and esteem. They were also very authoritarian. I remember house calls when I was a kid. The family went into a hushed whisper in their conversations when you were in the home, not because they were trying to be quiet so you could listen with a stethoscope, but because the family thought you deserved that kind of honor.

The doctor was the kind of a guy who said without words, I'm the boss, I'm the authority, and you're the passive patient, and when I want you to tell me anything, I'll ask you a question.

I think that the doctor-patient relationship has deteriorated over the last three decades, and with all the technology that comes in, you could say it's pushing patient and doctor further and further apart—but I think the Internet and e-mail is bringing them closer. One of my great concerns about my profession is that because physicians have not remained professional, because they have not policed themselves, because they haven't concentrated on being communicators in the age of communication, we stand in danger of becoming just journeymen, and the profession will be gone.

■ **Dr. Lundberg** The drive toward autonomy for patients has been under way for about twenty-five years in this country. The Internet simply is one medium that can foster and promote that drive.

When I was a medical student, it was commonly believed that you shouldn't even tell patients they have cancer because you might freak them out; there was a stigma attached to any kind of cancer back then. That's hard to believe today, but we were counseled as medical students, if you get a diagnosis of cancer in a patient, "Don't tell the patient. Consult with the family and decide with them whether you'll even bother to tell the patient."

What You Don't Know Can Hurt You

■ **Dr. Koop** I see the Internet as a way to pull back the deteriorating patient-doctor relationship. First of all, I believe that doctors like an informed patient. If you know something about your problem and I can talk to you at a more advanced level, then we've got a different rapport than we otherwise would have.

Second, the Internet actually empowers patients not only to take charge of their health but to be better patients and better decision makers. Any doctor

> "Doctors like an informed patient."

worth his salt wants to make decisions for a patient—both diagnostically and therapeutically—in tandem with that patient, because a doctor who makes a decision with a patient automatically sets up a barrier to malpractice. If something goes wrong, it's not, "You told me to," and it makes a tremendous difference.

An informed patient, who is empowered by our new knowledge, also aids the doctor in the following way. Suppose that you called me as an old patient and said, "You know, I've been having pain in my chest today, and I think it's worse when I'm active, but, of course, it was after I ate." Well, I make the judgment that you're not in any serious trouble from what you've told me. I say, "I'll see you at eight o'clock in the morning, and what I want you to do tonight is look up coronary heart disease on drkoop.com. Then when you finish that, look up gastroesophageal reflux or GERD, and I'll see you at eight o'clock."

Right now in this country I'll bet there are 5,000 doctors who are saying the same thing to a patient, "Your heart's a pump and it's got these two valves in it and all these vessels on the outside." Well, if you had looked at the Internet, I don't have to start at kindergarten level. I can start talking to you right away about angina, about unstable angina, about the choices one has in finding out if there is an obstruction. We can do this noninvasive technique, we can do an angiogram. If the angiogram shows an obstruction, we can do ballon angioplasty, we can do a stent, we can do a cardiac bypass. The patient's a graduate student to start with.

The Internet could also be a way of knitting together the frayed doctor-patient relationship. Let's take your mother. She's been to the doctor and she's got a lot of questions that he didn't answer because she's on managed care and she had eleven minutes with the doctor. She's home and she's a little despondent, so she sits down and types a question to the doctor. At his leisure, he can answer the question and put in a word of comfort. She can read it and reread it and do whatever she wants with it, but it's a connection with the doctor she never had before. It also saves playing telephone tag with your doctors.

■ **Dr. Lundberg** How do doctors feel about Internet-savvy patients? Well, there are nearly 700,000 physicians in the United States. They're all individuals. In 1996 when I would ask doctors around the country how many of them have ever accessed the Internet, the numbers were under 5 percent. In 1998 my informal polling showed it was close to 85 percent. The hard data from researchers shows that about 55 percent of U.S. physicians have used the Internet.

So the average doctor has been on the Internet and understands at least something about it; some of them know it and like it a lot. If you have a doctor who's savvy about the Internet, then the doctor may welcome your accessing the same information source they have for medical information. It can establish a patient-physician partnership about searching out good information.

Having said that, there are physicians who still don't want their patients to know much about their own diseases, but that's a diminishing group. Most physicians in this country now believe that patients should take charge of their health.

The problem with patients bringing their doctors a bunch of stuff they collected from the Internet is that a patient might have gone on sites that are nothing but garbage. They might have found all kinds of stuff that just isn't true at all or is scary or is excessively hopeful or is simply off-the-wall. In that situation a physician should understand that the patient is trying but he didn't know where to go, didn't know how to interpret the data, and was made afraid by it or was given excessive buoyancy by the information.

The Doctor Will E-mail You Now

■ **Dr. Koop** Some doctors don't take to e-mailing easily, but if you have the right culture and it becomes part of their lives, they take to it immediately. Dartmouth is a perfect example of the right culture. It was the first nontechnical school that demanded that every incoming student, not just medical students, have a computer and be adept in its use.

Dartmouth has 5,000 students, including the graduates; it has a faculty to support it of about 1,200; and there's a little town that supports both of them. Now how many e-mails do you think are sent in that little town per day? Two hundred fifty thousand.

The doctors in Hanover e-mail all the time. When I want a prescription to be left someplace for me to pick up, I e-mail the doctor, he e-mails back and says he did it. The first thing that almost every doctor does when he comes into his office is go and look at his e-mail and answer it. So the patient at home gets answered, I get my prescription, he talks to another doctor about setting up a consultation, and it just flows like this because the culture is established. In three or four years, that culture will be all over.

■ **Dr. Lundberg** In my opinion e-mail is a wonderful communication method, but it's only words. As such, it's even less effective and clear than the telephone. Humans communicate in a wide range of ways, of which words are only one method; e-mail is sharply constricted by being only that one method. Many physicians are using e-mail to communicate with patients who they know, patients whom they're taking care of, using e-mail as a replacement for the telephone and, sometimes, a replacement for a patient visit to the doctor.

Where it's bad is when e-mail is used as a substitute for having originally established a patient-physician relationship. My view of that is an absolute no-no; that is, it's verboten, it should be forbidden, is forbidden by law across states, and is unethical to the extreme.

I believe that the use of e-mail should be confined to doctors and patients who know each other, who already have a patient-physician relationship in which both parties are familiar with the other person's circumstance, communication nuances, and foibles. They should be able to use the words on an e-mail exchange to come to the right answer without voice language, without face language, without physical examination, without smell, without touch, sight, all of these other things a physician uses when dealing with an individual patient.

In the next few years doctors will be paid for these e-mail interactions just as they are paid now for an [in-person] interaction, or are paid on a capitated basis. If you have an online consultation with a doctor you'd be billed for it.

E-mail Bonding

■ **Dr. Koop** Should you look for a doctor who will answer e-mail when you are looking for a doctor? I really never gave that much thought. I have never suggested to a patient, be sure your doctor's on e-mail because I just figure it's going to happen

"Maybe I should start saying, 'Get a doctor who has e-mail.'"

eventually, and everybody will have it. You know, I get asked by hundreds of people what to do about this. Maybe I should start saying, "Get a doctor who has e-mail."

I've had doctors at Dartmouth who joined the faculty three years ago who say, "I was dragged kicking and screaming into the situation. I didn't want to do e-mail, but I don't know how I practiced without it before." In the right culture it works. Eventually, it'll work in all cultures.

The Web Makes House Calls

■ **Dr. Koop** If you are a patient looking for help you can go to drkoop.com, and you can look up children's health, children's immunizations, travel health, women's health, men's health, sports health, and get some general ideas broken down into categories.

You can now search out your problems in one of two ways. You can either say, "I know that I've been diagnosed as having Graves' disease, so I'll look up Graves' disease," or you can say, "I have this palpitation. My friends say that my eyes are more prominent, and my skin is very dry all the time." You look up symptoms and figure out this could be, among other things, Graves' disease. We tell you in each of these instances this is what you have, this is how you got it, this is the usual course of events, this is why it's important to take control of it, and this is what you can expect in the future. It's a pretty good summary.

We don't answer your specific question. You might say, "I got this thing on my elbow." We say, "Most people who have this find that if they do so and so, this happens." Whenever we think there's a chance that a patient's going to say, "Oh, boy, I can handle that," we say, "Don't deal with this problem without talking to your doctor." We don't practice medicine on the Web.

■ **Dr. Lundberg** Here's an example of how someone might use the Internet to get health information. Let's say your mother called last night to say she's been to the doctor, and the doctor's concerned that she might have a cancer. Of what? Well, he's not really sure, but he thinks it might be in her lymph nodes. Your mother's panicked, she has a good doctor, she trusts the doctor, but she calls you to ask what to do. You could go to the Internet and start looking around for lymph node cancer, cancer in general, and become familiar with the field and what you can find. There's a wonderful University of Pennsylvania site called Oncolink [oncolink.com] that just deals with cancer. And the American Cancer Society has a site [cancer.org] with a lot of cancer information, as does the National Cancer Institute [nci.nih.gov].

You can come to the Medscape site [medscape.com] and

look up words in the medical dictionary that involve cancers of any kind, lymph node cancers and so forth. When you call your mother the next morning you say, "The doctor may be right or the doctor may be wrong, but you can arm yourself with information by beginning to learn what the possibilities are on the Internet." Since it's not an emergency, it's a great place to learn all manner of things about cancers and lymph nodes.

Finding Sites You Can Trust

■ **Dr. Koop** We rate between 1,200 and 1,400 of the almost 20,000 health sites, and we give them one to five stars. Now you'll say, "Well, who are you to do that?" Well, the one thing that has been remarkable about my life is that my eight years as Surgeon General established in the minds of the public that this is a guy who shoots straight, he's never led us down the garden path, and we can believe him and trust him. So if drkoop.com says that the Mayo Clinic Web site [mayohealth.org] is worth five stars, people think, I'm going to look at that. And if a site only has one star, doesn't it make more sense to look at three-, four-, and five-star sites?

■ **Dr. Lundberg** There are no simple ways to navigate the Internet. It's grown so fast it's completely disorganized. There are more than 15,000 health sites on the Internet. I have a friend in Copenhagen who monitors this and says that it's more like a million health sites with thousands being added every day. If one counts every doctor's home page as a health site, well, he's probably right. So what's a consumer to do?

I believe it's sensible to remember the kind of places one might trust information from in your everyday life: brand names that have been there for a while, that have earned respect, maybe even earned some loyalty, are reasonable to visit. That would include things like the best medical journal sites, good medical association sites, and government health sites.

From a consumer standpoint you can pretty much trust the Mayo Clinic for most things, they have a site called Oasis [mayohealth.org] for consumers that is quite decent. I think InteliHealth [intelihealth.com] that is done by Johns Hopkins is credible, sensible, and reasonable.

The American Medical Association's own site [ama-assn.org] is uneven in quality, but the professional journal part of it is wonderful. *The New England Journal of Medicine* [nejm.org] provides free, limited information, but what's there is useful.

The *British Medical Journal* is freely available on the Internet [bmj.com], full text, and really quite good. It has a British twist, but it's good science, good clinical medicine, ethically done. The other really big journal is *The Lancet* [thelancet.com], which is very old and very respected. Its Internet presence is variable, and getting anything you want on a given subject from one journal is a problem.

The National Library of Medicine has run *Index Medicus* since the late 1940s, and the computer searchable element of it, Medline, has been up since the middle 1960s [ncbi.nlm.nih.gov/PubMed or it can be accessed through medscape.com]. It currently has about 3,900 medical journals worldwide freely available to anybody, but all you get is the titles, the authors, and the abstracts. You don't get the full text.

If one can get on one site that tries to be a full-service health site to serve physicians, to serve the health professionals, to serve the public, and then learn how to navigate that site and trust that site, and that site can link to all sorts of other places, that's probably the best thing for a consumer to do.

Buying Drugs Online

■ **Dr. Lundberg** The prescribing of medications on the Internet by a doctor for a patient that the doctor has never established an in-person relationship with should simply not occur.

However, at this time there is a substantial amount of prescribing by physicians on the Internet. The Internet, of course, is international. The license to practice medicine is a country-by-country distinction, and in some countries a state-by-state distinction. It is illegal for me as a physician licensed in Illinois to practice medicine in Indiana. If the patient's in Indiana and I'm in Illinois and the Internet is used for the prescription, that's in violation of law if such a prescription is written. I would imagine it's just a matter of time before the state licensing agencies in this country jump on that big time.

As with everything else, patients need to be educated. In the editorial that we wrote about this in 1997 in *JAMA*, we used the phrase *caveat lector, et viewor,* meaning let the reader (lector) and let the Internet user (viewor) beware.

■ **Dr. Koop** What you can do at our online pharmacy is renew your prescription. So let's say you take Cardizem and you get sixty at a time, which is a two-month supply, and you have five refills. When the time comes and you need a refill you go to our site, select the pharmacy you deal with—we have contracts with companies like CVS and others—you write in your prescription number, pharmacy store number, your name, e-mail address, push an icon, and that goes directly to the pharmacy. The pharmacies with which we have a contract guarantee that your prescription will be ready to be picked up in one hour, and if they have a delivery service, they will deliver it within two hours.

The pharmacy at our site also allows you to find drug incompatibilities online. For example, you see your internist on Monday, and he gives you a prescription. You see your cardiologist on Friday, and he gives you a prescription. But neither one knows what the other's doing, and you happen to take them to two different pharmacies to be filled, which is quite common for patients to do. If you took them to the same pharmacist, his computer system should alert him to tell you you've got two drugs that are incompatible. But under these circumstances, you can come home, type in your two drugs, and, whoosh, you get a red flag. Then you call one of your doctors and say, "I'm taking two drugs that I shouldn't take together."

Locating the Best Practitioners

■ **Dr. Koop** Many states have report cards on hospitals. For example, in Pennsylvania, all surgical heart patients in all hospitals are rated as to outcome, and not only that, but you can find out that Dr. Sikes, when he works at St. Francis Hospital, has a mortality of 7 percent, and when he works at Harrisburg General, it's 13 percent or vice versa. You can also find out that he charges patients differently in these different hospitals too. So it becomes an open book, which is, in a sense, good.

A lot of that information can be misinterpreted, and I hate to see *New York* magazine or *Philadelphia* magazine come out with a list of New York's or Philadelphia's 100 best doctors. How do they know? I mean, who do you rank those by? And it's not because I wasn't on the list or that it's sour grapes, but a lot of people are on that list because they used to be on the list or they've been around the longest time or they're the most glamorous or the most innovative. I just think it's very hard to do. A hospital might be the best to have your knee replaced, but you'd hate to have a baby there.

■ **Dr. Lundberg** How to find a new doctor is always a problem. It is possible to get a lot of information on doctors from the Internet, no question. The American Medical Association's master file is on the Internet. You can go on the AMA site and you can search for doctors by name, by location, by specialty location. If you're in the Bronx and you want an ophthalmologist, and you don't have an ophthalmologist, you could punch up the AMA site and punch in New York, ophthalmologist, and on the screen you'd see dozens of ophthalmologists' names and addresses.

You look for one in your neighborhood and punch that one up. You can find out if the doctor is a member of the AMA, if he's done continuing medical education recently, where he went to medical school, where his office is, what his office hours are, whether he takes Medicare patients, whether he takes Medicaid patients, whether he's in managed care or not, what his telephone number is, what his e-mail address is. You might even get a picture of the doctor. All that, right on the Internet.

There are other doctor finders as well. Some states are putting out information about the doctors who have licenses in their state when the information is adverse. If there have been many lawsuits against specific doctors or there have been questions about whether the person should lose his or her license, the state is putting that out. Massachusetts is the only state I know of that is putting that information up on the Internet now. You can find that by going to the Massachusetts Board of Registration in Medicine site [massmedboard.org].

The Spin Doctors

■ **Dr. Lundberg** Online outcome data is coming, but is not here yet. When it is present, it is often jaded by marketing spin. Medical institutions in America are in extreme competition with one another, and they've hired all manner of marketing experts to help them put their best face forward so that patients will come to them for their liver transplants instead of going across town.

Today you can punch up a medical center, punch up a medical school, a hospital, and you can find something online from them. They'll have a home page, and they'll give you a lot of information about what's there. Some of it will be outcome data; whether it's trustworthy, that's another question. Now some states—Pennsylvania is a leader—provide outcome data by hospital. New York provides it by doctor for certain kinds of common procedures. The future is providing patients with the kind of information that a savvy consumer would want in order to decide where to go to have an operation or which doctor to have perform it.

You should know that most patients do not avail themselves of outcome information even if it's available. Most patients, once they receive that information, still don't use it and are influenced by other things when deciding what doctors they choose or what hospitals they choose. They are influenced by what their friends said or what their mothers said or how close is it or is the hospital the right religion or did my sister go there and did she feel good about it or does my brother work there or can my husband visit easily without having to get off work? All those human considerations are elements that really drive patients to the doctor and hospital they select. For most people, the outcome data seems to be almost irrelevant to their decisions.

Dare to Compare?

■ **Dr. Lundberg** For about thirty years I have thought we'd see comparison shopping in my field, which is laboratories. I expected to see the posting of prices for lab tests and patients shopping for value. In fact, it's hardly ever happened at all. A major part of the problem is that the market approach doesn't generally work in medicine since a third party pays for most of the expenses.

Comparison shopping, in terms of the quality of care, is so nebulous and so difficult to define that I think we're a long way from that. I would like that to happen, but the whole business of quality care and how you evaluate it is very complicated, and the average patient hasn't the foggiest notion of how to do that when provided with a mass of data.

Shopping for prescriptions online can save you some money, if you have the time to do it; because of the volume of refills, prices tend to be not only competitive but lower for many things. Of course, this means that the local pharmacy business is likely to be in great turmoil. On the other hand, the big pharmacy chains like Walgreen's have the advantage of being conveniently located for the patient and they give good prices. But if you're away from such convenience, then the Internet's wonderful for ordering things.

Using the Web to Save Money

■ **Dr. Koop** Informed patients, interacting with their doctors, can help to bring down the cost of care. Here's how it works. Suppose your mother has been diagnosed with osteoporosis, and now you realize that your mother could have prevented

> "If you could make prevention glamorous, you'd get the Nobel Prize."

osteoporosis but she never took estrogen after she went through menopause, she never took any additional calcium, and she led a very sedentary life. You are old enough now to correct that before it happens to you. If you have the beginnings of osteoporosis, you can correct it pharmaceutically, but you can raise your daughter so she never even gets into that situation. You're not only treating one generation, but you're practicing prevention for yours that will keep you almost out of trouble, and you can raise your daughter so she has no trouble at all. It's not only something that is applicable to each patient, but you can make it multigenerational.

The thing about prevention is it's cheap, it's effective, but it's not glamorous. If you could make prevention glamorous, you'd get the Nobel Prize.

■ **Dr. Lundberg** The Internet can help people save money by smart shopping, by learning about their own health without having to go to a doctor for many things, by staying healthy, by doing the kinds of things that a good wellness site can teach a person to do and can try to enforce by reminding a person, "Did you weigh yourself today? Punch it in and we'll tell you whether you're okay or not." It's kind of a fancy variation on the talking scale. It tells you, "You better not eat too much today because you ate too much yesterday." The Internet can do all sorts of stuff like that.

Taking Ownership of Your Online Medical Records

■ **Dr. Koop** We have a pilot launch planned of the first ever free medical record owned by the patient. Now most medical records are owned by insurance companies or managed care companies. The idea, under the best possible scenario, would be that this would be your total personal medical record and you own it. It is triply encrypted so that you have to have three passwords to get in. Now you'd want to give your password to your internist, you'd want to give it to your gynecologist, you'd want to give it to your urologist, you'd want to give it maybe to your orthopedist who replaced your knee, but you would also like to give it to the doctor in Aspen when you break your leg skiing because you'd like him to know you have diabetes and how they're treating it. But it's up to you to decide whom you give it to, and of course, you give your pharmacy the ability to gain access to the record.

So the way it works is, again, under the best of circumstances, your internist sees you and he puts on your record, or his nurse puts on your record, what your chief complaint was, what the recommendation was, what the medications were. Then you don't see anybody, say, for two months, but in the meantime you've gotten enamored of herbs for the treatment of whatever, so you're now going to a health food store and you're sort of treating yourself for depression with some St. John's wort. You come home and record that on your personal medical record. You also had a little heartburn, and you heard that Tagamet over-the-counter will get rid of that, so you bought that. Well, you put that in.

Next time you see your doctor, he knows before he sees you that you've been taking herbs, he knows you've been taking Tagamet, and he has your history. I think that is going to make everything so much better for both the doctor and the patient because there are no secrets anymore.

The other thing about the personal medical record is that suppose you had your own chart in your hand while you're waiting to see a doctor, and you're thumbing through it and you see HIV positive and you're not HIV positive. You have a terrible time changing that. But on your personal medical record you can change it. If you want to falsify your medical record, you'll be able to do so, but it's not to your advantage to do that.

■ **Dr. Lundberg** I think medical records on the Internet are perfectly fine as long as there's informed consent and the patient understands that there are risks involved, but the benefits may exceed the risks. A lot of patients don't care that much about whether people know that they have high blood pressure or not. They may care if people know they have HIV or not, and they likely care that people will know they had an abortion or haven't, or if schizophrenia is diagnosed in their family or they're taking medication for depression or if they've had psychiatric care. It might mean that when they come up for a promotion in a company, somebody else gets promoted instead because a lot of supervisors, managers, and companies will use whatever information they can for or against a person.

Course of Action

■ **Dr. Koop** John Baldwin, who is the dean at Dartmouth, has always wanted to have what he calls a "community medical school." In other words, he's interested in educating the patient using the classroom.

In the springtime, on eleven consecutive Tuesday nights, we will have a two-hour session that people can sign up for and get credit for the class. We're not trying to make them medical students, we're trying to empower them with knowledge so they'll be better patients.

I told John that this is a great idea. I said let's take this on the Internet, and we'll call it the Dartmouth Community Medical School. The syllabus will be published on drkoop.com, people will take your exams at the site, and they'll get their certificate from us. We're going to try that and see what happens. We have to have a registration fee, but it'll be minimal. I'm not looking at it as a money maker. I'm looking at making the courses available to the whole country, to the world.

Community Online Centers

■ **Dr. Koop** People who don't have computers have places they can go to get online. For example, the Administration on Aging of the Department of Health and Human Services has 1,200 sites around the country where elderly folks can go to learn things. They also have computers and they have somebody on hand who helps the users.

The other thing that is springing up is called a CHIC [community health information center]; the first of these, that I know of, was in Philadelphia at the College of Physicians. It has a room with a bank of computers, three librarians, books on the wall, all kinds of video, and you walk in there and say, "My child has this, I have this, I'm looking for so-and-so." They'll say, "Here's a book you can take home and read, and why don't we look on the Internet and see what we can find for you? Let's download the information. You can take it home."

The Centers for Disease Control and Prevention came up and looked at it and said this is something that they'd like to see spread around the country.

The Problem with Alternative Medicine

■ **Dr. Koop** I give a lecture currently called "The Ten Major Health Care Issues That We Cannot Avoid Taking with Us to the Next Century." Some are good and some are bad. When I talk about number five, I talk about the explosion of knowledge on the Internet. Then I follow it up by saying many of the people who surf the Internet are looking for alternative or complementary medicine.

The problems are these. One is that the average doctor

knows little about alternative medicine. And although at the present time 30 percent of people are already engaged in at least one form of alternative medicine, only 30 percent of them tell their doctors they're doing it. So 70 percent of the people who are taking herbs and doing other things keep their doctor in the dark, and that's not good.

My plea is that we ought not get rid of alternative medicine out of hand, but take a position of caution and subject every alternative medicine that's suggested to scientific scrutiny and separate the wheat from the chaff. If it's good, let's keep it; if it's bad, let's, for heaven's sake, get rid of it. The difficulty is that all the information on the Internet glows with the same intensity. So you can't tell the difference.

■ **Dr. Lundberg** You can buy alternative medicine books at almost any bookstore. You can go see movies about alternative medicine. But there is more readily available information on the Internet, and that's the main thing with the Internet: at your fingertips there's a library for the world.

I would encourage you, for example, to do this yourself. Go home, punch up "shark cartilage" and find out how many sites there are. The last time I looked, there were seventy-nine sites, and that was about a year ago. My guess is there are 300 Internet sites that are selling shark cartilage. Well, shark cartilage is good for sharks because if they don't have cartilage, their skins collapse. But shark cartilage is good for nothing else that I'm aware of except for selling stuff that people make money off of. There's no evidence that it helps people in any way.

Don't Believe Anything You Read . . .

■ **Dr. Lundberg** For the unsophisticated online user, the panache of the computer and the panache of the Internet are such as to potentially place value on the information that it doesn't deserve.

If there was any point that I'd try to make in this book, in addition to being aware, it is don't attach significance to the

> *"Don't be dazzled by the technology . . . The medium is not the message. The message is the message."*

information you get on the Internet just because it's on the Internet any more than you would if you were hearing it from somebody in a bar, or seeing it on a signpost as you walk to work. Don't be dazzled by the technology. Be appreciative of the technology, but the information is the information. The medium is not the message. The message is the message.

. . . Unless You Follow These Rules

■ **Dr. Lundberg** Number one: Demand that the site tell you who wrote what you're reading. If you can't tell who wrote it, don't read it. Are you going to borrow a book from the library if you don't know the author? When you look at *The New York Times*, most articles have a byline.

Number two: Does the person who wrote the article have a real job? Where's that person from? Is there an e-mail address somewhere in the Atlantic or does this person work at New York Hospital? Who owns the site? A publishing company owns the *Times*; who owns the site you're looking at? Who paid for the information that's up there? It didn't get there for free. Somebody supported it. Who supported it?

Number three: When was the information put there? Is it current or is it from 1843 without attribution, put up in 1995, and shown to be invalid in 1847? If you can't tell when it was put there, when it was updated, don't read it. Are you looking for information or are you looking for entertainment? If you want entertainment, go to the Internet. You can be entertained infinitely. It won't cost you much money, just your connect time. Don't believe any of this stuff unless you can go through that list.

The Next Ten Years

■ **Dr. Lundberg** Ten years from now all credible primary medical information from researchers will be available full text on the Internet for free. The peer review process for validating information as a filter will continue. Developed countries will be Internet savvy and will be using it for whatever purpose. E-commerce will be massive, replacing retail stores en masse for all manner of things, including pharmaceutical products. Doctors and patients will routinely communicate by e-mail once they have an established relationship, replacing visits, replacing telephone calls to a large extent, unless a visit is necessary for a physical examination. Hospitals will be fully automated to a much greater extent than they are now.

There will be consolidation of Internet companies, far fewer than there are now. Many will fail, others will be bought, assumed, merged within all fields, including health information. The internationalization of medicine will have proceeded to an even greater extent.

In some ways the world will be a better place because of better communication, but those people who say that poor communication is a source of most human conflict and who believe that improved communication is a solution for most human conflict will learn that that isn't true. It's simplistic. Ill will, when communicated more effectively, is still ill will.

I believe the quality of medical care in the developed world will continue to be assessed in more and more sophisticated ways, and I believe pressures for the better doctors to become better and the poorer doctors to become better or stop being doctors will, ten years from now, be very substantial.

I believe that consolidation of hospitals and groups of hospitals, and even some medical schools, will continue and that the improved communication brought about by electronic transmission of information will be part of the reason they can consolidate in more efficient ways.

I think we will have extended our average expected life span by another two years, maybe even three or four years, as we hack away at the problem of aging. The Internet is helpful in all of that by improving communication of information so that it can be put into practice faster by doctors and by patients after validation.

Suggested Web Sites

allhealth.com	mayohealth.org
ama-assn.org	medscape.com
cancer.org	nci.nih.gov
drkoop.com	nih.gov
drweil.com	oncolink.com
healthfinder.gov	onhealth.com
intelihealth.com	webmd.com
kidshealth.org	

THREE

MILLIONAIRE TOOLS AVAILABLE TO ALL

I was downsized out of my $125,000 annual income, twenty-six-year career in mid-1995. I was forty-nine. I was computer illiterate and had been diagnosed with Parkinson's syndrome. I was scared, but I had the time to learn the computer and the Internet. I read up on computers, bought the equipment, and researched stock investing. I started with mutual funds and then got into stocks. I made $248,000 my first full year and I'm on track to double that this year.

—**Bob Williams, Pennsylvania**

"In the fall of 1997 I bought Mom a seafood cookbook from Amazon.com. She liked it and wanted another about Italian food. I showed her how to order it from my PC. She said it was fun. Mom was a housewife, raised four kids by herself, and hadn't graduated from high school. She heard about Amazon's stock market activity on TV; since she was familiar with the company, and liked it, she asked me to get money out of her savings and buy 250 shares. In the following two years, the stock skyrocketed, split several times, and gave riches to Mom that she never had before. Recently she bought another book from Amazon; it's about retiring in Palm Springs. She can afford it now.

—**Javier Medrano, California**

When I was a kid financial matters were strictly for grown-ups. Parents didn't talk about money in front of their offspring, at least not *real* money. You might have had a discussion or two about whether it was time for your allowance to be increased from $5 a week to $6, but Mom and Dad were mum about their investments; never mind how the stock market worked.

In school we learned to count using different-colored

plastic chips, each representing the ones, tens, and hundreds column when you were doing calculations. Then came slide rules and later calculators to help us get through numerical challenges. More recently I've felt like I was at the mercy of a stockbroker or loan officer or insurance salesman as they pitched me their service. They functioned in a dual role—expert and salesman—which for me was an uncomfortable combination.

With the advent of the Web and a vast array of financial sites to choose from, we now have new options for managing our finances, and money is no longer a taboo subject. Not only are adults using the Web to manage their budgets, plan for their retirement, and guide their investments, but even schoolchildren are learning the laws of economics and finance by setting up mock investment portfolios that they can track online.

What's making all of this possible is the accessibility of online tools designed to take the trauma out of complex calculations. Want to know how much money you'll need to reach your retirement goals, but unsure of how big a bite inflation will take out of your nest egg? Online calculators let you change parameters as easily as changing TV channels. Arthur Levitt, the Securities and Exchange commissioner, wanted to make it easier for investors to calculate the total costs of their mutual fund investments: Is it better to pick a no-load fund with a low fee or one that charges a high load, but a low expense fee? To help you figure it out, the fund cost calculator is now available on the SEC Web site (sec.gov).

Steven Swartz, president, chief executive officer and editor in chief of *SmartMoney,* is the first to admit that without these sophisticated modeling tools, he wouldn't be doing these calculations either. "Obviously, if you paid attention in calculus class, then you could do it," he laughs, "but who did that and who remembers?" Fortunately these new online tools are there to do all the work for you and, more important, to give you the confidence to create a plan you can follow. Everyone now has access to the tools that were previously used mainly by the rich.

Not only is the Internet making it easy to be a prudent planner, it also makes it possible to create and lose vast sums of money in a single day with just a click. In the last quarter of 1998, one of every seven stock trades in the United States was entered over the Web. This has helped fuel a frenzy of activity, especially in the shares of newly public Internet companies, as some online "day traders" buy and sell 100 or more stocks a day.

More changes are under way to move us closer to the day of global round-the-clock stock trading. Fueled in part by the growth in online investing and the development of electronic trading networks, E*Trade Group, a major online brokerage firm, and Instinet, a stock trading network for institutional investors, announced in August 1999 that in September they would offer small investors the ability to trade stocks between 4 P.M and 6:30 P.M. E*Trade is not the first to take this step; several weeks earlier, Datek Online Holdings announced plans to offer additional trading hours between 4:00 P.M. and 5:15 P.M. for its online customers. Other firms have announced plans to jump into after-hours trading, while Datek has indicated it has plans to offer before-hours trading. For his part, Dick Grasso, chairman of the New York Stock Exchange (NYSE) predicts that "in our lifetime" stock trading will be a twenty-four by seven product—taking place twenty-four hours a day, seven days a week.

And it won't be long before you'll see people in restaurants with wireless, hand-held computers conducting trades, tracking accounts, and receiving real-time quotes. Not everyone, however, will gravitate to these devices. As Charles Schwab, chairman and co-CEO of The Charles Schwab Corporation, says, "Some folks can make these kinds of decisions on the fly. Others need to be sitting at a desk and giving it some thought."

Is it time for you to use the Net to invest or make financial plans? What are the new rules for getting the most out of your money in the Digital Age? Swartz and Schwab have plenty of solid advice to offer to help you thrive in this fast-paced, electronic financial marketplace. And author Alvin Toffer, Bob Pittman of AOL, Ellen Pack of Women.com, George Bell of Excite@Home, and George Gendron of *Inc.* magazine add their thoughts on how the Internet is shaking up the global economy, as well as personal finance.

The New Economy

■ **Alvin Toffler** Overall, the Internet is going to have just an absolutely stunning impact on the economy. If I think about e-commerce, I believe at every step, practically from inception of the idea through production, to advertising, marketing, right on down to delivery, all those costs are going to be cut rapidly. As a result, I think it's going to have a profound impact on the economy and will be a great wealth generator; it's going to make things cheaper for ordinary people, and it's also going to allow ordinary people to become global entrepreneurs.

■ **Dick Grasso** We're very fortunate in this country. We've got 70 million Americans who own equity securities directly, and when one adds indirect ownership, we're probably just a touch above 200 million Americans who participate in the market. As you broaden the reach of the Internet and as you deploy what I'll term the "democratization of capitalism around the globe," I think equities are the tool of the new millennium, the fuel that will build economies, that will restructure economies, and that will raise standards of living to the betterment of the whole world.

We're in a period not unlike a time a hundred years ago. We're in a secular economic shift. A hundred years ago this country went from an agrarian economy to an industrial economy. Today we're going from an industrial economy to an information/technologically driven economy. And that really is a whole reinvention of the American dream, which is based on the Internet and will be very broad in its reach, not only to people here in the United States but also to people around the world.

■ **Bob Pittman** Going online adds a great productivity element to the commerce chain; thereby, I think, improving the economy. The only long, sustained periods of economic growth in this country have been when productivity has made a major jump. The last one was probably the turn of the last century and ushered in about a twenty-year bull market. This is the next jump in terms of productivity; by adding this kind of technology to the commerce chain, we're fundamentally improving productivity, improving earnings, and making life better for everybody.

The Democratization of Consumerism

■ **Dick Grasso** What the Internet has done, fundamentally, is shrink, if not all but eliminate, the separation between producer and consumer. Thus, all of the traditional intermediation models of commerce have to reinvent themselves or recertify the value they add. If you look at the Internet as an enabling tool, there are many who speculate that we will buy books, stocks, suits, as well as read our newspapers or periodicals all through the advent of the Net.

Whether you're in the newspaper business, my business, or the department store business,

> *"Technology has allowed us to reinvent the American dream."*

we're all going to be challenged by the Net to produce that point of added value or to reexcite the consumer to a very different model. Fundamentally that's great for the consumer because it's an empowerment that takes away the artificial separation of oceans or national boundaries or time zones.

The Net will reposition business in terms of products and services and, frankly, it's going to add great value in some places and define where commodity exists in others. That will have a huge impact on pricing, and will have a very positive impact on the global Gross Domestic Product.

Take telecom, for instance, it's like saying for those emerging markets that do not have the wire-based infrastructure, there is no need, necessarily, to build it in a wireless world. So the Net will have a positive effect on emerging markets, but also a very positive effect on us.

We've reinvented America in the last fifteen years. There wasn't a periodical in the mid-1980s that wasn't forecasting the end of America's ability to sell automobiles or to manufacture computer chips or for that matter predicting that financial services were going to be capitalized in any arena other than the United States. Technology has allowed us to reinvent the American dream, and it's still in an embryonic state for us. So while emerging markets and newly developing countries will have a jump-start on their economic models being matured to success, I think it gives America a whole new frontier of opportunity and one that's very exciting.

■ **George Gendron** It's conceivable that one long-term implication of the Internet is that it will accelerate the wealth gap. I don't buy the idea that access to the Internet alone democratizes wealth creation. In fact, I think if anything it can accelerate the distortion. The real question will be whether or not other countries develop the infrastructure required to allow and encourage their citizens to participate in the wealth creation that takes place as a result of the Internet.

We're blessed in this country with an economic system that in elegantly simple ways not only allows and permits people to take risks but encourages and rewards it. We take that for granted; in Europe that is just not the case. There are legal and cultural consequences for failure in different parts of Europe that send a very powerful message, which is, don't try—if you fail, you can lose everything.

We also have the world's most sophisticated capital markets, which means that if you have a good idea, there will always be money to help you get that idea to scale. That's why we have so many companies that didn't exist twenty years ago that are globally dominant players today.

By the Power Invested in You . . .

■ **Steven Swartz** I don't think there's been a more transforming thing for investors than the Internet. The dynamic nature of the Internet allows you to customize advice to your own needs so you are able to figure out, at a moment's notice, how much home mortgage you can afford. Then you can change the parameters and see that if interest rates go to 7.5 percent, you won't be able to afford this house.

It's amazing to be able to go onto the Internet and see how much you have to put in your 401(k) and then see, both graphically and numerically, what you'll have at age sixty-five, based on various inflation parameters. You can even put Social Security in or you can take it out. You can also do an asset allocation and see historically how much money you would have had in any one year or the most you'd have lost or gained in a year.

It's a phenomenal tool, not only for its immediacy but for its ability to allow you to do mathematical equations that none of us really can do, seamlessly, behind the scenes, and to get the results right in front of you. It builds confidence. It gives people the chance to have a plan for themselves, to know whether they're following it or not, and then to visualize where they might be in the future.

■ **Charles Schwab** It used to be that there were three parties when it came to the relationship you had with your finances: you; your money; and your banker, broker, or agent. Technology changes that. No more is there someone standing between you and your finances. Instead, your broker or banker stands beside you for assistance, but you can be firmly in control.

■ **Ellen Pack** Women are taking control of their finances. The way I see it, women spent the seventies gaining social equality, they spent the eighties getting career equality—not that we're done with any of these things yet—and we spent the nineties gaining financial equity. It has only been in this last decade that we have seen women truly take charge of their money.

Women have incomes now that they never had before—the data shows that 48 percent of working wives bring in at least half of their household income. For the first time, women are really focused on: How do I plan for my family? How do I plan for my financial security?

Banking at Home

■ **Steven Swartz** My wife and I use Citibank, and my wife pays most of our bills through the Citibank online program. She stays home with our young son, but she runs all of our finances from the apartment.

We don't pay all our bills online—some stores aren't yet set up to handle online transactions, so I still end up dropping some checks in the mail. While you can't do everything online, more and more this is where we're headed. For the majority of monthly bills that you get, you can even set them up to be paid automatically each month.

Another thing people can do is keep track of their finances online. There are some excellent software programs that you can buy and load on your computer. As long as you're willing to input things like how much you're spending on gas, or what you just paid when you come home from the supermarket, you can track every dime you're spending. These days, with online banking and the ability to download, you don't even have to input as much as you used to because you can download things directly from your online banking account right into your software program.

This is particularly helpful for people who are either retired and on a fixed income or starting out and needing to save. People can be shocked at how much they're spending in restaurants, or for gas, because they have this idea in their minds, I already paid for the car, so the car doesn't cost me anything. Too often people tend to think, only the wealthy people have a need to really track their spending, but actually the rest of us have more of a margin of error.

■ **Charles Schwab** Most people are concerned about future expenses, such as paying for college or their own retirement, and part of their problem is often that they don't know the specific costs or have a specific plan in place to be prepared.

With the Internet you can use an interactive goal planner to identify the issues and put together a specific plan, down to the monthly amount to save.

> *"The Internet is a great tool to empower the individual investor."*

The interactive planner on the Web will do calculations for you, store the information, or allow you to try different "what if?" variations. For example, "What if I save more each month? What if I earn less return than I'm hoping for?" You can even use the Web to set up automatic investments so that the money is being withdrawn and invested regularly. Then, using the tools that the Internet provides, you can monitor the results of your investments and see if you are on target to reach your goals. If not, you can make adjustments.

As for managing an investment portfolio, by using the Internet you have a very direct relationship with your portfolio, knowing why you made decisions, exploring your own ideas, and having the confidence to follow through. It's a great tool to empower the individual investor.

Maximizing Your Savings

■ **Steven Swartz** There are a tremendous number of online tools to help you save. Online calculators help you see how much you'll need for retirement. You can look at your 401K and see graphically how much you'll have to put in to have enough for retirement. You can even see how long your nest egg will survive and when it would run out, based on different spending and inflation levels.

To calculate your kid's tuition there are worksheets online

and recommended portfolios. On our site, you can click on icons with children of different ages; you click on your child's age and you can see a recommended portfolio of how to allocate your funds or stocks. There's a worksheet to check your progress to see if you're putting enough away. You can also find out how to get the most financial aid and then click through to other sites for information on college scholarships and to find the financial aid requirements at different schools.

Ten years ago the modeling tools were available to do many of these calculations, but almost no one could use them because of the math behind them, including me.

The ability to change assumptions is so easy; if I'm saving $10,000 a year and getting 5 percent on that, how much money will I have by the time my son is in college? That's an incredibly sophisticated calculation if you do it with a calculator, but online you just plug it in and the computer does it for you. Maybe a couple percent of the population used to be able to do a calculation like that. Now anybody can go online for free and figure all that out with very well-presented, step-by-step worksheets and calculators, and all the work is done for you.

There's another way of saving money on the Web—through shopping online. I would say there probably hasn't been a better medium yet invented that could save you more money than the Internet regardless of area: finance, travel, regular shopping, you name it.

Not only will you save money, you'll also save time. If you live in the suburbs and you want to buy something for your child, you probably have to drive twenty minutes to the baby store; whereas when my wife orders something online for James it takes her minutes, and certainly no more than the twenty minutes it would take her to drive to the store.

Portfolio Power

■ **Steven Swartz** The portfolios have become so sophisticated they can keep track of your tax liability based on when you made an investment. Most stocks obviously aren't bought on January 1, so the portfolio services can now calculate what your investment return is on various stocks or funds that you bought and take into account when in the year you bought them.

Many financial sites offer tools to help track your investments. On our site, for example, we have two separate features. We have a watch list that allows you to load in the stocks that you are interested in; all you have to do is put the symbol in, and it'll tell you every day whether they're up or down. Then we have a portfolio where you can load in multiple portfolios and track everything, from what your tax liability is to what the gain is on that portfolio since you bought the stocks. You can chart it, you can graph it, you can get up-to-date information on any of the companies or funds that are in your portfolio.

You can also track the Dow or you can track individual sectors. You can visually track the whole market with only a fifteen-minute delay. There's virtually nothing you can't do. But the fascinating thing about the Internet is that it allows you to make your own investments, your portfolios, and your tracking as simple or as sophisticated as your interests would dictate.

Trading All Day, Every Day

■ **Dick Grasso** On an average day, the New York Stock Exchange trades about 770 million shares. More than 90 percent of the orders, which produce about 52 percent of the shares that trade on this exchange, are done on the Super Dot system, our version of e-commerce.

Here's how it works. If you were to call, for example, a Merrill Lynch broker and place an order to buy or sell Lucent Technologies, that broker is online with the NYSE. The moment that order gets entered at the broker's workstation and he or she hits the Send key, my network—which is embedded in the Merrill Lynch network and virtually all other broker-dealers who are members of the NYSE—takes that order from the broker's terminal and delivers it to the mailbox where Lucent happens to trade. There it gets exposed to the auction process, executed, and it's back on your broker's terminal. The total elapsed time for that transaction to take place is 15 seconds. In 1999 more than 90 percent of our orders, producing more than 50 percent of the shares that trade, trade on that electronic model.

As you begin to look at the extension of the trading day and the extension of our e-commerce model, clearly stocks are going to be a twenty-four by seven product. Maybe not in the next two or three years, but certainly in our lifetime because the economy doesn't stop on weekends. The valuation process of all the participants in the marketplace is a continuous one. So our business is going to become a continuous one. Whether a retail investor or an institutional investor, eventually such an investor will have virtually instantaneous access to the NYSE on a twenty-four-hour clock.

Will this create greater risks and rewards for investors? What it does is allow the valuation process to be continuous and, therefore, you do not necessarily have the artificial separation of the market's valuation from a company's performance. Today the NYSE operates only between the hours of 9:30 A.M. and 4 P.M. Eastern time. The companies that we trade are virtually continuously in the commerce mode and, therefore, why should their stocks not be continuously evaluated?

It'll give individual investors, particularly in the near term, the opportunity to stretch their trading day. I think that becomes important when you remember that many of the 70 million Americans who own the 3,100 companies we trade are not sitting at screens, as I am, continuously watching the market. They're out teaching classes or driving buses or flying airplanes, and when they come home, the opportunity to rebalance their portfolio or to add a different mix of risk into their investments will be one that I think they'll be very happy to have.

When will this happen? I think the trading day itself is going to be extended by the primary markets—us and NASDAQ—early in 2000, but certainly no later than the fall of that year. And once you've taken the action to extend the trading day, it's a matter of incrementalizing it to the demand of the marketplace. In other words, if we thought there was a business case to be made for going twenty-four by seven, we would do that. It is important to remember that this is all driven by customer demand. So we will measure the customer demand for the extension of hours, and we will fit our supply (or services) to the demand of the marketplace.

We're not a gate, if you will, of technology. We run the engines twenty-four hours a day, seven days a week. We never shut the system down. We stop trading, but we don't unhook the system. The system is continuous.

Taking Stock of Online Trading

■ **Charles Schwab** Certainly the transaction cost is considerably less expensive online, but that is just the icing on the cake. People don't make the decision to go online based simply on cost considerations. A tremendous amount of time is saved, as well as the long-term benefit of having more control and a more proactive role in their finances.

■ **Steven Swartz** If you want to execute your transactions online, you definitely get a lower commission rate than if you were going to do it over the phone. The most costly way to do a transaction, whether it be a stock or a fund, is to go through a stockbroker. The second most expensive approach would be to go to a discount firm, but to talk to a real person and have him or her do the transaction for you. The third would be to go to a discount firm and do a push-button phone transaction. The least expensive method and thus the best way to save money is to execute all of your transactions online.

The Highs and Lows of Online Trading

■ **Charles Schwab** Have I been surprised by the speed with which online trading has caught on? Yes, we were surprised by the pace at which investors adopted the Internet. In fact, the pace was so fast that some of our customers suffered through occasional technical glitches that resulted when we added additional capacity to deal with the rapid growth. It's been pretty amazing.

Look at the length of time it has taken radio or even TV to reach a mass audience. The impact of the Internet has grown so much faster and, with that, the growth of online investing. But looking back, it's not so surprising the way the Web has captured people's imaginations—it's just such a fabulous tool, especially for investing.

The benefits are clear: the Internet offers access to great

information and research tools; it offers greater ways to empower people; it puts the individual in the driver's seat and levels the playing field. The risks are the same as before, investors need to understand themselves before they take any actions. Investing is about the long term, about having goals and setting up a plan to reach them. The Internet doesn't change that—it just gives you tools to help plan and execute.

Is online trading for everyone? No. There will always be a place for very personalized one-on-one advice and money management.

■ **George Bell** I really was surprised, though probably shouldn't have been, by the phenomenon of retail stock trading on the Internet. Just the magnitude of it, how many people are doing it, and with what frequency, was unexpected. If you take the daily trading volume averages of Excite@Home and Yahoo! together, just picking two public companies, they would exceed the daily trading volumes of all the broadcast networks, and that includes General Electric as a parent of NBC. And both these companies are less than four years old.

■ **Steven Swartz** Right now active online trading is still for people with a very high-risk appetite because there are still problems with the system. I find it's easier to make a phone call. There's such a Wild West nature to the online brokerage game; they're all expanding faster than they should be just

> "I haven't seen a teller in my bank in probably fifteen years and that's the way purchases of mutual funds and stock will go."

trying to grab market share. So we've seen systems shutting down and some horror stories where somebody thought they bought 100 shares and they ended up buying 1,000 shares.

The savings for the average person aren't worth it until the systems improve, but they're going to fix those problems over the next couple of years. It will be just like the way we went from seeing a teller to using ATMs. I haven't seen a teller in my bank in probably fifteen years and that's the way purchases of mutual funds and stock will go.

Day Trading

■ **Dick Grasso** You have to separate the risks of online trading from day trading and online applications of financial services. Day trading is, in fact, the shortest format of risk one can assume in the equities marketplace. Some do it well and some do it very poorly, but the marketplace is a great arbiter of that—if you do it poorly for long enough, you won't be doing it. That differs from the online application of financial services, which is simply an enabler and, I think, broadens the category to many more consumers.

> "Day trading is, in fact, the shortest format of risk one can assume in the equities marketplace."

Junk Bond Junkies?

■ **Charles Schwab** Just because people have access to something does not mean they will abuse it. At the same time, there is no question that investing online can be fun and exciting. Investors have to temper the fun of it with an appreciation that investing has very serious implications for their future. It's not a game.

■ **Steven Swartz** Is there a risk that some people will get addicted to online investing? Absolutely, but I think that the naysayers of the world can take that too far. Potentially, anything's addictive. Good food is addictive, and then people get fat. But I believe the benefits far outweigh the risks.

Financial Data for All

■ **Charles Schwab** A lot of online data that is available is free and will continue to be free. The data will become more of a commodity. But good useful information is different from data; it has a layer of interpretation or a layer of intelligence added. Some of that kind of information will go for a premium. Fortunately for the investor, the technology is forcing the industry to reevaluate the old model of hoarding information.

> *"Fortunately for the investor, the technology is forcing the industry to reevaluate the old model of hoarding information."*

Picking a Site

■ **Steven Swartz** There are a lot of sites that let you enter your stock portfolio and then track your progress. So, how do you know which one to use? Well, I think that you'll find that some sites are aimed at different investors. Let's say you're a trader, you really want to trade every day, and you want news minute-to-minute about small stocks. Well, there are a couple of sites like cbs.marketwatch.com or thestreet.com that would probably take care of your needs. If you just want the most sophisticated portfolio out there, I would say the Microsoft site [moneycentral.msn.com] is the most sophisticated.

We would position our site largely for a baby boom audience, for people who want sophisticated information on stocks and funds, but who also have a lot of life questions at the same time about 401(k)s, retirement, or taxes. There's a site called the Motley Fool [fool.com] that mainly aims itself at the younger, generation X crowd. Their approach is very irreverent. They'll go into such basics as paying down credit card debt and things that we might leave aside.

Are Brokers an Endangered Species?

■ **Charles Schwab** Someone still needs to know the needs of the customers and help them when they have a problem or need advice. Technology will never replace that.

■ **Steven Swartz** Any intermediary business is threatened right now, whether it's a retailer coming between the maker and the consumer or a translator like journalism or a broker coming between the stock and the client. Some will find a way to win and to use the Internet as an even more powerful vehicle.

Right now on the Internet we're selling over a thousand subscriptions a month to our magazine. To the extent that this keeps growing, that's a powerful aid to the profitability of the magazine versus what we have to spend mailing out millions of pieces of mail to try to get people to subscribe. Realtors are running an ad campaign currently where they stress that you could be at work while they're selling your house. Obviously, they're feeling the threat from the Internet where you can buy and sell without the intermediary.

Do Your Homework

■ **Dick Grasso** If an individual is going to be a direct investor without the guidance of a qualified financial intermediary, then that individual had better do his or her homework because while the Net becomes a great facilitator, it also becomes a potential threat to the financial shenanigans that can go on in chat rooms and places where services may be offered that are not consistent with the objectives of that individual. The Internet is an enabler, but it also creates an obligation on the part of the consumers to be educated consumers, to do their homework, and to make certain they are not the target of some fast-buck artists who operate anonymously through technology.

Finding an Online Broker

■ **Charles Schwab** Know your own needs first. Are you just shopping for the lowest cost? Do you trade often? Are you looking for a complete package of services? Do you need the support of people on phones and in branches? Find a broker that will best suit your needs and whom you trust.

■ **Steven Swartz** A number of sites rank brokers. At our site, for example, you can look at our overall favorite or use an application we provide that allows you to select the characteristics in a discount broker or an online broker that are best for you, and then it will reshuffle the order to show you what would probably be the best choice for you.

The New Rules of Investing

■ **Steven Swartz** Years ago something positive would happen to a stock and it would have moved up 20 percent over the course of a couple of weeks. In the first move it would be up a few bucks and you could think it was probably a positive thing, and I might recommend that stock. Now not only do you get the full run-up, you get the overreaction. So something positive happens to a stock and it may be deserving to move that stock 20 percent, but it'll move 40 or 50 percent in one day. Of course, the same thing happens on the downside.

■ **Charles Schwab** No doubt investors have come to expect more and expect it instantly. The bar has risen and will continue to go up. At Schwab, we've been doing a lot to help investors understand both the strengths and the limitations of Internet trading—and it's important that investors see both sides. The government regulators, like the Securities and Exchange Commission, have been talking about this too. For example, we think investors need to have a better understanding of what happens when they invest online and adjust their expectations accordingly. Another example, quotes on the computer screen do not necessarily reflect the price that will be confirmed once a trade hits the floor of the exchange. Investors should be aware of the various tools available to them, such as stop and limit orders, and the repercussions of market phenomena, like fast-moving markets.

■ **Dick Grasso** Some things never change. In the Digital Age prudent investors are investors who do their homework, who understand, first and foremost, why they're in the marketplace and what the horizontal objectives of being a risk taker are. Are you investing for the education of your children, your retirement, to buy a home? Whatever the fundamentals that cause one to be in equities need to be defined, need to be constantly reevaluated.

And most important, once that process and the selection of investments that fit the risk profile to those objectives is elected, the importance of staying the course, not being in any way what I'll call a knee-jerk reactor to the market of the moment, is imperative.

Bill Paying Will Get Easier

■ **George Bell** One of the new things that's coming is bill presentment and the manipulation of certain types of vendor relationships online. In the same way that you have an Excite start page—with modules such as My Sports, My Stocks, My News, My Weather—why can't you have My Communication Services? Then you can manage your pager, your cell phone, and your home telephone lines, change bill presentment, as well as features of each one of those agreements that you have through a start page.

For example, I've got a bill this month from AT&T, and it says I owe them forty-five bucks for some long-distance services, and I agree I'm going to pay that bill online. But I click on the bill and I see that, based on my long-distance patterns, I'm buying the wrong program from them. I shouldn't be buying the unlimited, all-you-can-eat model, I should be doing something different. In the future, I'll go in, look at their rate plans, alter my plan, verify that I've altered that plan to conform to my telephone use, and then have that become part of my bill cycle in the next month on my start page. That could be done with many different things: you could change the features of your mortgage or the features of your auto loan or your lease.

With a persistent connection into the home, as you get with a cable modem, there will be no reason that the Web can't begin to operate the day-to-day workings of your house from the "always on" connectivity. We've already looked at software that would allow you to turn your lights on and off, open and close the garage door, turn on the washing machine or your coffee machine—things like that. Because the cable modem connection is persistent and always on, it becomes another aspect of personalization that you could build right onto your start page, a module labeled My House.

When will this happen? There were a million broadband subscribers at the end of 1999, just on the @Home service. It'll probably be three years before 10 million homes have broadband. To get adoption of the broadband platform to accelerate, access costs will have to be driven down. Vendors and advertisers will underwrite that access to get consumer loyalty and then will make the higher margin off the services offered to consumers.

The Future of Financial Markets

■ **Dick Grasso** Increasingly it is the individual investor that is the staple of this marketplace. While people oftentimes say institutions are the bulk of the day-to-day trading volume, which is true, it's important to remember that institutions simply represent a collective of individuals. So putting that aside, individual investors' direct participation is now at an all-time record level, almost 70 million Americans, unlike any country on the face of the globe.

In trying to envision what the market structure will look like ten years from now, the one thing I can predict with certainty is—nothing like it does today. And I say that because if you look back ten years ago, the NYSE averaged 150 million shares a day; we were the world's second largest market to Tokyo; and we had fewer than 90 non-U.S. companies traded on this exchange. Here we have left the decade as the world's largest equities market by a factor of almost five and we have almost 400 non-U.S. companies producing almost 9 percent of our average daily volume, which is approaching 800 million shares a day.

Technology has become a strategic enabler for us, and who's to say what the technology will be ten years from now? I think it's most important that we embrace technology as a tool for the constant rebuilding of any form of commerce to better serve consumers. Those who do that effectively will have business models that will flourish 10, 20, 100 years from now. Those who deny it will simply be a part of history.

Most Popular Web Finance Sites

(Source: Nielsen//NetRatings)

americanexpress.com   discovercard.com   nextcard.com
ameritrade.com   etrade.com   novusnet.com
bankofamerica.com   fidelity.com   quicken.com
bigcharts.com   firstusa.com   quote.com
bloomberg.com   fool.com   schwab.com
citibank.com   marketwatch.com   smartmoney.com
cnbc.com   multiexinvestor.com   vanguard.com
cnnfn.com   newsalert.com   wellsfargo.com
datek.com

10 Sites to Help You Save Money

(Excerpted from *SmartMoney,* April 1999)

Autos:	carpoint.msn.com
Credit cards:	bankrate.com/smm
Gardening:	garden.com
Gourmet food:	greatfood.com
Homes:	realtor.com
Mortgages:	E-Loan.com
Insurance:	insuremarket.com
Long distance phones:	trac.org
Wireless phones:	Wirelessdimension.com
Travel:	biztravel.com

THE EDUCATION REVOLUTION

After my senior year of high school, I was extremely nervous about starting life at a new school. I thought it would be hard to adjust and meet new people. Two weeks before starting school I decided to instant message another incoming freshman who also came from a small high school and was going to study journalism. Chase and I stayed in close communication, even after we arrived at school. We didn't meet until he surprised me by suggesting we go for a walk. I knew from the moment we met that we would continue to be friends. We became each other's support system for surviving the first semester of college.

—**Lauren Gusman, Ohio**

My nursing career took a downward spiral when nerve compression in my arms forced me to give up hospital nursing, my job for almost twenty years. I had no bachelor's degree, so my options were limited. I decided to pursue a degree and enrolled in a program for nurses. Financial restraints made it difficult for me to pay for school, but through the Internet I found a scholarship site. I received a scholarship that will enable me to continue classes in the fall. Thank you Internet!!

—**Susan Bagaglia, Rhode Island**

For many of us, school recalls a time when learning meant repeating the multiplication tables over and over until you could recite them in your sleep; memorizing the dates of the major battles that took place during two World Wars, along with the names of the generals that led them; and practicing cursive writing until the teacher was satisfied with the slant of our letter *S*. The school day ended promptly at 3 P.M., followed by milk and cookies when you arrived home. Afterward you'd undergo some more drill and practice with your mom to prepare you for a spelling quiz the next day.

Learning was largely confined to brick-and-mortar buildings and was controlled by teachers, librarians, and parents. The system worked reasonably well, and generations of students educated in this fashion went on to become leaders to yet another crop of kids eager to follow in their footsteps.

As we enter the twenty-first century, the educational system is being turned upside down as educators search for new ways to prepare students to become knowledge workers, able to seek and find answers independently and perform in an unstructured environment. Futurist Alvin Toffler says, "Education itself has to be completely reconceptualized. It's not what we call education today." For his part, Halsey Minor, founder, chairman, and CEO of CNET, notes that while change in education has been slow, it is coming. He speculates that one day, school ratings might be widely available on the Internet, forcing underperforming schools to get their acts together. And Bob Pittman of AOL believes going online will be "the great equalizer" for education.

The public school system has come under attack for failing to educate our children for the Information Age. School systems are scrambling to outfit students and teachers with computers and Internet access, but many teachers are ill-prepared to incorporate these tools into their lesson plans and overcrowded classrooms. The old methods just don't cut it anymore for a workplace that's increasingly built on the ability to make quick decisions under intense pressure.

"The whole world is filled with wild cards and when somebody deals you one, your capacity to handle that, to play it effectively, is going to determine your success," says David Thornburg, Ph.D., expert on educational technology and director of the Thornburg Center for educational research. "An educational system that's built around showing people how to deal with wild cards effectively looks very different from an educational system that is based on a glamorized form of Trivial Pursuit, where you're given a whole bunch of disconnected tidbits of information for the sole purpose of giving them back on a test at the end of the year."

Through his center, Dr. Thornburg conducts research and provides staff development in the areas of educational futures, multimedia, communication, and learning through multiple modalities (including language, movement, images, sounds). His extensive experience has led him to rethink how schools, teachers, parents, and students need to prepare to meet the challenges of the future. He goes so far as to suggest that textbooks could be eliminated for some subjects and the savings, in part, used to purchase laptops for every child.

Thornburg is not alone in thinking about how to revamp education. Linda Roberts, director of the Office of Educational Technology and special adviser to the secretary of the U.S. Department of Education, thinks about little else. Roberts, a former teacher, knows it's not enough to provide Internet access to all the schools, a job that will be completed in 2000. She knows that to get the most educational benefit, every classroom also needs to be connected.

Rapid progress has been made, with 51 percent of classrooms linked to the Internet at the end of 1998, up from only 3 percent in 1994. However, schools with a minority enrollment of 50 percent or more lag behind, with only 37 percent of their classrooms networked. Now that students and teachers are gaining access, the next pivotal step is to focus on how technology is integrated into the curriculum. And to that end, school budget money must be set aside to provide teacher training and support.

The most recent Department of Education budget placed a great emphasis on teacher education. In fact, a new program was launched called "Preparing Tomorrow's Teachers to Use

Technology" with $75 million budgeted in 1999 alone. Says Roberts, "It's an amazing amount of money to get in a first-year program." But when compared to the progress that other sectors of the economy have made with technology investments—such as banking, insurance, or medicine—Roberts notes the investment in education is still at the "bare margin."

Roberts travels frequently to schools across the United States and more recently to other countries to see how educators are tying technology and student achievement together. She weaves a fascinating tale of hope and progress below, even though she knows that much more still remains to be accomplished.

In addition to changing how and what people learn, digital technology is also being used to transform test taking and other processes involved in higher learning. For example, college applications can now be sent in bulk over the Internet to a student's schools of choice; number two pencils are not needed for the Graduate Record Examinations (GRES), which are now taken on a computer; and if you or your child is applying to business school, expect that at least two essay questions on the Graduate Management Admission Test will be scored by both a human being and an electronic robot called the E-rater.

And if you thought schooling was over once you got your diploma, think again. We're about to enter a new era of life-long learning, fueled by easy access to virtual classes and universities that believe education should never stop.

24-Hour School Day

■ **David Thornburg** If we take a look at the tremendous number of computers that are coming into children's homes, and the large percentage of those that are connected to the Internet, we can see that students of all ages will have access to educational resource materials twenty-four hours a day, and their learning time is going to far exceed the time they spend in school. The potential is for learning to become an anytime, anywhere experience.

That's very positive. Some children really get excited about a subject and want to pursue it in some depth, and suddenly

> *"The potential is for learning to become an anytime, anywhere experience."*

the bell rings at school, they have to go home, and they are deprived of the people and materials they needed to explore this particular topic. With the Internet they have the capacity to support their learning interest a little bit more. I think that's one of the greatest potential impacts of the Internet on education.

Let's say that you're a history student, the Library of Congress has a site called the American Memory Project [memory.loc.gov/ammem/amhome.html] that is making digital copies of their historical collection available for free to anybody who wants access to them over the Internet.

What makes this access tremendously powerful is that if you're a child living in Washington, D.C., you're not allowed into the Library of Congress unless you're 18 or older. Electronic access, which is available to anyone in the world, provides the opportunity to use materials that you couldn't even use in person.

For example, I was fascinated to look at the correspondence between Alexander Graham Bell and his fiancée around the time that he was beginning his demonstrations of the telephone. Suddenly, this historical event took on a very human face when I saw the documents written in his own handwriting describing how people were reacting to his demonstrations. It made the history of science come alive.

The volume of material that is available, of absolutely

incredible quality, is just mind-boggling. In addition to the Library of Congress, you've got the National Archives, which is doing a similar sort of a test [nara.gov/nara/nail.html]; NASA, which has done an amazing job in earth sciences [earth.nasa.gov and earthobservatory.nasa.gov] and planetary sciences [nasa.gov]; and the U.S. Department of Education [ed.gov/free], which has made available, for free, complete lessons that tie into just about any subject, at any grade level, that a student, teacher, or parent would want to explore.

Access = Achievement

■ **Linda Roberts** There is a growing body of evidence that is being collected in the United States, and from other countries as well, that points to positive effects with technology when the teachers know what they are doing, when they are trained, when the content and the applications mesh with the educational objectives, and when the quality of the content or software is high.

There's been a long-term study (focused on reading and writing) of students in West Virginia who have had five years experience in their classrooms with computers. Overall there are gains in student achievement that can't be attributed solely to technology, but the technology impact is clear. The gains are on the order of 10 percent a year, but what's particularly significant is the greatest gains are being made by the students with the lowest achievement.

There's another study that's just been done in Idaho that looks at mathematics. This study actually has what we all would love to see more of—experimental and control groups; there were classrooms that had computers and classrooms that didn't, but they all had the same curriculum. The kids who had computers show very, very significant post-test gains.

The question is, What's happening here? First, the students spend more time learning, they're more engaged. Second, teachers have a way to help kids understand concepts that go beyond print or simply telling them. Mathematics is a very interesting area because you can present simple concepts (like addition or subtraction) and advanced concepts (like algebra or calculus) graphically. I remember how I learned algebra—I did endless numbers of equations and rarely drew a picture of what the equation represented. With graphing capabilities and software applications linked to key concepts we can give students new ways to master skills and acquire a deeper understanding of concepts.

Who Will Teach the Teachers?

■ **David Thornburg** Once you bring the Web into the classroom, the fundamental model of education shifts. The teacher now has the opportunity to become a facilitator of the learning process rather than just the content expert, someone who can be more involved in asking questions than in providing answers.

That's different from what has historically been asked of teachers, and so they will face new challenges. First is making sure that our classrooms are properly wired for Internet access, and that there is ample technology so students don't have to wait in line to gain access to information. But even more important than that is making sure that educators have the requisite staff development to be able to do their job effectively. You can't just bring technology into a classroom, turn on the power, and expect that anything is going to change—except the electrical bill—unless you provide really good staff development.

That means working with the educators, acknowledging

their expertise in terms of curriculum, in terms of teaching methodology, but then saying: You're going to need some new skills to use this new technology. We've done an adequate job doing this, but I don't think we've done as good a job as we need to do. A lot of that comes down to funding.

■ **Linda Roberts** What's really encouraging to me over the last decade is that there is a growing sense that technology isn't something you do in a laboratory. In other words, you don't go to the computer lab and expect that the skills that you're developing or the way you're thinking about information carries over into the classroom. From what I can tell around the country, there's a growing effort to get resources, computers, and connections to classrooms, which means the real burden is on the teacher. Our focus then has to be on professional development.

I am convinced that we really have to redouble our efforts in this area. Not just to help the teachers in the classrooms today, but to focus on the teachers who are coming into the classrooms tomorrow, because tomorrow the technology is going to be there.

We were able to convince the folks at the Office of Management and Budget and at the White House that if we didn't act now, and invest in professional development, we'd really be missing a very important opportunity since we expect to replace about 2 million teachers over the next ten years, out of a total of 3.5 million teachers currently in the system.

Education Begins at Home

■ **Alvin Toffler** Where do kids actually learn? They learn from the media, they learn from their experience, they learn in the streets, they learn from each other, they learn from parents, they learn from all over the place—the school very often being the least of it. It seems to me that one model that we might think about for education in the future is to somehow bring together the media and the computer, not so much in the classroom as in the kitchen where the whole family has access to it. While I don't oppose

> "We are, in effect, cheating our children of a relevant education because we are still preparing them for the factories that aren't going to be there."

wiring of the schools, I think putting it in the kitchen is much more important, where you have the economic and technological levels to make that possible.

I would like to bring together media, the computer, the family, and distributed intelligence from the community. Every community has people in it who know things. There's a carpenter who knows how to make things out of wood, retired pilots, accountants, doctors, and there are nurses. These people have knowledge they can share with kids, but they're not allowed to because they're not teachers. What we need to do is harness that distributed intelligence in the community and bring it together with a teacher—who by this time is trembling about losing his or her job—becoming, in effect, the coordinator or facilitator.

It's kind of a utopian model I suppose, but I believe that replicating the factory-style schools that we now have is wrong. The schools we have were a magnificent, humanizing, democratizing step forward, but they really prepare kids to work in a factory: to do repetitive work all day, to show up on time when the bell rings because when the whistle blows at the gate, they have to be on time. You're measured going in and you're inspected like toothpaste coming out. The function of education is to simulate the future the children will live in, but what happens if the adults don't know what kind of future kids are going to make?

We did a book called *Learning for Tomorrow* in which we used the example of a tribe that has lived on the bank of a river for 1,000 years. The parents have educated the kids over the generations and taught them to build canoes, to fish, to cook that food, and to grow the kinds of plants that grow on the banks of the river. The entire culture, the entire way of life is built on that river. What they don't know is that 500 miles upstream somebody's building a dam. Now, how relevant is everything you've just been teaching your kids?

I believe we're in that situation. We are, in effect, cheating our children of a relevant education because we are still preparing them for the factories that aren't going to be there.

Grading Schools

■ **Halsey Minor** Ultimately I believe that the advantages the Internet offers both consumers and businesses in many different areas is sufficient to compel virtually anybody or any institution to change. I'm watching them fall one after another, and education is one of the institutions that is very, very difficult to change and slow to change.

Some of the ways it will change are apparent, others not so obvious. For instance, using the Internet to connect students and teachers is a pretty clear opportunity to get parents to see what other kids are doing. Another less obvious way would be if somebody went in and just compiled statistics about how good schools were and put that up on the Web, so that parents and the press could come in and get information about the schools in their area.

I've been party to some conversations where people have talked about doing in education what has been done with pollution; where the press, for example, can very easily find out the major pollutants in their area and who's generating them. All of a sudden the people who run the companies that are generating the pollution become a whole lot more serious about trying to cut down when it becomes public knowledge. The ability to distribute that kind of information, and make it available to a degree that's never been done before, will create a whole new level of accountability.

Integrating the Internet into the Curriculum

■ **Linda Roberts** How do you prepare and support teachers? The best strategy puts the technology tools or the software applications or the online resources that one would consider using in the context of what you're already teaching. It's not preparing to teach technology as a separate subject, but preparing teachers to think about where the Internet resources fit into their teaching of history or geography or the arts.

The really well-designed programs recognize that this is a new set of tools in the teacher's toolbox, and that there's a progression that teachers go through in gradually incorporating more resources and ideas into their teaching.

States, like Ohio, talk about teachers who go through three stages: the novice stage, then the practitioner stage, and finally the expert stage, where teachers are actually thinking about software or applications they want to develop. I would guess that about 10 percent of the teachers in this country are at that expert stage. Another half of the teachers already have some knowledge of technology, but a vast number of them are really only at the beginning; this is where we ought to be focused.

How Parents Can Help

■ **David Thornburg** There's a lot that parents can do to help. Parents need to realize that their child's teacher has their child's best interest at heart. Parents can work closely and supportively with teachers, and if a parent has a particular set of skills that could be of use to the teacher, don't be bashful, let the teacher know about your skills and whether you've got some time to help out. It's very hard in a classroom, even with twenty-eight children in it, for one teacher to provide the sort of support needed for somebody working on the Internet.

Three Fundamental Skills Everyone Needs

■ **David Thornburg** Sometimes we confuse the ability to use technology with knowing how to use it effectively. Kids seem incredibly facile with computers, but just because they know how to log on to the Internet or know how to install software or get the machines up and running, doesn't mean that they know how to use them effectively in an educational setting.

In order to use the Internet effectively in education there are three fundamental skills that everyone needs to have, and this includes parents, teachers, and students.

First, you need to know how to find information. The amount of information available on the Web is staggering. Knowing how to pick out the morsels that are of interest to you is very, very important and has to be taught.

Second, you need to be taught how to determine if what you've found is relevant. Let's say, for example, you're interested in studying the moons of Jupiter. Once you start getting into NASA's Web site, you might suddenly find yourself fascinated with what's happening with the international space station. The next thing you know you've spent two or three hours exploring something that isn't relevant to your task.

The third, and most important, skill that everyone has to acquire is to know how to figure out if what you've found is accurate or not. There's a tremendous amount of misinformation on the Web just as there is in many parts of our lives. In the physical world we have ways of knowing, or at least suspecting, that information is accurate. Sometimes when we see something on a computer screen, we automatically give it credit that it may not deserve at all.

How to Search

■ **David Thornburg** It's important to realize that there is no complete search engine of the Web. But there are some search engines that really do a good job of helping narrow down information in a particular subject area for you. There are really two types of tools that I think are valuable.

Directories are organizations of sites, and one that's absolutely wonderful for helping younger children do research is Yahooligans [yahooligans.com]. Yahoo! [yahoo.com], the parent of Yahooligans, is also a terrific directory. What's nice about these directories is that the sites that are listed in them have already been screened by somebody for relevance. It doesn't necessarily mean that they're the most up-to-date or the most accurate, but at least they're germane to your search, and that's a big plus.

When you want to get more specific, and you can also use Yahoo! in this way, I like to use AltaVista [altavista.com]. When it does a search it ranks the results in such a way that, from my experience, it guarantees that you're going to find something relevant to the question that you asked within the first screen or two of responses. AltaVista also has a specialty photo search that allows you to bring up a whole bunch of thumbnails [miniature representation of images], and when you find one that you like, you can click on it and get the original picture, which you can download and use.

Is It Relevant?

■ **David Thornburg** If you want to be sure your kids are using the Web effectively, especially the younger ones, you want to be with them as they're doing their research. This is assuming that they're doing it from home. That way, when a child goes down a path that doesn't appear to be relevant, before the child clicks the mouse to go someplace else, you could say, "Tell me what you're thinking when you see this site. Is this helping with your project or is it not helping, or how did you get here?"

By doing it in the form of a question rather than just saying, "This doesn't have anything to do with your project," it forces the student to think about what he or she is doing and not just react to what you're saying.

By the way, recreational Web surfing is a lot of fun, and I think there's a place for it. I'm just talking about the situation where a student has a specific project and some time pressures for completing it.

One of the pieces of advice that I give educators is to be sure that kids do not even gain access to the Web on school time until they have written down why they're going onto the Web, what they hope to find, and what strategy they'll use for finding it.

Is It Accurate?

■ **David Thornburg** In many cases it's very, very hard to figure out whether information is accurate. What I like to do when I'm working with teachers is take them to a Web site that has obviously incorrect information in it; usually a satirical or parody site. People will see a fake news story and they'll laugh because they know that it's fake. Then I'll ask them to tell me why they know that the story is wrong, and they'll tell me how it stretches the realm of plausibility too much or that a story of this magnitude would have appeared in another medium. I'll write that down—lack of corroborating evidence. Someone will say, "I've never heard of this particular source of information." Okay, unverifiable source. We start coming up with a set of criteria that would apply to evaluating the veracity of any information. It's just a matter of common sense—can you check the source, can you see if you find corroborating evidence, do you have a way of contacting the author to get some background on this piece of information?

It turns out that you do have some Web tools available to you that you may not have with a printed document. With a newspaper you can call and ask to speak to the reporter who did the story. With a Web page your browser usually has on one of its menus something called page information (in the case of Netscape Navigator it's under the view menu). This gives you background on that particular page of information and tells you when it was posted so you know if it is current, and in some cases it will give you more information about who did the posting.

A Tale of Two Classrooms

■ **Linda Roberts** We need to give students an opportunity to be critical users of information. We could easily be drowned by the weight of all the information that is available and "garbage in, garbage out." It's what we choose to do with the technology that is so critical.

I'll give you an example. I was in two high schools recently, and I was struck by the difference in these two schools. In one school the biology and environmental science teacher was an expert on Web-based learning resources. Before students were free to search the Web, they were clear about their assignment. The question was whether some environmental indicators have improved over time or have they gotten worse? She didn't just say to the students, "Go on the Web and find out." She very deliberately said, "I have bookmarked the sites I want you to go to and your job is to evaluate the data, and with your team, write a status report."

Now there was a lot of controversy. The students were getting mixed information from these various sites, but they were credible sites, and one of the parts of the assignment was to evaluate the reliability of the information.

I was in another school, in the same state, on the same day, and the students had been given an assignment to use the Web to find information on a number of different topics. I stopped at one student's workstation and said, "What are you doing?" He said, "I'm looking up information about wetlands." I said, "What have you got?" He said, "I've gotten lists." I asked him, "What are you going to do?" He was really great because he was very honest, and said, "Well, I don't know what to do. All I have is thirty minutes. I'm going to try to look down this list and figure out if there's anything that looks more promising than anything else, but to tell you the truth, it's going to be pretty random."

I said, "I think you're going to learn something in this process, and I want you to think about whether or not you ought to have a different set of searching strategies by the time you're finished."

Then I went to his teacher and said, "How have you pre-pared these students to use the technology?" He said honestly, "I'm worried about it. I don't know if this is the right way to do it. I think they're overwhelmed." I said, "I think they are too. Are you overwhelmed?" He replied, "Yes, to be quite honest. This isn't the right way to do this."

I suggested to him that he look at a couple of Web sites that were focused on areas that he was interested in and that were geared for teachers. The second thing I told him was he was paired with this other high school I had just visited that had more experience. I suggested he e-mail a couple of the people and ask them for advice about how to introduce his students to the Internet in powerful ways. But before that, I told him he should leave some time, either that day or the next, to talk to the students about their experiences, and make something out of their stories, not just leave it as a random event.

How Young Is Too Young?

■ **Linda Roberts** I've been in schools where young children are using the Internet effectively with strong guidance from their teachers. Recently I visited a first-grade classroom at Portage Path Elementary School in Akron, Ohio, where there was one computer and a large screen. Students were gathered with John Bennett, their teacher, to talk about the morning's weather. John led the discussion as the class watched the weather patterns on the National Weather Service Web site. They talked about the direction the rain was coming from.

I was pretty amazed because these were first-graders who understood cloud patterns and could track directions—north, south, east, and west. I remarked, "John, when I taught kids this age, I was lucky if we could put up a little cloud on the daily calendar." He said, "We do that too, Linda, but my kids understand how to read a weather map." I said, "You could do this with television too." He said, "Yes, we could, but with access to the Internet, we can go to the weather when I'm ready to go to the weather, and we can make this useful."

Does this mean that young children should spend all their time on computers? Not at all! The children in John Bennett's room are engaged with books, crayons, counting blocks, musical instruments, plants, animals, and all sorts of tools that help them understand their world and learn to read, to write, to do math, to draw, to enjoy music, and to think!

■ **David Thornburg** People often ask, "At what age should a child be allowed go online and how much time should he or she be permitted to spend there?"

I think that any time a child can do something in the real world, as opposed to doing it on the Web, they really ought to. I would hate to see a kid visiting a Web site that had a simulation of kite flying on it when it was a lovely windy day outside and the child has the resources to go and build a real kite and fly it. It's important that kids interact with other children and with the physical world. I don't think that it's a good idea for kids to have virtual experiences to the exclusion of physical ones.

That said, some kids are more introspective, more self-directed as learners, and for them the Web could be a very powerful tool from a fairly young age. Generally, if toddlers know about the Web it's because one or both of their parents are engaged in using it. There are some wonderful places that kids can go and develop some of the skills in navigating and clicking around on the Web.

So where is the crossover point? I think you need to take the question on a case-by-case basis. When I was a kid in high school, we didn't have the Web, but the boys had cars. A lot of

> *"I would hate to see a kid visiting a Web site that had a simulation of kite flying on it when it was a lovely windy day outside and the child has the resources to go and build a real kite and fly it."*

my friends spent every spare minute working on their cars, and that meant to the exclusion of having a social life, to the exclusion of dating, to the exclusion of hanging out.

Parents are always concerned when we see our kids get sucked up in something that we may not have as deep a grasp of as we'd like. We want to be sure that our kids are having an experience that's going to be beneficial to their overall life, not just as a student or as somebody who's interested in technology, but as a balanced human being.

Are there things that little kids could be doing on the Web that are good for them? Yes, probably so. I would say that the increased likelihood, though, is that the effective use of this technology with children increases with the age of the child. Certainly by the time you get to middle school and high school the educational resources available are so compelling that kids really need to have access to this tool, and they need to know how to use it effectively.

Do You Know What Your Child's Web Page Looks Like?

■ **Linda Roberts** Parents ought to be with their children at all ages monitoring their use of the Internet. It's a good idea to engage in family-centered activities and bring the computer and Internet out where everyone is apt to be.

When kids are in high school, it's a little different, but even then it's important to know what they are doing. If you have a child who's created his or own Web page, and you haven't looked at it, I would be concerned. It's the same thing as your high-schooler's compositions for English class. Wouldn't you want to read what your kids are writing about?

> "If you have a child who's created his or her own Web page, and you haven't looked at it, I would be concerned."

Keeping Kids Safe

■ **Linda Roberts** Schools, by and large, have very clear policies about Internet use and Internet safety. They have rules of the road that they ask students to agree to and often ask parents to sign a permission slip as well before they allow students to have access to the Internet. Most teachers do not encourage unlimited access to resources, and many school districts filter sites that students can access. It's not foolproof.

> "We're dealing with a highway with no lights and no lanes."

This is an area where the education community, the government, and the Internet service providers could work together more deliberately. This will happen over time, but we're dealing with a highway with no lights and no lanes. It's vast. I think the good stuff outweighs the bad, but at the same time we have to find a way to protect our kids better from totally inappropriate material.

I was in a fifth-grade class at Mantua Elementary School in Virginia and students were studying a unit on the history of the Roman empire. This class used CD-ROM encyclopedias, books from the library, and online resources. When I arrived, all of the students were engaged in their research and writing projects. Several students were online, using the five computers hooked up to the Internet.

All of a sudden one student called to his teacher and asked her to look at a Web site he had found in his search. He pointed to a Web site and said, "I don't think I should go here." The teacher looked at it, and said, "I don't think you should either. Good job. You know, you're really thinking about this." Mantua Elementary does not use filtering software; the student and this teacher believed that "the best filters are clear policies and responsible students."

■ **David Thornburg** Schools have special obligations to make sure that children's privacy is honored. Many times when I visit a school's Web site, I see a picture of the entire class. I think it's wonderful to have, but there should not be one-to-one identification of the children with their pictures.

This gets into another domain: chat rooms. I don't think that children, especially children who are in elementary school, should be using chat rooms unattended. If it's decided that a child should for some academic reason go to a chat room, then a parent or other responsible adult should be by the child's side to monitor the process, to make sure that the child's going to be treated with dignity and treat others with dignity, and to ensure that the conversation is appropriate to the subject that's being explored.

A Fresh View of Homework

■ **David Thornburg** As teachers come to understand that kids have access to some of these tools at home, they could start working that into their curriculum in a meaningful way. For example, if a teacher knows that every child in the classroom either has access to technology at home or through the local public library, then it becomes appropriate for the teacher to give some homework assignments where the student would use the Internet. You can't do that if there are children who are excluded from these resources. But if every child does have access to them, then I think teachers can give different types of homework assignments than they were able to give in the past, and I see that as a positive change.

Does this give an advantage to students with access to home computers over those who have to go to the library? Well, there are pros and cons to both. I don't know that there's a downside to either of them.

There are a couple of benefits from gaining access at a library. One of them is that libraries tend to have faster access to the Internet than most homes. This is starting to change as we're seeing cable modems and high-speed phone lines come into the house.

The second thing that libraries have going for them is that they have librarians, and librarians are fantastic human beings because they know how to address those three questions that I said we all need to know: How do you find stuff, how do you determine if it's relevant, and how do you determine whether it's accurate? Having a librarian on call when you're doing homework can be incredibly helpful.

On the other hand, libraries may have a half a dozen machines available for the general public, but if you're in a community where there are twenty-five people waiting for those six machines, you may be out of luck for a while. The benefit of having technology at home is that it is available to you any time you want to use it.

Within a few years, we're going to see such an influx of Internet appliances that we'll have access to the Internet any place that we want it. We're in a transitory period right now where we have to go places to gain access to information. Certainly within five years we'll be able to gain access to information wherever we happen to be. These technologies already exist, but in the future what's available to a minority will be available cheaply to all.

Redesigning the Classroom

■ **David Thornburg** We've got a couple of challenges for the educator in the classroom. One of them is that most of our classrooms are not nearly as well equipped, technologically speaking, as many teenagers' bedrooms. Most of our schools don't have meaningful access to the Web on the classroom level.

Also, the layout of schools is wrong. A traditional classroom is set up with three or four electrical outlets around the walls of the room. The desks are all generally facing the front because our schools were designed for the idea of teaching largely as a telling experience. The students may do some work on their own or with their peers in small groups; a lot of the small group interaction is a fairly recent development in education, within the last thirty years or so.

■ **Linda Roberts** I think we need to think more about redesigning the classroom. We have gone at it very intuitively and, for the most part, have not really thought about what the classrooms of the twenty-first century should look like. What about the schools themselves?

This is an important time to think about school design, in part because many communities are building more schools right now and others are renovating schools that were built at least twenty-five years ago. In newer schools wires and electrical outlets are being installed all over classrooms and throughout the building to make computer access ubiquitous. The idea is to be able to use the resources wherever you are.

There is also a greater focus on having longer periods of time for learning, because learning doesn't end at the end of a forty-five-minute class. I've been in schools that are also multi-disciplinary—math and science and art and music are to-gether—particularly in middle schools and in high schools.

The other big difference I see in some places is that when you talk to teachers about the classroom, you have this image of the walls going down, that the classroom is here physically, but there are virtual connections with other classrooms and other resources. These virtual connections are as important as what's going on in the physical space; they enrich the physical space.

What's important is that there are options. Students in Alaska said this to me when I was talking to them on the phone, after poor weather conditions had prevented me from reaching their school in Whittier. There were 100 kids in this bush school, K through twelve, and they were totally isolated. I asked them, "What's the biggest change now that you are connected to the Internet?"

One of the students said, "We really have more options than we ever had before." One of the teachers popped in and said, "What has changed the most for us is that we're not lim-ited by where we are, what's here in this building, and who we are." I think that's what we're really talking about for the fu-ture.

The Ideal Student-to-Computer Ratio

■ **David Thornburg** What's the ideal ratio of students to com-puters? The ideal would be for every child to have his or her own machine so that access to information was available on demand. That's the honest answer to that question.

However, there is a lot of very effective work being done

with a ratio of two children to a computer, and the benefit of having two kids gaining side-by-side access to a machine is that they can talk to each other about what they're doing, which provides some focus to the task.

The reality is that you can also do wonderful things, even if you have only one computer in the classroom. It's not just the technology, it's how it's used that matters. If the technology is just being used to perpetuate an old curricular or instructional model, then the number of machines you have isn't germane.

We used to get very caught up with this whole idea of student-to-computer ratio, but that's like saying, "What's the ideal ratio of students to pens?" The answer, probably, is two pens per kid because they're going to drop one. But you can tell me all about the ratio of pens to children and not have communicated a thing about the quality of the writing program at the school.

The Singapore Model

■ **Linda Roberts** There are some important lessons to be learned from other countries. I had the chance to meet the Singapore Ministry of Education and visit some schools in Singapore. Singapore has an Information Age economy. There are no natural resources in Singapore—it's an island—and they have put all of their focus on both quality education and putting technology into the schools.

By 2000 there will be a computer for every two students in Singapore, every teacher will have access to computers, and all will have completed extensive training. Furthermore, in every school there will be sufficient technical support to keep the technology updated and maintained so the teachers won't have to do it.

It's a very impressive strategy, not just because of its scale and comprehensiveness but because the focus of the use of technology is on teaching and learning—"Learning to think; thinking to learn."

Will Textbooks Vanish?

■ **David Thornburg** There is a move to make textbooks available online, but I don't think that we should do that because I don't believe we should be using textbooks at all for some subjects. Let's take the sciences, for example. Developments are happening so quickly in the scientific domain that by the time a textbook gets published it's already out-of-date. I would prefer that kids had access to project-based learning where they get to explore these scientific principles using information that's current and up-to-date and to move away from textbooks.

> *"Textbooks are an artifact of education, based on the best technology of the time. If we'd had computers before we had books, I don't think that the modern textbook would ever have come into existence."*

Textbooks are an artifact of education, based on the best technology of the time. If we'd had computers before we had books, I don't think that the modern textbook would ever have come into existence. It's not at all clear to me that we need textbooks, as you and I have known them, especially in subjects like history, science, even mathematics.

■ **Linda Roberts** Could textbooks vanish? Sure it's a possibility for some subjects. For some teachers these new electronic resources untether them from texts, but textbooks really do serve an important function in many classrooms. Rather than replacing them, I hope that we will see textbooks becoming the anchors for the curriculum, to be used as guides, but from the textbook you go out into other resources.

There's a very interesting example that involves the National Association of Science Teachers and a number of textbook companies who, in addition to the text, are building Web site addresses and connections in the text that students can scan and literally link to as they're doing their studying.

In Texas, there's been some talk of giving every student a laptop computer and their texts on CD-ROM; that way the text can be readily updated. I don't think the idea of the textbook goes away, but maybe its physical format changes.

Connecting Homes and Schools

■ **David Thornburg** The results of the longest running project in the country on the home-school connection have been absolutely breathtaking. The project's been in place in Indiana since 1988 and is called the Buddy System.

The project was launched in five schools, with all fourth-graders provided with computers, printers, and modems—about 300 families in all. In addition, the schools were each outfitted with labs. The following year the program was expanded to include fourth- and fifth-graders, and the year after that the sixth-graders were added. This way the teachers knew that the kids had universal access to technology and access to a special section of the Internet, basically what we call an Intranet, that was operated by this particular project.

What they found was that the technology took the place of kids playing with video games. In other words, kids could come home from school and instead of turning on the Nintendos and things of that sort, they would log on to the Internet and start doing their homework assignments and, in some cases, doing collaborative projects. You'd have kids in Indianapolis doing collaborative projects with kids in Terre Haute. At the end of the year, kids had spent the equivalent of thirty additional days of classroom time doing schoolwork without spending one extra minute in the classroom itself. Now that was an incredible payoff for them.

Parents are a critical part of the home program. They discovered that parents who had not come to school visits and events of that sort were suddenly getting far more involved because they were sending e-mail to their child's teacher. If you go to their Web site [buddynet.net], you'll see all kinds of projects that are for parents, teachers, and students. The parents, for example, are given recommendations on books that their children might be interested in reading or activities for them to do with their kids relating to academic assignments.

It's just beautifully designed, and it started out as a little research project, doodled out on the back of an envelope. It has gathered force and now has well over 9,000 students involved in it, in sixty schools across Indiana. I see it as the prototype of how the Internet can bring parents, teachers, and students together for education.

Once again, the critical component was staff development. The summer before the project started all of the teachers were brought together so that they could redesign their lesson plans based on the reality that all the children in their classes were going to have a computer, printer, and modem in their homes.

■ **Linda Roberts** Building the home-school connection is important in every way possible. There are a number of really nice examples of school districts, schools, and even teachers who have figured out that it is really important to reach parents, if they can, e-mail them, and give them an update on their student's progress. Some schools have found ways to reach parents who don't have access to a computer at home, working with public libraries, community centers, as well as local employers.

In Colony Middle School in Palmer, Alaska, a rural area about 50 miles from Anchorage, all the classrooms are connected and 75 percent of the children, according to the principal, have computers and Internet access at home, the result of a cooperative effort among the local phone company, the school district, and the local government.

In this school, not only do the students share their work and talk about what they're doing in school on the Web, but there's a rotating team of students that reports every day on what happened in math, science, and language arts classes, and also lists the homework assignments on the school's Web page. Nan Whitmore, the science teacher, is delighted with the quality of students' Web projects. She is ecstatic that when students are absent, they come back to school with their homework done!

The Great Equalizer

■ **Bob Pittman** Going online is going to be the great equalizer for education. I grew up in a small Southern town and went to one of the worst schools in America. It wasn't a lot of fun and you weren't going to attract great teachers to come to this little town. But online you can get access to everything anybody else can get: great teachers and tutors. As a matter of fact, Homework Help is a very important area for kids on AOL because you're able to get teachers to help you no matter where you're going to school.

It will also solve one of the great problems we've had, which is getting parents connected to the schools, to the teachers, and to the administrators. They can do it all online very seamlessly. That will give them a better understanding of what their kids are doing and what help and support the kids need in order to help them grow and flourish.

An Explosion of Home Schooling

■ **Alvin Toffler** Home-schoolers are struggling with the traditional methods—sit down at the table, open the textbook, and so on—but give them the support of all the power that's going to come down that broadband box, and I think you're going to see an explosion of home schooling.

> "Today you give your kids to teachers who may very well be less educated than you are."

The assumptions on which the mass education system was built are no longer there. When we created the mass education system most people lived in rural villages. That meant that you gave your child over to the most educated person in the village; it might be the only one who knew how to read or the one who had gone twenty miles away to visit a big city. Today you give your kids to teachers who may very well be less educated than you are. That stands the whole thing upside down. Not very nice to say, but it's true, depending upon what community you're in.

The underlying assumptions of the system have to be totally torn up and reconceptualized. I would like to see education demassified. If the rest of the society is becoming more diverse, then the education system has to prepare kids for that diversity, and I'm not just talking about ethnic diversity. I'm talking about diversity in occupations and in everything.

I have wanted to see diversity occur within the public school's framework, but after waiting for twenty or thirty years and seeing precious little of that, I now will support anything that increases diversity of educational forms available to American kids. If that's vouchers, that's okay by me. I don't want the vouchers to promote racist policies. I don't want them to favor the rich, but if the vouchers are large enough and distributed properly, I think that those dangers can be eliminated. I don't think that's the solution to the problem, because there's a much bigger structural problem, but anything that creates diversity in the system, at this point, is a plus.

Virtual Universities

■ **David Thornburg** There are several pros and cons connected with virtual universities. To start with, we are social creatures and a lot of our learning takes place physically in the company of other human beings. Even in the case of a virtual university, I would hope that there would be a way that people who are studying similar topics, at similar institutions, would find out about one another, so that they could meet in coffee shops and talk about their educational experience.

> "There should always be room for one more in a virtual university."

If you think about the benefit of a virtual university, you don't have to deal with physically locating where the university happens to be. It's an absolute godsend for somebody who is going to school part-time because you don't have to take off work at a particular time to go attend a class. You don't have to deal with enrollment restrictions or the limitations of a physical campus that causes somebody to say, "Well, we're going to cap our enrollment and, sorry, you didn't make it." There should always be room for one more in a virtual university. I think it is going to be useful because it's going to extend educational opportunities to even more people.

A Radical Approach to Lifelong Learning

■ **David Thornburg**   Peter Drucker said that the brick and mortar university is a dead concept. Basically he was saying that the old ivy-covered walls are going to come down. In some cases the universities are bringing this on themselves because they don't see themselves as being in the business of supporting lifelong education. This is where the virtual universities have the potential to do something really spectacular.

> *"I'm sorry, but allowing a professor who used to bore fifty students to be boring to hundreds of thousands simultaneously just doesn't cut it for me."*

All of us who graduated from college receive letters asking for money. In exchange you're offered nothing. I would really love to have an ongoing relationship with my college; in exchange for a few hundred dollars a year, I'd have library privileges at a campus close to where I live, I could attend lectures and there'd be exchange privileges among schools. But schools don't do that. They see you as a student, then you graduate and you're a donor. In business everyone knows that it's a lot cheaper to keep a customer than to get a new one.

The market for lifelong learning is huge. There's no question that this is going to happen. My fear is that some of the virtual universities think that distance education means taking what they used to do in a traditional classroom and putting it onto the Web; so you end up with old wine in new bottles. I'm sorry, but allowing a professor who used to bore fifty students to be boring to hundreds of thousands simultaneously just doesn't cut it for me.

We need to acknowledge that the online world provides us access to new types of media, new ways of interacting with peers, new ways of doing things that we couldn't do in a physical campus, and allows us to take advantage of those in some meaningful way.

Does the Net Make Us Smarter?

■ **David Thornburg** Forty years ago, "smart" was defined by the stuff that you knew. Take a look at the popularity of game shows like *Jeopardy!*, where people are rewarded for knowing decontextualized facts—that used to be how we defined smart. If you knew that Columbus discovered the Americas in 1492, you were viewed as smarter than somebody who didn't know it.

In a world where we are just drowning in information, the definition of smart needs to be replaced by another one. The Internet gives us raw information. The real challenge for us is stepping beyond it and knowing how to apply that information and, in particular, finding a context in which to use it.

I wouldn't say that the Web makes us smarter. I would say that it facilitates our capacity to make ourselves smarter, and that's a slightly different statement.

The 100-Year Challenge

■ **David Thornburg** We're not going to wake up one morning and find the whole system has been transformed. It's a change that's happening like the spread of a new species that just migrates around the planet.

Parents have an important role to play in this because every parent wants his or her child to be successful. The question is, What's the definition of success in education? Quite often parents measure it against their own experiences when they were in school. When parents see a teacher doing something with a child that would have gotten the parents in trouble when they were children, they say, "Wait a minute, you call this cooperative learning? The child's collaborating with somebody else. When I was a child, we called that cheating."

If you take the long view and you realize, for example, that there are children who are being taught today by teachers who entered the teaching profession in 1960, and some of these children are still going to be in the workforce in the year 2060, that's a 100-year gap. You've got to take the long view and say: What can I impart to these kids that's going to have lasting value to them?

I think it's keeping their creativity alive, helping them acquire the skills to know how to have tolerance for ambiguity, for ill-formed questions, and to know how to get answers to those questions.

Suggested Web Sites

altavista.com	infoplease.com
askjeeves.com	jasonproject.org
collegenet.com	jonesinternational.edu
collegeboard.org	loc.gov
discovery.com	nasa.gov
ed.gov/free	nationalgeographic.com
ed-x.com	onelook.com
fastweb.com	sil.si.edu/newstart.htm
historychannel.com	

Most Popular Web News/Information Sites

(Source: Nielsen//NetRatings)

accuweather.com

cbs.com

cnet.com

cnn.com

deja.com

encyclopedia.com

familyeducation.com

harrispollonline.com

homearts.com

homefair.com

intellicast.com

marketwatch.com

msnbc.com

npdor.com

nytimes.com

oxygen.com

pathfinder.com

personalogic.com

priceline.com

realtor.com

salon.com

sidewalk.com

thestreet.com

usatoday.com

washingtonpost.com

weather.com

webhelp.com

wunderground.com

zdnet.com

FIVE

A GREAT TIME TO BE AN ENTREPRENEUR

I spent almost twenty years as a systems analyst in the defense industry. Although the work was challenging, I never felt like the formal lifestyle fit my easygoing personality. Five years ago, I quit to create my own Internet business: a nationwide online directory of antique stores. The response was tremendous. Now I spend two-thirds of my time administering the directory, and the other third traveling, promoting my service, and visiting members. Recently, I even turned a profit!

—Carolyn Lilly, California

After my seven-year-old daughter was diagnosed with diabetes I decided to stay at home full-time. I was using the Internet mainly to research diabetes information, but started to look for a home business. I was offended by all the scams aimed at at-home moms. I started a web design business and published columns on my Web site. I soon heard from thousands of women in the same boat. Now my site [WAHM.com], the Online Magazine for Work-at-Home Moms, receives over 100,000 page views a month and is my full-time business.

—Cheryl Demas, California

Americans savor the stories of successful entrepreneurs almost as much as they do the exploits of famous actors and athletes. It's part of the American dream to bootstrap a new business, work like crazy for a few years, take the company public, get rich, and go off and start another venture—or never work again. The boom in high-flying Internet start-ups in the late 1990s that has created instant millionaires and even a few billionaires only fuels that fantasy.

In fact, the number of Harvard Business School graduates

who say they plan to start their own businesses has been rising recently. An informal student poll of almost half of the class of 1999 showed that 8 percent of them planned on becoming entrepreneurs, owners, or partners in their first year out of school; that's up from 3 percent the year before. Moreover, 25 percent expressed an interest in high-technology businesses, up from 11 percent in 1998. Stanford M.B.A.s seem endemic to Silicon Valley start-ups.

Not all students are lured by a desire for riches. Some are motivated by a desire to escape the corporate rat race or to build something new that doesn't exist today. And you don't need a Harvard or Stanford M.B.A. to think you can have a shot at it. After all, Bill Gates didn't even graduate from college.

Today's corporate chiefs have taken notice of these young hopefuls breathing down their necks. George Gendron, editor in chief of *Inc.* magazine, recently attended a dinner at the Harvard Business School for about eighty technologists. "Every single CEO at the dinner said they live in fear these days, not of a German competitor or a Japanese competitor, but of some twenty-one-year-old college dropout who's working on some Internet-based competitor that's going to come in and clean their clocks."

Big-company CEOs are keenly aware of the need for an Internet strategy. Booz·Allen and Hamilton, along with *The Economist*'s Intelligence Unit, did a study of 500 CEOs and business leaders worldwide and found that these leaders strongly believe the Internet economy will either transform the world marketplace or have a major impact on it within the next three years (a total of 92 percent of respondents). Moreover, 76 percent said the Internet would improve customer satisfaction, 67 percent said it would reduce costs, 56 percent said it would globalize their operations, and 56 percent said it would foster innovation.

Whether you're part of a big corporation, or a small one, just starting out or thinking of getting out, anyone can follow the American dream and launch his or her own online venture. The initial barriers to entry are few, the independence enticing, and there's always the chance of succeeding beyond your wildest dreams; like Susan Polis Schutz and her husband, Stephen, whose Blue Mountain Arts site [bluemountain.com] has become one of the most visited sites on the Web. Two years ago they had a small card-and-book-publishing company in Boulder, offering feel-good messages to a small customer base. The Web site was launched in 1996 and now the privately held company reaches about 12 million people on the Web who like to send the company's free electronic greeting cards. In the fall of 1999, Excite@Home bought the company for about $780 million in cash and stock.

Of course, not everyone who starts a business online gets off to such a promising start. But the Internet makes it easy for anyone with a product to sell to find someone who wants to buy it. Perhaps the simplest way to test the waters is through an auction site like eBay [ebay.com] or Amazon [amazon.com], which offers a steady stream of customers through their cybergates. Locally newspapers are on the cusp of starting auctions around online classified advertising.

One entrepreneur who decided to give auctions a try is Ross Wright of Thousand Oaks, California. Wright, an independent sales representative, had his interest in auctions piqued after meeting a kid at a restaurant with a Beanie Baby killer whale purchased on eBay. Wright's wife collects stuffed killer whales, which are very hard to come by, so he decided to log on that night and check out eBay. What he saw was enough to convince this seasoned salesman that online auctions offered a great new sales tool.

Less than two years later, Wright is running anywhere from 400 to 800 individual auctions a month. Mostly he sells guitars that he buys as factory seconds or returns, books, and video-tapes. Prior to selling online he supplemented his other sales income by selling guitars from his house. When he saw what was happening on eBay, he thought, This is going to be great because I could sell guitars and not have to deal with having a bunch of strangers coming to my house every weekend. Well he got his wish. "Nobody comes to my house now. I have my own privacy, but my house has turned into a warehouse." Wright, who's an avid reader and collector of books, now stocks 2,000 books in his second bedroom, which has turned into his warehouse.

The Internet has made it possible for Wright to realize a life fantasy at forty-two, instead of waiting until he was fifty to open up a combination bookstore and music store. Up until now he was too busy to pursue his dream and didn't have enough money to open a retail store. The Internet, he says, "has given me the ability to sell retail without having a real storefront. Now I can garner profits on deals I wouldn't have touched before—deals that yield only two or three dollars." It's also given him the upside on transactions that can yield several hundred dollars in profit per sale.

In the pages that follow you'll find out how Wright turned a pastime into a serious business; get seasoned advice from *Inc.*'s Gendron about how small businesses can navigate the Internet to their advantage; receive valuable tips from experienced Internet entrepreneurs like Halsey Minor of CNET, Peter Friedman of Talk City, Mark Cuban of broadcast.com, and Esther Dyson of EDventure Holdings; and get guidance from *SmartMoney*'s Steven Swartz. And David Bohnett, founder of GeoCities, explains how his site provides the tools to help you get started with an e-commerce site of your own.

More Opportunities, More Risks

■ **George Gendron** It's not an overstatement to say that ten years from today, everyone who has a business will find that the business has been dramatically affected by online commerce. I don't think it's going to happen in the next year or two, it's more likely to take ten years for things to play themselves out. Anybody who's awake these days—who has a business or has assets that he or she is thinking about building or protecting—has to be thinking about both the opportunities and the threats that the Internet poses.

■ **Esther Dyson** The Internet's greatest impact on people is giving them more options, more choice, and therefore, more responsibility . . . which isn't always welcome. Now you're responsible for what you choose instead of saying, "Ah, couldn't help it. I had to take this job because I didn't know about any others."

Now you can be a producer. You can now go into business competing with other people whether you're selling cookies or becoming a journalist or being a consultant. You can control your own life, not just as a consumer but, in some sense, you become a producer of labor rather than an employee.

Not everyone will take advantage of this. There are three sets of people: People who, no matter what, are going to go out and define their own lives for themselves. Then there are people who, no matter what, are going to be victims. In the middle there are people who, if you give them the tools, will take advantage of them.

Get Online or Get Lost

■ **George Gendron** What are the implications of the Internet for people who already have a business? I'll give you an example. We run a program at *Inc.* magazine called the Birthing of Giants; it's a continuing education program that we run jointly with MIT for people who are in their twenties and have very successful businesses. They meet once a week over the course of three consecutive years. This year, for the first time, the audience of sixty-five chief executives and founders reported that they really think of themselves as having two businesses. They have the business that they started, in most cases six, seven, eight years ago, and then they have a second business that they think of as the business that's helping them adapt to the digital economy.

It is not an overstatement to say that you've got to figure out how to adapt to a new world in which everything is digital. However, if you were to take a survey of the population of existing businesses, you'd find that some people find the popularization of the Internet to be extraordinarily exciting and a lot of other people find it terrifying and think they've got a lot to lose.

■ **Halsey Minor** Five years from now, successful businesses will be those who have a multidistribution strategy. If they're a store, they're going to have to figure out a way to sell online; whether you're a grocery store or you're Barnes & Noble, I think that's pretty clear. It doesn't mean that there can't be Internet-only retailers, because there can, but I don't think you can just be a physical-world retailer because you won't be able to grow your business. Even if Internet businesses don't cannibalize your existing sales, they will certainly cut down on your growth, if not eliminate it. That's true for CDs and books and all sorts of things.

A Golden Age for Start-ups

■ **George Gendron** For someone just starting out, the Internet means there are more opportunities than ever before and almost all of the traditional barriers for entry for new businesses are disappearing or have already disappeared. For example, twenty years ago if you were going to launch a magazine like *Inc.*, it would have required somewhere between $5 and $20 million to get the magazine to break even. That is a huge barrier to entry, in terms of access to capital. Today you can launch an online competitor to *Inc.* or any existing magazine for probably less than $1,000. I'm not arguing you'd be successful, but the capital barriers to entry that have kept really smart people out of industries have just about disappeared, thanks to the Internet.

The capital required is increasingly being driven down to almost zero, and people starting businesses today have an incredible advantage that the rest of us don't have, which is they have no assets to protect. They're starting with a clean slate.

■ **Esther Dyson** It's much easier to do a start-up now, not just because there's more capital but because there's more outsourcing available. There's an infrastructure that will support you: people who will rent to a small company without established credit or people who will buy from you even though you're small. You see that infrastructure much more broadly in the United States than elsewhere.

It's not just the Internet that's making this possible; everything works together. It's social changes. Women say, "I don't want to work in this corporate rat race. I want to do something on my own." They find that the support's out there. The Internet is one incredibly useful tool, but there's everything from your mother-in-law, who no longer thinks you're nuts for wanting to start your own business, to finding a lawyer who's willing to deal with you as a small business. Women see this more because, for them, the change has been greater and they also tend to find the corporate structure more stultifying and probably have had a less easy time in it.

The same thing is happening in Eastern Europe where there's a limited culture of small business. So it's not just money; it's not just the Internet; it's culture too. There are some people who are born visionaries and entrepreneurs, and it doesn't matter where they come from. They say, "I'm going to build something." There are other people to whom it wouldn't occur, but if their neighbor does it, then they say, "Maybe I could too."

I'm actually a pretty good example of this. I came to work for Ben Rosen, who owned this newsletter company, and we decided that it didn't make sense for him to be involved because he had a conflict of interest. So we thought we should find someone to sell it to. I remember thinking, "Well, if Ben Rosen can run this company—he's a wonderful guy and he's very smart but he's human—I could do it too." It was because I had a living example in front of me. Without his example I wouldn't have done it.

Self-Examination Time

■ **George Gendron** Entrepreneurs and founders can't afford to sit by passively arguing that because they're in a particular niche their business won't be affected by the Net. I think it's hard to make an argument that there is any niche anywhere that won't be affected.

On the other hand, we see a lot of examples of *Inc.*-size companies that are overreacting; reacting in the wrong way, walking away from all of the strengths that they used to build their successful company in the first place. I think that's a huge mistake. People need to step back and ask themselves, once again, the question for this ter-restrial, non-Internet business they have: What is our business? What are our competitive strengths? Why do people do business with us? What makes us different? And then try to fig-ure out how you enhance that difference using the Internet as a tool. Very often the solution is to be found in areas that are surprisingly mundane.

> *"Entrepreneurs and founders can't afford to sit by passively arguing that because they're in a particular niche their business won't be affected by the Net."*

Whiz Kids Versus Biz Kids

■ **George Gendron** How does a company find an adviser to help with its Web strategy? That's the $64,000 question be-cause, of course, every major technology company in the world now claims that they're offering advice to growth com-panies, small companies, and start-ups. In every neighborhood in America there are now hundreds of people who have hung a shingle outside their front door saying: We Do Web Site De-velopment. Now, sorting through all that, to find the people who possess that rare combination of business know-how and technical savvy is extraordinarily difficult.

I think the best way to do it is the way would-be entrepre-neurs and founders navigate most of the time, to network. I would not go out and hire some hot young kid, which is what so many companies are doing that it's becoming a cliché. I would find other companies that have similar opportunities online, that are not competitors, and ask them what they're doing, where they are getting their guidance.

The one thing I would be unbelievably wary of are people

who come in and either don't know my business or don't know business at all. You can eliminate 95 percent of all the people who claim they're doing Web site development by asking them some really fundamental questions about business. If they don't understand business, then they can't do Web site development. Maybe they can do graphics, maybe they can do HTML [Hyper Text Markup Language, the programming code read by Web pages], but they can't do Web site development for businesses.

Turning Hobbies into Gold

■ **George Gendron** The Internet is a very simple and not terribly elegant tool, but potentially a very powerful one for bringing together buyers and sellers in a way that's much more efficient than ever before.

So if you have a hobby, collecting clocks for example, the Internet allows you to test, in an inexpensive way, whether or not you can turn this into a business. You don't have to do expensive direct mail. You can go out and inexpensively test the market for what you're selling. You can find out if customers exist, and if they do, who they are, what they are willing to pay, and how many of them exist.

In fact, there aren't really that many questions beyond those that determine what I would call the viability of a business. That's really all you care about in the starting stages: Are there people out there willing to pay real money for clocks? The Internet today, even in its infancy, allows people with money to buy the clocks and the people with clocks who want to sell them to get together in ways that are much more efficient than ever before.

You could conceivably go out and log on to inc.com, or any one of hundreds, if not thousands, of sites like this that allow people to create a basic home page for free. Literally within twenty-four hours you could have a site; a primitive one, but you'd be up and running and you wouldn't need to know anything about HTML coding to do it.

Cheap 'n' Easy Tools

■ **David Bohnett** GeoCities, as well as other online sites, provide tools that make it easy for a mom-and-pop shop to create a virtual store online. We call our service GeoShops and it's available to all GeoCities members. Here's how it works.

There are two different ways for members to set up a shopping site. The first one costs $24.95 a month and allows people to put their store online in order to promote their business on their personal home page.

The next level is a fully commerce-enabled Web site. That service starts at $99.95 per month. In addition to the same benefits as the $24.95-a-month service, people can actually sell goods and services over their Web page. We provide all the back-end technology that allows them to do this—credit card processing, shopping cart convenience, and so forth. It's really a turnkey operation; they don't need to know anything technical to make it work. A person could have it up and running within a few hours.

In addition, we offer tools to help people build their personal Web pages; specifically, we provide prebuilt templates for all kinds of Web pages. So, for someone who's not very Internet savvy and doesn't really know how to build a professional-looking e-commerce site, we provide templates that are prewritten and predesigned based around specialty businesses, such as a florist or an attorney or an accountant. These templates have multiple pages with professional-looking graphics and prewritten text based upon that individual business.

Now your accounting site is going to look quite different from someone else's using the same template because you're going to add your own graphics, pictures, and you're probably going to change the text to better reflect your own individual business.

The templates allow the average computer user, who can drag and drop with a computer mouse, to build a fully commerce-enabled Web site on our site. The shopping cart, which allows an individual to purchase goods online seamlessly, is also integrated into the package.

We also offer fully secure, online transactions. All you have to do is provide us with your banking information, your account information, and so forth, and it'll all be set up for you.

Getting Started

■ **George Gendron** There's a guy I know in Los Angeles who has a fantastically successful chain of three small retail stores, and all he does is sell imported Italian pottery. He's got a very affluent and urbane population that really appreciates his product. He is developing a Web site now that will offer him an opportunity to take his company national and multinational without having to build any more stores.

If you were to ask this fellow, if he were starting his business today would he open a retail store, I think his answer would be no. Why would he need to? His real expertise is that he's one of the world's leading experts on world-class ceramics and pottery. I think the chances are good that he would probably think about starting, let's call it, ceramicmug.com tomorrow. He wouldn't have to worry about the store, wouldn't have to worry about finding retail locations, or theft, which has been a problem for him.

He's also in one of the earthquake capitals of the United

States. Now imagine the implications for a store that's selling coffee mugs, some of which sell for $120 and $150 apiece, when it goes through an earthquake? It's just been one headache after another, all of which would have been eliminated if he were selling direct and were really more of a distributor.

On the other hand, I've had really interesting conversations with him, and other retailers, about why he would still start one retail store and have an online presence; the retail store would serve as an R&D facility, a place where he gets to meet his customers face-to-face, watch them handle the pottery, and see what's selling.

A Customer Base of Millions

■ **David Bohnett** There are a lot of individuals who probably never thought of starting a business in their own backyard, but with the Internet they're now able to gain access to millions and millions of potential customers worldwide. For as little as $100 a month, you can reach millions of potential customers. There are a lot of people who are gearing up to sell their wares on the Web because of this phenomenon, and if you've got a great product or great service, there's no reason why you can't be highly successful.

It Pays to Be Unique

■ **George Gendron** I don't think we'll necessarily see fewer stores in the future, but we will see different kinds of stores. We're now seeing the proliferation of unique, one location, retail operations.

Let's go back to our mythical clock expert who decides that

not only does he or she want to sell clocks online, but in fact, wants to have a clock shop that will be appealing enough, idiosyncratic enough, unique enough that it will actually drive traffic into the store. We'll see more of that, and as shoppers, we still want to have that live retail experience; we still want to touch the merchandise. There's a certain part of shopping that is serendipitous; we don't know what we're looking for until we see it.

■ **Steven Swartz** The Net offers some small players a chance to be more successful because it is a great distribution route. The more unique your product is the better your chance for success. If you're truly a craftsman and make great high-end chairs, for example, and people can find you through search engines, then the Internet becomes attractive for your business.

Right now we're in this weird transition where some of the commodity sellers have made themselves the biggest players, but the question in the long run is: How do you make money selling a commodity product when the Internet always allows somebody to come in with a lower price? I don't know the answer, but I have to think that the less commoditized your product is, the better your future is.

■ **George Gendron** Most of what really differentiates a business from its competitors resides in the minds of the people who work in that business. This is where the real opportunity for existing businesses lies right now.

For example, there's a traditional retail store in New York that was very successful selling cigars locally. The company has unbelievably knowledgeable people who work in the store, a very attractive inventory, and loyal clientele. People would come into the store for the first time and be dazzled by it and keep coming back for more. But you had to be in New York.

Then somebody persuaded them to take this incredible know-how and see if they could embed it in a site. We heard about it because people in Hollywood started buying from them online. Stars would be on a set shooting a movie and it would be eleven o'clock at night and they'd have some time to kill. So they'd go online; they were really into cigars and suddenly, this little store in New York became very hot in Hollywood. It became a national business at little additional cost.

Auctions: The Customer Is King

■ **George Gendron** Auctions are in their infancy and I believe they will proliferate. In fact, I wouldn't be surprised if there comes a day when almost every major Web site in the country will have an auction component to it.

Today you can go online and basically dictate to the airlines the terms under which you're willing to buy a ticket [a reverse auction, such as priceline.com]. I can indicate that I want to go from Boston to Houston on this date and at this price, and wait and see whether, in fact, an airline is willing to meet my demands. This turns the relationship between customer and supplier on its head.

> *"I wouldn't be surprised if there comes a day when almost every major Web site in the country will have an auction component to it."*

On the other end of the spectrum, Bill Hambrecht, who spent his entire life in investment banking, is doing the same thing for initial public offerings [openipo.com]. The Ravenswood Winery went public in the spring of 1999 with what I believe is the first reverse IPO. Instead of the company saying we're issuing X numbers of shares at $12, they actually said to the public, what are you willing to pay for a share of stock in

Ravenswood Winery, and held a Dutch auction of the company's stock [bidders indicate the highest price they're willing to pay for a given number of shares, the price is then set at the highest price at which there is sufficient demand to sell all the shares]. The company raised $11 million in this offering.

The Internet is really putting a lot more power and control into the hands of consumers. Consumers are beginning to dictate the terms under which they're willing to do a transaction, which is really fascinating.

■ **George Gendron** Unlike starting your own Web site, where you have to lure customers to you, the auction model offers an entrepreneur a built-in customer base and some guaranteed traffic. You've also got the infrastructure to conduct secure transactions online, which someone starting out may not be able to afford on his or her own. You've also got the reassurance, if you will, of the brand name of the auction site. Most people already know somebody who's bought something from eBay, for example, and no one ripped off their Visa card number.

In a way it's similar to a question that entrepreneurs historically should have been asking themselves anyway. You come up with an idea for a great new product, ceramic mugs for example, and you have to ask yourself: Is my idea worth building a company around? Do I want to start the Ceramic Mug Corp. or do I want to go to somebody who's already in the business of marketing and manufacturing ceramic mugs and say to him, "I have a novel concept. I'd like you to manufacture and market it, and I want to license the idea to you."

Demand for Almost Any Supply

■ **Ross Wright** I'm finding that virtually anything can sell online. It's really amazing what people will buy. I do a lot of surfing and skimming to see what other people are selling, and I talk to a lot of other different sellers; it's a pretty close-knit community. Sometimes my mind boggles when I see what other people are selling.

I tell a lot of people about what I'm doing, but not everyone jumps into it. A friend of mine really got into selling on-

> "I'm finding that virtually anything can sell online. It's really amazing what people will buy."

line. He lives in a very small town in Illinois, in the middle of nowhere, and he started going to garage sales. He bought a bunch of dishes and glasses for a dime a dish, and ended up selling several of them for $50 and $60. The first thing he did was send me an expensive bottle of liquor to thank me. He said, "I had no idea that this would be so much fun."

Why does this concept work? Well, the sellers at garage sales and thrift stores don't really care about the price of the items they're selling to you. And if you get the right two people bidding on an item online, you'll get what the market will bear. Of course, the very next week, the items that you just sold for $40, might sell for $5 or $6.

It's really the American market system at work—supply and demand moving action on a day-to-day basis—all depending on how many of these items are up for auction, what auction sites they're on, what the prices are, and who's willing to buy them. I just had a video that closed out at $30, when my cost on videos ranges from $3 to $15. I had no idea that it would close out that high.

What Skills Do You Need?

■ **Ross Wright** You don't need to know about technology to do this. I'm fairly knowledgeable because I've been online for a long time, but I talk to other sellers who sell as much or more than me who are virtually computer illiterate. It does help, however, if you know HTML code because you can make your auctions more readable, but it's not necessary. You have to have relatively good typing skills and it helps to have a certain command of the English language, but I also see people who can hardly spell a single word still selling stuff.

Clearly there's a benefit if you can write a good description of your merchandise and if you include a photo. I've been in sales and marketing all my life, and I believe it helps if you can make your copy sizzle. This can be time-consuming; there's a lot of thought that goes into the descriptions and a lot of typing. I save time now by using a template that I've created, so I don't have to retype the sales terms and clickable links. Then I just have to plug in the description of an item, which usually runs a paragraph or two in length. All my auctions look pretty much the same, with the title and author in bold type, followed by a couple of paragraphs of text and then the terms.

There are tools available online that allow you to plug your descriptions into a ready-made template, for example, Auction Assistant 2 by Blackthorne Software [blackthornesw.com].

Using Auctions to Drive More Sales

■ **Ross Wright** Not only are my auctions in themselves a revenue stream, but I'm also using them to point to my other fixed inventory and generate additional revenue. Let me explain. I already have a searchable inventory of about 1,800 books. So, if you go to one of my book auctions and you see an interesting book, you can click on a link that will take you to my online inventory. Once there you can inquire: "Do you have another book by this author in stock? What's the condition? How much do you want for it?" I sell the books in inventory at a fixed price.

There is a physical limit to the number of auctions I can run, but I have so much other stuff in inventory that I don't want to limit myself to just selling what I can handle in 100 to 200 auctions a week. After all, I want to make every penny that I can.

The Inside Scoop on Pricing

■ **Ross Wright** I try to do research for each individual piece that I sell. Usually, I start the auction at somewhere near my cost or somewhere near half the current book value, and sometimes I just throw a bunch of auctions up and see which way the wind's blowing. I don't like to start at current book value because you won't get the auction started. People want to have an auction, they want to see something that feels like a deal.

It's funny, but sometimes if an item doesn't sell the first time, I'll assume that the market has changed and throw it back up for under cost. I do a lot of cost averaging because I buy a lot of books, maybe 300 or more at a time, so I may need to sell only 30 or 40 of those books to recoup my investment. From then on, anything else I sell from that lot is pure profit.

Oddly enough, sometimes there'll be more action the second time I list an item and it'll end up selling for more than book value. Other times there will be no action and I'll have to relist it a third time. It's all about the whims of the customers. It's all about time and place, the right two people bidding on what you're selling. Sellers also have to pay a fee to eBay and Amazon; their rates are very similar.

Turning $1 into $100 or More

■ **Ross Wright** I've sold a lot of books for over $100 that I paid a dollar for at a garage sale. I've done that about six times in the last year and a half, but I only expected to do that well once, when I listed a rare, limited-edition reprint of the Chaucer *Canterbury Tales* that was published in 1958. I paid a dollar for it at a garage sale and sold it for $125.

I also sold a boxed set of *Dark Shadows* paperbacks for $180 that I picked up at a garage sale for a dollar. I just kept watching it climb and climb and climb. I generally watch my auctions once an hour. It's like watching the stock market.

Dealing with Customers

■ **Ross Wright** You do have some customer hassles, but it's nothing that's insurmountable. For example, I try to write accurate descriptions, I even try to play down my descriptions, but you are going to run into people who feel like they didn't get what they expected. When that happens I'll try to make some kind of amicable offer. I might say, "Look, you paid $10 plus shipping for this item, how about if I just send you $5?"

That knowledge comes from my wholesale sales background, where I've learned that if a customer is dissatisfied for any reason, it pays to cut an extra 10 percent off the deal to keep him or her happy. Of course, if someone was totally dissatisfied, I'll give a full refund, but most of my items say sales are final; especially with musical instruments, they're bought as is.

The way the deal works is the money comes first. I never ship anything out unless I have already been paid. I haven't accepted credit cards yet, but I'm looking into it. I accept checks, money orders, and cash. A lot of overseas customers will send cash, and I'm always surprised that a lot of domestic customers do too. I get about $50 to $100 in cash a week.

Tips from the Trenches

■ **Ross Wright** If you want to sell online, try to stick with what you know and what you like. If you like to collect books, if you like to collect movies, if you're in the music business or if you've sold electronic components, there's a market for everything. That's my main advice, stick with what you know because it's safer that way. You'll know what the value of items is, and you'll know when you're getting a good buy and when you're not. Otherwise you could make the wrong buy at the wrong time, and that can really hurt you.

Buying and selling online is as risky as anything else. I'm putting my money out front every time to buy the goods I sell. It's similar to investing in the stock market, but not as risky because you're putting your money into inventory and it will remain inventory if you don't sell it.

You don't need a lot of inventory to start. I began with my own personal collection of books, roughly 300 to 400 books, and four or five guitars. But right away I wanted to push it and started doing a lot of buying.

Full-Time . . . and Fun

■ **Ross Wright** Originally, I thought that the money I made on online auctions would be secondary income, a mad money kind of thing. It's turned out that it's outperforming all my other commissioned jobs and now represents about 50 percent of my income. All in less than two years.

In fact it's gotten to the point where my wife quit her job and is going to work with me full-time in this business. She'll be doing a lot of the data entering of back stock. I'll still be doing the auctions, the buying, the marketing, and the shipping.

The Net certainly has exceeded my expectations. I have friends who call and ask me about retirement. I say, "Why?" To be able to make that dollar on an item and be happy . . . I never thought that day would come until I was retired. Now I don't have to wait.

Spreading Seed Money

■ **George Gendron**   There's been a proliferation of sites claiming to give small businesses access to capital and there's been a lot of talk about how eventually the Internet will democratize access to capital. In other words, it will do the same thing that the auctions are doing, put together people who want to invest in small companies with people who have ideas for companies they want to create.

As of right now, the track record for that is absolutely appalling, but it's early. Who knows, within the next three to five years, parts of the capital market might change dramatically. I suspect the parts that will change most dramatically and most quickly will not be the parts that are of most interest to people starting a company.

The overwhelming majority of people that start a company think they want to raise capital, but more than 95 percent of all businesses are started with personal savings, a loan from a family member, or cashing in a life insurance policy. I don't think that's going to change substantially.

I think what might change dramatically is access to equity, especially with a company like Wit Capital out democratizing the world of initial public offerings. They are using the Internet to create a virtual stock market that will put together investors and, at least initially, smaller companies looking for investors. This will make it more efficient and less expensive for companies to go public than on NASDAQ. The people launching this all have very solid experience on Wall Street, so it should be taken very seriously.

The New Challenge: Getting Noticed

■ **George Gendron** While it might require less capital to get started today, it's also much harder to get and keep people's attention. It's even hard for multinationals to do that. The distractions for people's attention and their time have proliferated dramatically and we're still in the infancy of the Internet.

Somebody said the other day that between now and ten years from now, the amount of information and knowledge that's

> *"While it might require less capital to get started today, it's also much harder to get and keep people's attention."*

available to you and me at home, through our computer, is going to multiply a hundred thousand times. So it's not going to be easy. It's very difficult to cut through all of that clutter and communicate a clear compelling message and, by the way, to get that message to a receptive person on the other end.

IPOs for Small Companies?

■ **George Gendron** Right now the vast majority of companies, even very attractive and profitable ones in the United

States, are not what we would call IPO candidates. The reason for that is the investment banking firms have high overhead and need to do deals of a certain minimum size in order to make money on those deals.

People like the guys at Wit Capital, and other companies, could create a stock market where you could do small deals. So it's possible that a healthy, viable company, which had a million dollars annually in revenue, could go public.

There are other online players like garage.com that are using a slightly different twist. They are attempting to use the Internet as the tool to put together founders of young companies—people looking for early-stage capital—with angel investors—wealthy individuals who want to invest in start-ups.

People estimate that there's as much as $35 billion worth of angel money invested in companies every year, but there's no real rational marketplace. You're going to see other attempts to match individual investors with entrepreneurs proliferate all over the country, and they'll proliferate, probably, by activity. I expect there will also be companies like this that are based on geography. For example, I'm sure there will be a bostonangel.com. I'm an investor living in Boston, but I'd like to invest in local companies because I'd like to be able to meet with them routinely face-to-face.

Execute, Execute, Execute

■ **George Gendron** In 1984 we asked the founders of that year's *Inc.* 500 companies—our annual list of fastest growing private companies in the United States—what's the one thing, more than anything else, that has led to your current success? Now this was a particularly hot class—Microsoft and Oracle were on that 500 list; these were companies that were destined to become multinational giants. Seventy-five percent said they had a really novel, unusual, proprietary idea for their business. Not surprising!

Ten years later, we asked the same question of the *Inc.* 500 founders, and 75 percent said

"When industries consolidate, entrepreneurs flourish."

they would describe the idea for their business as ordinary or mundane. So we said, "If the idea for your business is ordinary, why the hell are you so successful?" They said, "Superior execution."

Basically they explained that the day when you can go out and build a sustainable company around a hot idea is over because you get copied so quickly. The only way to build a sustainable company, they said, is to take an idea and execute it better than other people, offer a product that has higher quality at a lower price and get it to market faster, with more customized features.

We realized back in 1994 that it was time to say goodbye to the age of entrepreneurial novelty and welcome to the age of entrepreneurial execution. That message is just as true today, even though we're going through a temporary period where companies that go public when they're six months old have billion-dollar valuations. The truth is that it won't last. This pattern happened before with the PC revolution; there were 200 hardware companies, now there are 7. It happened with biotech; it happens with everything.

A lot of what's being written about the Internet makes it seem as if we're going to end up with five portals that will dominate the world. So much attention is being focused on the AOLs, the Amazons, the eBays, and the Lycoses of the world. There's an impression that the Internet is accelerating the rate at which every market is consolidated.

Well, one thing that you learn really quickly just by hanging around *Inc.* is that when industries consolidate, entrepreneurs flourish. As companies consolidate, they can't pay attention to the niches the way they used to anymore. They just get too big. What ends up happening is that all the headlines focus on the consolidation, while tens of thousands of niches are being opened up. You can almost predict now where a lot of start-up activity will be by looking at where there's a lot of consolidation going on. You can have two apparently conflicting trends occurring simultaneously, and that's what's happening right now. The rate at which new opportunities will be created for entrepreneurs on the Internet will be breathtaking.

Instant Communication

■ **Mark Cuban** Every company in the world can benefit from real-time communication of a message. That hasn't existed before. It could be the conference call of a public company communicating to their shareholders. It could be the CEO of a major corporation communicating his ideas to his employers. For instance, Motorola's gone through a lot of change in their organization. We put a camera in front of Chris Galvin's face, the COO, and enabled him to broadcast to the entire company. People who were in different time zones or who were on vacation and couldn't make it, could either watch from home or listen to the replay. We enabled it so that they could ask questions in real time, and Mr. Galvin could respond to them. This is real-time communication. There's not one company in the world that can't benefit from it.

■ **George Gendron** Another benefit of having your business online is, if you're keeping track of your transactions you're getting unbelievable information in real time about what people want and what they're buying. It's not like waiting for the inventory report at the end of the month to find out what people bought; you come in the morning and see what happened in the prior twenty-four hours.

The other advantage is you become smarter about the way your site is structured. You can invite people to request things that they'd love to buy from the store but the store doesn't stock. Now your customers can begin to help you determine your inventory, and they can do it in real time. It's not fragmented and anecdotal data, it's information that you can capture in real time and archive.

You can reach a point, as we said earlier, where customers can dictate the terms under which they'll want to conduct a transaction. They can also begin to tell the retailer what they'd like the retailer to sell them. All of this helps to create a sense of community, which really smart companies want to do.

Profitability Still Counts

■ **George Gendron** We're living through a period right now that is an aberration and creates the impression that a lot of people are starting businesses, taking them public or being acquired, making a fortune, and then doing it again. The problem with that idea is that for every Amazon, there are tens of thousands of people who have tried to do it and failed. They just don't get much attention.

When you get beyond the hype, people are going to end up making money and creating value on the Internet the way they always have—by creating viable companies that add value to the economy and end up being profitable, and then, eventually, could be sold. We'll discover sooner, rather than later, that when it comes to profitability, the old rules still apply.

Act on What You Love

■ **George Gendron** I give the same advice today that I've been giving for every year that I've been at *Inc.*, which is, there has never been a more exciting period to be in business. In fact, there's never been a more exciting period to start a company, and it seems as if the conditions for doing it get better every year, not worse. If you want to be an entrepreneur and try to start something on your own, and you could have been born anytime, the best time to be doing it would be right now, here today. And it will only continue to get better.

> *"There has never been a more exciting period to be in business."*

My advice, particularly for young people, is a lot like the advice that Hemingway used to give to young writers: Write about what you know. I'd say, start a business based around something that you know or something that you love. When you're young, that's where your strengths lie. As you get older and get more industry experience, your options start to multiply.

Garden.com, for example, had a group of people who were seasoned enough and sophisticated enough to feel that they had developed a bunch of management talents that were transportable. They could do garden.com, but they could also do somethingelse.com. When you're just out of college, that's not the case. You don't have that knowledge, you don't have the Rolodex, you don't have the access to capital, you don't have real-world business experience. But that doesn't mean that you don't have something that you can use to build a business.

When you've got a hunger to go out and do something on your own, I think you should do it. The longer you wait, the harder it is to accomplish because you end up with more financial responsibilities. I don't care what anybody says, it's a lot harder to start a business when you're thirty-five.

Suggested Web Sites

all-biz.com	morebusiness.com
financehub.com	nbia.org
hoaa.com	sba.gov
inc.com	smallbizhelp.net
moneyhunter.com	vfinance.com

PLAYING BY THE NEW CAREER RULES

I spent the first thirty years of my life without a career focus, never able to settle on a choice that would inspire me. I met a remarkable man during a random chat one day. His obvious dedication to his work gave me the desire to find that passion for my life. Through our daily interactions I realized I had to follow my strengths and use my "bulldogged determinedness" (his description of me) toward a journalism career.

—**Colleen Ebel, Alberta**

I first began accessing the Internet in 1995 when I was working at The Good Housekeeping Institute as the dining services coordinator. My love of food led me to the eGG forum (Electronic Gourmet Guide) on AOL. I applied as a message board manager, answering food and cooking questions. I took classes to learn HTML so that I could publish my own food and travel Web page. One thing led to another. I am now the Miami for Visitors guide on About.com [gomiami.about.com], where I am paid to write and maintain the site. My life has not been the same!

—**Audrey Parker, Florida**

Looking for a job? Interested in testing your employment prospects elsewhere? Don't just reach for the Sunday classified section, now you can join the millions of people who are clicking their way to new career horizons. The online job industry is taking off. Job postings were up 60 percent from early 1998 to early 1999, according to data from *The Industry Standard*, an industry news magazine. And Forrester Research expects that jobs posted online will represent close to 20 percent of classified advertising employment budgets by 2003. A report from Nua Internet Surveys notes that 82 percent of students graduating from college in 1999 will search for jobs online, according to a survey by SBC Internet Services. The Internet goes beyond the electronic posting of jobs and sending of résumés. It enables savvy users to manage their careers in ways that were heretofore impossible.

> *"Middle management has a much more important role now than it ever did before."*

The time to explore new options is not when you've been laid off. Instead, electronic tools enable you to stay on top of management trends and industry news, network with others, and receive the training that can make you more valuable in the workplace, all while you are actively employed. Moreover, if you are planning to relocate to another city or state, the Internet can help you research companies in the area, explore housing alternatives, and look at the local paper to get a feel for the new community—all without leaving your house. If you do find yourself out of a job, pounding the virtual pavement will broaden your search options and save wear and tear on your shoes.

Man Jit Singh is president and chief executive officer of Futurestep, an online executive recruiting service from Korn/Ferry International and *The Wall Street Journal*. Korn/Ferry is an executive search firm that recruits for positions with annual compensation of over $150,000; Futurestep is focused on middle-management jobs with annual compensation in the $75,000 to $150,000 range.

While many middle managers have seen their jobs trimmed in recent years, Singh does not believe they are an endangered species—although their roles will change. "Middle management has a much more important role now than it ever did before." This is because these managers are charged with managing teams of generation Xers who act as "contract workers." In this environment, he adds, "middle management is the custodian of the corporate strategy and must provide continuity in vision as teams form and dissolve." Senior management will have to readjust, he adds, becoming more computer literate than ever before.

Jeff Taylor, founder and chief executive officer of Monster.com, the number one job board site with close to 7.6 million monthly visitors, was an early convert to the Internet. He launched the site in the summer of 1994, before Internet mania set in. In fact, Monster.com (previously known as the Monster Board) was only the 454th commercial Web site launched. Taylor started with 30 clients and 200 job postings and has since seen his career hub site grow to more than 100,000 clients; 210,000 job postings; and 1.3 million résumés, which keep growing by about 40,000 résumés a week.

How do Taylor and Singh suggest you employ the Internet in your career management efforts? Do firms prefer electronic or paper résumés? How are electronic résumés scanned? What does it take to succeed in the twenty-first century? Whether you're seeking a job or looking to hire someone, whether you're at entry level or occupy the executive suite, you can't afford to miss out on their seasoned advice for job seekers and employers.

The New-Age Classifieds

■ **Jeff Taylor** For a hundred years the place for job seekers to go look for a job and for employers to go look for people has been the newspaper. What we've done—in a five-year transformation—is provide a new resource for job seekers and employers.

This new resource is easier. You can look for a job anytime you want, twenty-four hours a day, seven days a week. You don't have to wait for the Sunday newspaper to get your help wanted section.

Instead of spending an hour flipping through the paper trying to find the jobs you're qualified for, the job search engine lets you find those jobs in about two minutes. Then you can spend the rest of that hour actually researching the companies you're interested in.

The ability to apply online means an end to typing laborious cover letters and sitting at home at your computer or typewriter, totally intimidated, trying to figure out what to say to make yourself stand out. Instead, in a twenty- to thirty-minute experience, you can find jobs you're qualified for, research the companies, develop a cover letter message, cut and paste your résumé, and apply directly to the company, all in one sitting.

Online job hunting also lets you speed to the best opportunities. Instead of having to wait until the Sunday paper comes out and applying the next week, you can answer the ad as soon as it's posted. This shows an employer that you're on top of things.

Less Work for Employers

■ **Jeff Taylor** The employer can also recruit twenty-four hours a day, seven days a week. People don't give their notice on Thursday at three o'clock to make it convenient for you to make the newspaper's deadline; people give their notice all the time. So it's nice to be able to manage the process and post the job right away.

Companies get a prequalified candidate from an online applicant, because a job seeker needs to know how to use his or her computer, how to use the Internet, how to traverse the Web, how to find a site like Monster.com, how to apply for a job online, how to get a résumé onto the system.

Employers also get to beat the competition to the best

prospect by posting a job earlier in the week rather than waiting for the newspaper deadline.

If you look at the human resources department in an organization, their customer is really the line manager. So if a line manager calls on a Tuesday and says, "Will you post this job for me?" and the HR person can get her the first responses in an hour instead of a week later, this reflects very well on the HR professional. Moreover, electronic résumés are easily rerouted to the managers without having to be scanned and formatted for their systems.

Finally, advertising online is a fraction of the cost of newspaper advertising; it's roughly one-tenth of the cost of advertising in major markets, and about one-quarter or one-half of the cost of placing an ad in a local paper.

■ **Man Jit Singh** Most large companies have their own Web pages set up to receive applications. They are encouraging electronic résumés rather than paper résumés, which they have to scan into their database.

At the same time companies are finding that instead of print ads, they can post jobs on the Internet and get people to apply to them directly from various job boards. It's opened up a whole new avenue for informing people about jobs and it's broadened a company's options.

■ **Jeff Taylor** When you place an ad in the *Chicago Tribune* you get anybody who can type a cover letter, never mind that—anybody who can lick a stamp and is within the circulation range of the paper.

There's an expression: You've got to kiss a lot of frogs to find your prince. The frogs you kiss in the traditional media are within the circulation range of the *Chicago Tribune*. On the Internet, it's just a different set of frogs because you can potentially get candidates from around the world.

The Weeding-Out Process

■ **Man Jit Singh** The issue that companies are facing is they're getting inundated with data. They are getting thousands and thousands and thousands of résumés when they do a posting on some of the popular job boards. As a result, they have discovered that they need to screen these résumés more effectively.

On our Web site, for example, we can process large volumes of people and come up with the relevant set of candidates that will be applicable to the company.

First, we have all candidates register. They provide background employment and education information, but most important, they fill out a profile of the kind of work environment that they're seeking. We find that the single biggest reason why a person succeeds or fails, especially at the midmanagement level, is culture fit. Do you fit the culture of the department in which you're going to work? Is your style going to work there?

Our clients fill out similar forms, enabling us to make better matches. We review their responses carefully to determine, for example, if they need to have a C.P.A. or not. And then we look at the environment of the department and the career opportunities it offers versus an individual's career motives.

Our assessment evaluates two things. One, it looks at what it takes to succeed on the job, and that very simplistically is a function of how you use information to make decisions. For instance, if you're someone who needs a lot of information before you make a decision, you may be the person to build a fighter plane but not the person to fly it.

Second, it looks at your career motives and what a company can offer. Take generation Xers, they want to come in and do interesting projects and then move on. Well, if you look at the research department of a major pharmaceutical firm, they may want you to come in and live and die oncology and be known for your expertise in a narrow class of cells over many years. Well, that may not suit a generation Xer, but the same company's sales department, which rotates people from sales to marketing to new product and postmarketing activities, is a perfect fit.

An Ongoing Relationship

■ **Man Jit Singh** This type of matching existed before the Internet, but the Internet allows us to reach out to the widest number of people because, at the mid-management level, companies are looking for the best and the brightest across all industries. Industry doesn't matter as much at this level, what matters is a cultural fit.

What the Internet enables us to do is go out and collect these people into our database, which

> *"In the old days it was one way. You sent in your résumé, you never heard anything."*

currently has 316,000 people in the United States. In a traditional search, I would start calling people, maybe I would make 300 calls, maybe less, but I'm never going to provide my client with access to 316,000 people. The Internet also allows me to keep that database up-to-date.

I know where people are because every two weeks I send them an e-mail. If their e-mail comes back undelivered, I send them a letter at their home while they're still getting their mail forwarded, so I can keep my database fresh and continue to help manage people's careers. In addition to a dialogue with people, the Internet also allows me to provide them with useful advice. They can come to the site, read articles, go to chat rooms and talk anonymously to other members.

All these things enable them to manage their careers more effectively, and it's only because of this communication medium called the Internet that that's possible. In the old days it was one way. You sent in your résumé, you never heard anything.

Today you are building a lifetime relationship with a company like ours. We might have a job for you today or next year or five years down the road, but, more important, you have a place to come anytime you have a question about your career.

Putting Employers in the Hot Seat

■ **Man Jit Singh** Our belief is all companies are going to have to find more intelligent ways to process prospective employee data because they're getting too much of it. The other fact is that the Internet is quite demanding. When someone sends in a résumé and applies for a job, he expects to be managed very actively, she expects to hear from the company, and many companies are ill-prepared to keep up-to-date with their candidates.

So two things happen. One, the candidate actually gets turned off by his experience, which is bad because on the Internet he can spread that information around. But, two, the companies lose the ability to keep their database fresh, so when the time comes and they could really use someone, they find most of their database is no longer current.

Keeping Your Confidence(s)

■ **Man Jit Singh** At the mid-management level you need to go to sites that are completely confidential so your résumé isn't shopped around and available for all to see. I would not go to a site that didn't guarantee confidentiality.

There are sites where you post your résumé and it's available for everyone to see. Personally, I think that that's cheapening yourself. You get a lot of people looking at you. I'm not sure it's the most effective approach.

Then there are sites that are hybrids that block your name, address, and phone number, but let people review your basic particulars. Then if they're interested, they'll indicate that to you, you can look at the job, and decide whether you want to respond or not. However, there is a danger that people can recognize who you are. Let's take, for example, a manager in the entertainment area at Price Waterhouse in Los Angeles. There's probably only one manager at Price Waterhouse in Los Angeles who's worked in entertainment. So people can start figuring out who you are, and that's not necessarily to your advantage.

We would recommend having people list themselves only where it's confidential, and instead of putting their résumé out, look at the job boards, such as Monster.com, CareerPath [careerpath.com], CareerMosaic [careermosaic.com], HotJobs [hotjobs.com]. If you're looking for a more junior position, look at the job boards, and if you see a job you like, apply for it directly. At the mid-management level there's a good job board at the Wall Street Journal [careers.wsj.com]. They're our partner and we send people there to look at those job lists.

There are a few job databases that are specific to an industry niche, such as Attorneys at Work [attorneysatwork.com] for lawyers. So almost every function and every industry is going to have a specialty board of some kind that you can register on.

If you know the company that you are interested in working for you can go to its site. If there's a job posted that you are interested in, click on it and respond. If there's not a job, you can send in a résumé electronically with a cover letter.

■ **Jeff Taylor** How can executives be comfortable that their search will be confidential? In the Monster.com résumé database, these are the three popular choices for storing a résumé: public, confidential, and private.

Public means your résumé is going to be in an open database for all of our member companies to be able to search, which probably means either you're active in your search or you're a contractor and you're always looking, or you've had a bad day at the office and turned your résumé on.

Confidential means that your contact information is hidden and just your skills are listed; your contact information is replaced by a résumé number. That way a company can e-mail your résumé number and it would get to you, but they don't know who they're e-mailing.

Private means that your résumé is being stored for free in our system, and when you find a job you're interested in, you pull your résumé out and apply online, but no one else can ever see your résumé.

One of the things that I would recommend, especially as you become more senior in your career, is that you spend more time making sure that the places where you place your résumé look at the ethical nature of their communications and the confidentiality of your particular résumé.

Now if you are the CFO of General Motors or of Disney, then you're going to want to be more careful about the way you use your résumé online. There is a part of the business where either the contingency recruiter or the executive recruiter will continue to have a very important job, and that's in moving gainfully employed executives from one position to another based on the needs and desires both of the candidate and the employer.

Are Online Job Boards for Everyone?

■ **Man Jit Singh** At this point there are not as many senior executive positions being filled through online means. Specifically, you are not finding the CEOs of major Fortune 500 companies coming through an online search. That will change as the generations move up.

But this is not a medium just for the young. Every age group is using the Internet. We have people of all age groups on our database, and the preconceived notion that it is only the young kids who are experimenting is just not true anymore.

■ **Jeff Taylor** The target audience for using Internet job searching is the Information Age worker, which is what I call somebody who spends at least an hour a week on a computer. That also includes some executives and a small group of blue-collar workers.

To get a clearer picture of this you could draw a pyramid, the top of it is the executive group, and a narrow band at the bottom of the pyramid rep-

> *"Not only is the Web appropriate for people at all levels, it should be measured as one of the critical tools to finding your next position."*

resents the blue-collar worker. Then the whole middle is what I call the Information Age worker. If you draw a circle within that pyramid it will actually cross over the executive area at the very tip and cross over the blue-collar workers at the bottom of the circle. That's the target for Internet job searching.

In 1994 and 1995, 90 percent of the positions posted online were technical; about 10 percent were the first experiments in general recruiting. If you look today, about 45 percent of the jobs are technical, whether it's engineering or information technology or what I call sundry technical, which is positions in marketing where you need an engineering background. The other 55 percent, and by far the fastest growing sector, is every other job you can imagine. So you'll see online advertising in insurance, for administrative assistants and executives—kind of a whole laundry list of career opportunities.

The Web has grown up enough now that I wouldn't say certain positions are easier to get online. The experience and opportunities around online jobs have grown to the point where there are real career opportunities and people looking for all levels in all fields. Not only is the Web appropriate for people at all levels, it should be measured as one of the critical tools to finding your next position.

Creating an Online Résumé

■ **Man Jit Singh** Honestly, there are a number of viewpoints on what kind of résumé should be sent by e-mail. There are people who will tell you to put a block at the top of your résumé that has the keywords for the kind of work you want to focus on. The block can be hidden in an HTML document by putting the keywords in the same color as the background; you have a résumé that looks like a normal résumé, but it has a block of keywords that the company's search engine will detect and then pull up your résumé.

There are also different views on how much formatting you should put into a résumé because a lot of this is being electronically processed. Increasingly, companies are getting more and more sophisticated; they can handle any format. You can send it like a paper résumé, looking nice, and they will be able to read it in that format and print it out.

■ **Jeff Taylor** I can remember very clearly coming out of college and thinking about putting an image of a high jumper on my résumé to show graphically the skills that I had as an entry-level candidate. I recall that one of the discussions that people had is what kind of paper are you going to do your résumé on? There was this cool, gray-flecked paper and all those great typefaces that I was going to use for my résumé.

All of that stuff is a disaster in today's workplace. You want to either format your résumé electronically and store it in

Word on your desktop so you can cut and paste it into a Web form or so you can e-mail your résumé in its entirety.

I'm told by internal sources, and by other industry contacts, that about a third of the résumés come in through the mail, about a third of the résumés come in by e-mail, and about a third of the résumés come in through a Web form. Two years ago it was about 80 percent paper and 20 percent electronic.

That doesn't mean that paper résumés will become obsolete soon. I think paper résumés are always going to be there, but people should know that many corporations are moving to an electronic file cabinet for résumés as opposed to the traditional gray filing cabinet. By doing that, they're actually taking a picture of your résumé and using a simple search system to match the words in your résumé to a particular job requirement.

What Do Recruiters Look For?

■ **Man Jit Singh** What happens to résumés that are sent and then scanned electronically? Well, it's very similar to what humans did when you sent them paper. People look at a résumé very quickly for key things. Just as an example, if this particular person was looking for M.B.A.s, he'd want to know: Does the person have an M.B.A.? Is it from a recognizable school? What is the person's work experience? Then he'd say, "Three pluses, it goes in one pile; three minuses, it may go in another pile."

It's very similar to what electronic scanning systems do. They look at whether you have the degrees they're looking for, or do you have the number of years of work experience they're looking for. It also scans for keywords. Is your experience relevant? But it also enables one to vary any criteria; for example, to look at candidates with two years work experience instead of five years. On our site we can also weigh any of these factors in considering a fit and, very important, include the cultural dimensions. There is no way to understand how an individual fits with your corporation from just a paper résumé. So it enables a much more intelligent choice to be made faster.

When you have hundreds of résumés to read, the fatigue factor sets in at a certain point, and unfortunately, if you're at the back end of the pile you may be skipped. Whereas on the electronic side you're not skipped. You will be considered.

■ **Jeff Taylor** The old rules for writing résumés suggested that you were supposed to use, in reason, some colorful adjectives that would describe your management experience or your skills in a particular marketing job. You would say things like, "I'm a people person" and that you are a "manager of a large staff." But now you would want to redefine those descriptions to use phrases that get at specific skills. Are you a good marketing person? Are you a good communicator? You would want to give the technical description or the specific words that describe the general skills you have.

This is hard for people to do, but you have to realize that times have changed. In the 1980s, for example, you would state on your résumé that you were computer literate and that would be sufficient. Today you want to state that you're proficient in the Microsoft Office Suite and Word and Excel and HTML.

Moreover, as an entry-level worker, you want to retool your objective. So instead of saying, "I want an opportunity that allows me to grow with a medium-size company," now you want to say, "I'm looking for marketing opportunities at an Internet company where I can learn HTML and publishing." That way you have the word *Internet*, the word *marketing*, the word *HTML*, and the word *publishing* all in your résumé.

Focus, Focus, Focus

■ **Man Jit Singh** In any job hunt you may get turned down again and again, but if you persevere and you know what you really want to do, you're going to find the right job eventually. The Net allows you to say, "Hey, there's a marketing job, let me try that. I'll tailor my résumé and send off one for marketing. Oh, there's a financial planning job, let me try that because I've got an M.B.A." It allows you to diffuse your job search so much that you barely know what you're doing. In fact, you lose credibility because you now have too many options.

It's much better to focus, and stick to what you really believe you want to do. You've got to keep trying and going back and taking rejections, if that's what happens for a while. Eventually there's a crest, and suddenly you start getting acceptances. But if you've applied to five of these electronic jobs and you said, "I didn't get anything back, let me try five in a different area," that's a mistake, and that is happening.

■ **Jeff Taylor** The goal here is not to pump up your résumé with words that would mislead somebody about your skills, but you do want to describe the kinds of positions that you're looking for, and you want to describe your skills in a way that will increase the chance that your résumé will be picked up by a keyword searching mechanism.

There's an expression "loading your résumé," and it doesn't take long before somebody realizes that a résumé has been loaded without the applicant having the skills to back it up.

It's so easy to apply online that you should customize your cover letter or message, which you can do right online, specifically to each job. With electronic résumés I would recommend not doing a résumé-blaster type of action, but instead doing a customized communication.

Taking Charge of Your Career

■ **Man Jit Singh** The Internet gives you, for the first time, access to a huge amount of information to manage your career. For example, our salary data is useful when you want to know whether you're underpaid or overpaid. Our assessment feedback is useful in telling you which area you should go into. There are articles at many sites that talk about career issues. There is so much information on the Web that will help you structure yourself and figure out what the trends are and where you need to develop your skills to keep up-to-date.

There's always been great secrecy about negotiations on salary, but it's becoming more and more transparent. You know what people are earning out there, you know what you're worth. You can manage yourself more aggressively. You know what skills you need to develop. You know where you can go and get them. Some of the sites are even linked to training programs. It is a tremendous opportunity to take control and be in charge of your career.

E-mail and the ability to network through the Net is just another tool at your disposal. Of course, you should also continue your in-person networking. But this gives you a fabulous opportunity to network even more deeply.

For instance, we've found that the members of our site wanted to send batch e-mail to other people at our site who were in their graduating class from university. Well, we can make that happen. They've lost touch with some of these people, but anonymously we can send this out, and the ones who want to get together can get together in a group. We can even set up a chat room. There are all kinds of possibilities.

In addition, more and more people are using e-mail to network directly into companies. They might even ask the human resources department to set up an e-mail relationship with someone in the company, so they can go back and forth on what's good about a company, what's bad about a company. It greatly expands your ability to get out there; that's the power of e-mail.

> "For the last fifty years managing your career has meant going to the local copy store, having your résumé typeset, making thirty copies, putting them in a manila folder, going home and cutting out ads, applying for three jobs, and thinking the whole process stinks."

■ **Jeff Taylor** For the last fifty years managing your career has meant going to the local copy store, having your résumé typeset, making thirty copies, putting them in a manila folder, going home and cutting out ads, applying for three jobs, and thinking the whole process stinks. That is a typical career initiative for everyone, from the entry-level person all the way up to a very experienced person.

With the proliferation of the Web, the ability to self-publish your résumé on the Internet is probably the most dynamic component of the career management process. One copy, always in distribution, easy to change.

Networking on the Internet

■ **Jeff Taylor** We have over 100,000 messages a week now on Monster.com in our chats and message boards, and we're seeing a whole marketplace forming of people saying, "I live in Boston and I'm a marketing person; does anybody know about opportunities?" What that tells me is there is a business opportunity, there's a marketplace forming that I'm not controlling, and that was a big part of why we decided to launch talent auctions online (allowing freelancers to announce and auction their services) because people are auctioning themselves without even knowing that's what they're doing.

With the popularity of online chat, companies have to be aware of the impact it can have on their reputations. For example, one of the things you can do online is go to your favorite stock listed on Yahoo! and then go to the message board area for that stock, where you are likely to find people talking about this company. Companies are very uncomfortable with this because people are saying, "This stock stinks. It's going to tank." And somebody else is saying, "No, this is a really good stock." And somebody else is saying, "I know somebody at this company and he's a real jerk." But this is a whole different kind of networking, and you can't control it.

I can't control what happens in our chat rooms either. There's a lot of quality career talk going on, but there's also a certain amount of dating that's trying to happen. That's just the way it is. Whenever you put people together it's going to happen. Someone is going to say, "What is your career? Can we meet?"

Tech Skills for the Twenty-First Century

■ **Man Jit Singh** I think the basics, in terms of technology skills, are still your spreadsheet, word processing, and probably some presentation package. Everyone's going to do his own presentations. You're not going to have assistants doing your presentations. Everyone's going to do her own spreadsheets, everyone's going to type her own letters, and so on and so forth.

I don't see us, as common individuals, needing to know C++ or Java or JavaScript or HTML. That's not necessary. It's all going to be point and click. So we're not going to have the need for having a huge amount of code knowledge in our heads, not at all. It's the other way, we're going to simplify that.

The Best Jobs and the Worst Jobs

■ **Man Jit Singh** I don't think the Internet has an impact on what the best jobs or what the worst jobs are. I think that those things will change based on where we head as a service economy as the population ages. Clearly the need to create content is going to be a growth business. Some of our smokestack industries are going to be less exciting. I don't think the Internet necessarily has a role other than that it is speeding distribution changes. In that sense, it is having an impact on every business, and there will be winners and losers.

■ **Jeff Taylor** A best job for you is a worst job for me. Jobs are a very individual challenge, but the business changes I'm seeing are that certain industries are really doing well. If you look, for example, at one of the hottest new areas, obviously the whole Internet sector has built up a new set of e-company activities. People who are wired into this industry are hot right now everywhere because everybody's trying to build up a Web presence and e-commerce initiatives.

I'm also seeing continued increase in health care participation online. A lot of the health care industry works on its feet and is not like typical computer users. As a result the health care industry has been slow to adopt the Internet, but I'm seeing it come on strong now.

How the Internet Economy Works

■ **Jeff Taylor** There is a business opportunity at every turn. It's the one thing that scares me about staying constant right now because the whole world is going to change owing to the way the Internet has penetrated what we do.

It's the difference between a Darwinian society and a Deming society or only the fit will survive versus quality, quality, quality. We've been in a Deming cycle for forty years where, generally speaking, we've been improving on the quality of our businesses without being at risk of the business changing like quicksand underneath us, at least in the major business sectors. With the Internet we've moved from a Deming culture back into a Darwinian culture. As a result entire business sectors are actually going to go away or get flipped upside down. There are examples of this phenomenon all over the place. I mean, if you look at convenience, you look at Amazon.com; if you look at price, you look at BUY.COM; if you look at deal making, you look at Priceline.com. All of these are examples of companies that have basically reinvented or flipped the model of the traditional bricks-and-mortar four-walls business.

I like to think of WWW [World Wide Web] as the world without walls, and the world without walls is, from my perspective, in direct conflict with the four-walls world. World without walls is about global business, it's about pricing structures that have fallen apart, and it's about the disintermediation of the middleman.

Now CEOs want to believe that WWW is the wild, wild West because then it feels as if a bunch of gunslingers, with very little substance, is out shooting things up, but they're not going to shoot me.

■ **Man Jit Singh** Internet companies are going to win in the long run. They are exciting places to be. They have a different work ethic, a different work culture, which is spreading to other industries.

The hierarchy command-and-control bureaucracy is gone. Now it is self-managed teams, it is enlightened teams, it is people with information, knowledge workers who use information productively to get things moving forward.

That said, I don't want to leave the impression that middle management is completely gone. Middle management has a much more important role now than it ever did before. In the past middle managers were the filters, the steps, the ladder.

> *"The executive who isn't computer literate is not going to survive in the long term."*

Now they are the keepers of the corporate vision, and as these teams assemble and disassemble, they're the people who guide the teams through a series of battles that eventually win the war of the corporate objective. Companies are going to have to restructure their information access and the technology to accommodate that flow of information.

The executive suite is going to have to be able to process the information they're going to receive. I think information is going to move faster, more efficiently, but I think they're going to have to process more of it. They're going to have to manipulate the data themselves rather than sending it back and forth. The executive who isn't computer literate is not going to survive in the long term.

Selling Talent to the Highest Bidder

■ **Jeff Taylor** The Internet is changing the way people are doing business. I see many more opportunities all over the Internet for the consumer to gain control of his or her experience. *Disintermediation* is an overused word but it is happening as the consumer wants more control over the transaction; the employment process is not immune to this either.

In fact, we're launching a new product called the Monster Talent Market, and we're challenging contractors and what we're calling free agents to declare their independence on an auction-style format. At our site, free agents can actually put themselves up for auction.

If you're a freelance writer and your desired rate is $30 an hour or $50 an hour, you can put yourself up in the auction and say, "I'm available to write freelance," and people can come in and bid for your services.

This service is for any type of free agent in any industry. There will be a fee to users, but not when we start. We've never had a fee before, but to put yourself up in the auction format there's going to be a micro payment of $3.95 a month.

We have plans to launch a college draft on the Internet where college graduates can register themselves. Everyone will put up a credential sheet, or draft sheet, with their work and school experience. We're going to do it with 100 schools and get all their college seniors to get in the draft. I guess you could say we're doing crazy stuff everywhere, but that's what businesses need to do today.

I also want to do a human stock market. We're starting to do the work right now on the concept of being able to develop a stock market for people. David Bowie led this charge with his Bowie Bonds when he packaged himself as a business and sold bonds. Ultimately we think that heads of companies have the potential of being traded. As our society moves from the employer or the corporation being in control to individuals really being in control, then we think there is the possibility of some sort of trading that could go on with human capital.

■ **Man Jit Singh** The company that is really going to win is the executive or group of executives who understand the impact of technology on their business. In the search business, for example, the impact is tremendous because traditionally what has been valued is finding people. With perfect information in the future, finding is going to be the least of the problems. What is going to count is assessing people correctly and placing them; that skill set is very different from having a Rolodex.

I liken it to the tax people in the accounting firms in the

1980s. They were valued for their knowledge of the tax code of 1954, a huge book they knew so well they could give you the answers off the top of their heads. Well, it became available on diskette in 1987 and they're all gone now because, first of all, they were terrible human beings to deal with; and second, the value of their knowledge went to zero overnight because you could do a keyword search for that information.

You've got to figure out how this technology is changing your business and what you need to do to change with it. At Korn/Ferry, for instance, we are now educating our people on how to use assessment tools and how to close a placement, rather than just finding people.

The End of Job Security

■ **Man Jit Singh** If people believe in today's environment that there is complete job security and they don't have to look and self-manage their career, I think they're in for a rude shock. The days of not being proactive about your career and expecting the corporation to look after you for life are gone. You have to take responsibility, and the Internet is a tool that facilitates your taking responsibility for your career and managing it. If you don't, you are likely to be disappointed, and you're going to be left behind. The Internet is a tool that you have to use. Are there other substitutes? Possibly, but this is the easiest tool, so why create unnecessary pain when you've got an easy tool?

> *"If people believe in today's environment that there is complete job security and they don't have to look and self-manage their career, I think they're in for a rude shock."*

The other message is pursue learning and understanding—learn what's going to happen, where you should be going, what issues managers are facing; keep yourself abreast of things; help manage yourself; help look at situations; be proactive. The Net can help you in that.

Suggested Web Sites

bestjobsusa.com	hotjobs.com
careerbuilder.com	jobsearch.org
careermosaic.com	jobtrak.com
careerpath.com	monster.com
dice.com	nettemps.com
headhunter.net	virtualrelocation.com

SEVEN

CONSUMER POWER

The milkman's coming back.

—Halsey Minor, CNET

I have been an avid horseback rider for several years and currently own three horses in Colorado. I found a new 1998 Logan Coach gooseneck, three horse, slant-load, horse trailer in my Web searches and ended up purchasing it. I saved $1,500—I'm so pleased! I also sold my two old horse trailers easily. What a happy ending to business between Colorado and Utah.

—Susan Hier, Colorado

The purchase of a Web TV changed my life in several ways. I am an invalid, and can't get around very much. I am now able to keep in touch with my family, who live in three different states on the East Coast. I also do all of my shopping for clothes on the Web. I had to get a new water kettle last week, so I shopped around on the Web, found one, and ordered it.

—Ruth Grant, California

There are many reasons for people to use the Web, but there is generally one experience that sucks you in and convinces you that this is not a passing fad. Halsey Minor, founder, chairman, and CEO of CNET—an online site offering technology news, product reviews, and comparative data, as well as auctions of computer and technology products—claims that most people can remember their first "gee-whiz" Internet experience, where they said, "Wow this is great, I can't do this anywhere else." For Minor it was discovering a dynamic virtual community that was a little democracy unto itself, at a time when there were very few Web pages in existence.

Today he sees two major kinds of "gee-whiz" experiences: getting information that you couldn't have gotten any other way, or even more important, commerce-related activity. People are often amazed to find products online that they can't get in their hometown or to discover the ease with which they can comparison shop and get the lowest prices. Ultimately, electronic commerce comes down to convenience, saving money, and making a more informed decision.

I remember my first "gee-whiz" shopping experience. It actually came about because of a frustrating experience at a neighborhood computer store. After wasting twenty minutes trying to discover if the printer I wanted was in stock, I went home, booted up my computer, and plunged into the unknown realm of e-commerce. In much less time than I had spent at the store, I shopped models and prices, clicked, and ordered. The order was placed on a Friday and the printer arrived on Monday. I was definitely hooked.

I'm not alone. Researchers disagree about what constitutes online shopping (does it include researching goods online but ordering them by phone or picking them up in the store?), which makes it hard to come up with just how much is being spent at virtual stores. According to research from Cyber Dialogue, $11 billion in goods were paid for online in 1998; however, if you factor in items that were ordered online and paid for offline, then another $15.5 billion was spent, and if you include offline orders that were influenced by the Internet, then you get another $50.8 billion worth of purchases, or a grand total of $77.3 billion in consumer spending in 1998 was affected by the Internet.

While electronic commerce is still in its infancy, the speed with which it is transforming traditional businesses is unprecedented. Amazon.com, for example, has demonstrated that a start-up Internet company can beat an established brand name like Barnes & Noble at selling books in cyberspace. Not content with just being a bookseller, Amazon wants to become a full-service electronic mall, the first place you turn to on the Web when you want to shop. As I write this, it is selling books, music, videos, gifts, electronics, and toys; offering free music downloads on its site to entice listeners to buy the CDs; has invested in sites that sell pet supplies, groceries, pharmaceuticals, and beauty and health care products; links to other sites on the Web that sell clothing, computer hardware, and travel; and offers customers the ability to buy and sell from its auction site.

If you enjoy going to yard sales or watching *Antiques Road Show* on television, you will be pleased to find out that millions of collectors have followed their passion for treasure hunting right to their computer. The largest auction site, eBay [ebay.com], has more than 1.8 million items up for sale every day in over 1,500 categories. In the fourth quarter of 1998, $306 million worth of merchandise was sold among individuals on the site.

Everyone seems to be getting into the electronic-commerce act: Nike, Sears, General Motors. Even Mercedes-Benz is offering to test Web sales of its used vehicles. Moreover, 20 percent of respondents to an NPD Online Research Survey said they've redeemed coupons they "cut" online. Even the U.S. Postal Service has gone digital. In August 1999 it announced the availability of postage that customers can buy over the Internet; the first new way of delivering stamps since the introduction of the postage meter seventy-nine years ago. Electronic business is growing so fast that it is now on the federal government's radar screen; it announced in 1999 that it will begin tracking annual online sales.

You can pretty much buy anything you want online, from homes to garden furniture, from new cars to used cars, concert tickets to airline tickets, diapers to toilet paper, books to CDs, videos to violins, wine to filet mignon, and on and on and on. Big-ticket items, like cars, are more likely to be researched on-line and bought offline, but consumers have discovered that knowing what a dealer paid to have a car delivered to the showroom gives the buyer considerable negotiating clout.

And with many investment dollars going toward figuring out the next great idea for e-commerce, you can bet there will continue to be many unique shopping models cropping up. For instance, Paul Allen, the billionaire co-founder of Microsoft, launched Mercata [mercata.com] in May 1999, based on the principle that goods will get cheaper the more people sign up to buy them. So the price of a color television could be $300 to start, but after 200 people each agree to buy a set, the price could drop, for all, to $270. Priceline [priceline.com] came to market with the unique idea of matching buyers and suppliers, but with a twist—the buyers are in control of the game. Here's how it works: Consumers get to name the price they want to pay on everything from airline tickets to hotel rooms, new cars, home mortgages, refinancings, and home equity loans. Priceline submits your request to suppliers and quickly notifies you if they have found a supplier willing to accept your price. Nice concept!

Booking travel is particularly popular online. Terrell Jones, president and CEO of Travelocity, notes that there are more dollars spent on travel on the Web than anything else. Travelocity [travelocity.com] has over 6 million members. In 1998 it sold $285 million in travel online, which, Jones says, put it among the top twenty travel agents in the United States in bookings. Travelocity is run by Sabre, the company whose airline reservation system is used by 40,000 travel agents in 100 countries around the world. In October, Travelocity announced plans to merge with Preview Travel.

When the merger is complete, Travelocity will be the leader in online travel.

Kathy Misunas is chairman, CEO, and president of brandwise, LLC, a new Internet company launched in early 1999 that takes comparison shopping to new heights. Key to the development of this Web site is the creation of a giant database with millions of pieces of data on various home-related consumer products that you buy infrequently, such as major appliances and consumer electronics. In the future the site will add other products, such as small appliances and lawn and garden equipment. Misunas is no stranger to database management and product distribution; as the former CEO of Sabre, she was responsible for huge travel databases used by customers around the globe. In our conversations, Misunas talked about the site's current services, as well as some future ideas.

Minor, Jones, and Misunas all believe the Web is empowering consumers and forcing suppliers to overhaul their businesses to better meet their customers' needs. They share their thoughts—along with additional comments from George Bell of Excite@Home, Ellen Pack of Women.com, and David Bohnett, founder of GeoCities—on this amazing new world of commerce and show how you can become one smart customer.

Home Shopping: What's in Store?

■ **Halsey Minor** My wife and I were talking the other day and agreed it just doesn't make sense for us to go to twenty different stores to buy stuff when we can go and buy it all over the Web and have UPS deliver all the products. Basically it's much more efficient to have one truck driving around dropping stuff off as opposed to having twenty families going out and driving to stores and buying.

But even people like me, who live on the Internet, are only buying a fraction of the goods and services that they will buy in a couple of years. Ultimately there's a lot of infrastructure that needs to be built

> *"Basically it's much more efficient to have one truck driving around dropping stuff off as opposed to having twenty families going out and driving to stores and buying."*

and local delivery services that need to be provided. Internet commerce could not exist without UPS and Federal Express. And some of the services are so new they haven't perfected the formula yet. But over time people will get much better at selling online, and more and more of our everyday transactions will migrate to the Web.

■ **Terrell Jones** Today's busy consumer is looking for convenience and often speed, and the Internet is a great place to answer those two demands. It's convenient in that the stores never close; they're available twenty-four hours a day, and there's this huge selection of products. People are also looking for low prices. Many innovative marketers have found ways to have lower prices because they don't have to have a storefront, and therefore, may not need to carry inventory.

People are beginning to reinvent their business in new ways, and that, in turn, is attracting shoppers. Take, for example, a site like garden.com where you pull up a little application, tell them your zip code, and you can start dragging flowers into your garden and arranging them. If a flower won't grow in your particular part of the country, it pops back out of the garden. When you get done putting all the plants where you want them, you can simply order your garden. They'll get all the seeds for you, they'll tell you how to water it, they'll order the fertilizer, they'll even sell you the tools. That would be very hard to do at a garden shop.

Amazon.com is doing a similar thing with recommending

books. I never had a bookstore say to me, "Well, the people who are buying this book are buying that book too." I've had them recommend books, but never on that scale.

■ **Halsey Minor** Loans are a great example of the kind of transaction that will migrate to the Web; you can do instantaneous comparisons of price and terms. Financial services are widely available on the Internet and people are getting pretty close to perfecting the experience of online trading. I think virtually any commodity that you buy can probably be merchandised better over the Internet.

An area where no one's done it right is groceries. That's probably the best example of where the infrastructure needs to be built. When my wife and I are really busy we use a service called Peapod [peapod.com]; it's for active families, particularly if both parents are wage earners and don't have time to go to the grocery store. The vast majority of stuff you buy is repetitive, like peanut butter and jelly for your kids. It would be great to buy all that online and have somebody deliver it to you.

Comparison Shopping Made Easy

■ **Halsey Minor** Of all the things that are in the advanced intelligence, shopping category, the one that we know works is price comparison because consumers do that already. You're not asking them to think some entirely new way about shopping. A lot of these intelligent agents, such as shopping bots [intelligent software programs that search for information], are a little more complicated. When you try to see what people who are like you like, that's not typically the way we think about shopping.

But every time we shop we do wonder whether we're getting a good deal. It's very simple for people to say, "I want to buy this, show me what ten or twenty or thirty people are sell-ing this item for." We see a lot of this on CNET. We have prob-ably over 100,000 people a day who come in and do price comparisons on products from our pricing database, so we know that it works.

■ **George Bell** One of the most powerful aspects of the Web, from a commercial perspective, is the ability it provides to make comparisons. Any comparison that makes sense from a consumer perspective—comparing mortgages, insurance, the price of cars, even the price of books—is so easily accom-plished on the Web that it reduces the consumer's resistance to comparison. You can even ask for comparative bids to be de-livered to your e-mail box from mortgage providers and insur-ance providers. I bought the mortgage to my home in Maine on the Web a year and a half ago.

I absolutely believe that, because of this capability, virtually everything on the Web is going to have to be sold at or near cost over time. The commerce sites are going to have to make their margin not from the consumer, but from squeezing the supply end of the chain.

Narrowing Down Your Choices

■ **Kathy Misunas** The Web allows us to empower the con-sumer by making use of the data we've collected in such a way that it satisfies *their* particular needs for a product. Let's say you live in an apartment with a small kitchen. You want to find a really quiet dishwasher because you know if you turn on a loud dishwasher that you can't use your phone!

There are hundreds of dishwashers in the brandwise data-base. As you begin your search, we ask you a series of questions that allow you to start narrowing down the number of products that will suit your needs. When you get to the question on performance, you can indicate that quietness is really important to you so we can weight it accordingly. We can also screen for other features that you desire (like color or capacity), as well as your preferred price range. We want to narrow down the response to a choice of three or four different products that match your needs—since that's what our usability and focus groups told us consumers want.

Once the choices are more focused, we provide you with more in-depth information about each product's characteristics. If you want to compare one to the other, there's a compare button so you can see, on one page, exactly what the essential differences of those products are. It's very tailored to finding the best product based upon your needs versus just what is on special or what other consumers have bought.

At the end of the search, we ask you if you're interested in buying and/or going to a retailer to see any of the products. If you want to go to the store, we then take you through a set of questions, which starts by your entering your zip code. We then indicate which retailers have that product available for you to see in their stores, within the travel distance that you specify.

You can also indicate your desired delivery, installation, warranty, and service preferences. If you want your new product delivered in the evening, as well as want your old dishwasher taken away, you can select those requirements and see a list of retailers in your area that offer those particular services. Either way, you can buy the product online through a merchant or visit a retailer that carries the product you want to see.

The Web: Vacationers' Paradise

■ **Terrell Jones** Travel is a great virtual product. It's an experience. You hardly ever buy the same thing twice, particularly on a vacation. Therefore, you have a product that needs a lot of research and has complicated pricing. The Web is a good place to do research and of course, the computer tools we offer will help get you through the pricing.

There are many choices in travel. It takes a long time to listen to all those over the phone, and a lot of people need time to study them. We also find that travel is a collaborative experience, particularly leisure travel. You generally go with a friend or a loved one and therefore you can't plan it by yourself. Usually that's done at home—when the stores are closed but the Web is open—or at work, when both parties can be online at the same time they're conferring on the phone.

Who's Shopping on the Web?

■ **Terrell Jones** It used to be that everybody would physically walk down and talk to Thomas Cook before going on the steamship. Nobody does that anymore, everybody uses a telephone. Most people, frankly, don't go to a travel agency physically anymore. They might go the first time, then once they've established a relationship, they never go again.

Well, the Web takes that one step further by saying, why don't you do the shopping part yourself, pick what you want, and use these tools that'll help you find the best value and the right schedule. Then it'll show you a picture of what you're going to buy and back that up with a series of trained people who will provide the service you're used to.

Most of the people who are using the Web today are people who like to do their own planning; if they're just buying an air ticket, they're probably in great shape. If they're planning the ultimate vacation and they're trying to do it all on the Web, and they're the kinds of people who don't plan normally; it's probably a reach for them today. I wouldn't recommend it.

■ **Kathy Misunas** Approximately 70 percent of major appliance decisions in the United States are made by women, and about 60 percent of consumer electronics purchases are made by men. Therefore, each of these categories has a different demographic that we're trying to reach.

At some point soon, we'll be expanding to a wider customer set, such as interior decorators or contractors—people who are buying on behalf of others. Realtors have also started getting into the act of advising their clients about who to contact in order to accomplish renovations after they move in. As realtors start to broker recommendations of good, reputable service people in the area, we will be working with them to use our site for product solutions.

Other types of potential users may be folks that like to buy as part of a shopping club or loyalty group. It's possible we can interact with those groups by being the "brandwise inside" for home-related purchasing.

■ **Ellen Pack** There's no question that women will be a powerful consumer group on the Internet. Offline, women are responsible for 80 percent of purchases. However, I have a theory that the Internet is actually going to make bigger shoppers out of men too. I think that they've really gotten into: "Oh, I can just sit at my computer and go shopping. I don't have to go out. I don't have to park. I don't have to deal with the crowds. I don't have to deal with salespeople."

■ **Terrell Jones** The number one travel purchase is a simple round-trip airline ticket, followed by cars and hotels, although vacations and cruises are a fast-growing part of our marketplace. Up until now, the way that we sold vacations and cruises has been shop on the Web, buy on the phone, because we felt someone spending $1,000 or $1,500 would be concerned about doing that on the Web.

We are moving up into online vacations; some of our competitors have already done that, and those are beginning to sell. We'll be bringing up online cruises later this year; 50 percent of cruisers are repeat customers, so we think that it makes sense. People might not buy their very first cruise that way, but perhaps a second or third cruise would work.

Getting off the Ground

■ **Terrell Jones** You can certainly go to a supplier directly if you know exactly what you want; if you fly only airline A and stay only at hotel B. But that's pretty unusual. Most leisure travelers are looking for a good value, and they want to go to an unbiased site. At Travelocity, for example, we have 95 percent of the world's airline seats, over 40,000 hotels, 50 car rental companies, vacations and cruises, and destination information all presented in a totally unbiased fashion. Travelers can be assured that we're not listing one airline over another or one hotel chain over another.

> "I went to Morocco last year and booked my air tickets myself, but I talked to an expert on Morocco to understand what to do on the ground."

Many people need expert advice; I do for some trips. I went to Morocco last year and booked my air tickets myself, but I talked to an expert on Morocco to understand what to do on the ground. I believe you should still consult an expert, even though there are people who don't do that today.

Now, clearly, you can come to us and say, "Alaska, seven days, about $1,500," and we'll give you a recommendation. We'll come back with what we think is the best, but we can't have a conversation with you about it, at least not yet.

Whom Do You Trust?

■ **Kathy Misunas** One of the things that we've done to ensure credibility of our site is contract with independent test labs to do rigorous testing on the products. Instead of just talking about functions and features, we can evaluate whether representations made in manufacturers' brochures have tested out as accurate.

The tests we are conducting and the results that come out of the lab are created and evaluated in concert with the Good Housekeeping Institute, which has over 100 years of this type of experience.

Not every product in the database is tested since many products use the same chassis, or consumers have told us that testing for a small appliance or some consumer electronics isn't really necessary. In many cases we have tested more than 50 percent of the products available.

■ **Terrell Jones** There are a lot of sites on the Internet, and it's hard to know when you're going to the wrong part of town. If you're driving around and you look at a physical place, you kind of get a feeling for what it's like. But on the Internet everybody sort of has the same size storefront. It's pretty hard to know if there's a big company behind it.

Because you do need to be careful, not so much from a security standpoint, but from whether this is a company that will stand behind its product. For instance, if you have a problem when traveling, is there a twenty-four-hour phone number to reach someone who has been in the travel business and knows what's going on?

Return to Sender

■ **Kathy Misunas** I was surprised to learn that of the major appliances that are returned to stores, more than 50 percent of them are returned because people didn't measure the space where it was to be placed and therefore bought the wrong size. One of the first things we actually ask the consumer is whether the product he or she is looking for is a replacement that has specific space requirements—if so, we suggest someone promptly go measure and then provide us with the dimensions, so we can list only those products that will fit the opening.

And speaking of returns, I think there are always challenges associated with returns, whether online or offline. Historically, if people get something delivered through the mail or overnight service, unless it is really dreadful they are much less apt to go through the trouble of repackaging it and returning it.

In the future, as more and more "Internet products" are delivered via the mail and overnight, I believe returns are going to cause all sorts of other businesses to be established and flourish. There's going to be what I'll call "the return store." Somebody's going to open local outlets based on the concept that consumers can return anything to a single location in their neighborhood and the "return store" will figure out how to return it and get your refund for you.

Fare Game

■ **Terrell Jones** We've just introduced a new product called "best fare finder." In the past you've always had to tell the reservationist your dates of travel, and then he or she would tell you what the best deal was. Well, we turned that around.

For instance, let's say you're going from New York to Las Vegas, we'll tell you that the lowest fare from New York to Las Vegas is $314, and then we'll show you a calendar and show you the dates that the fare is offered. The lowest fares in that market today happen to be on a Tuesday, Wednesday, or Saturday only departure. That might not work for you. You might say, "I know what the lowest fare is, but I can't do that," or you might say, "Well, that works for me. Tell me if there are any seats on the seventeenth of July." We'll go out and do that, and if there are seats, we'll show you the flights where you can get that fare.

Now, again, some airlines don't offer the most convenient flights for the lowest fares. You might look at it and say, "No, I don't want that," but you might say, "That's exactly what I want," and flex your schedule a little bit in order to get the lowest fare. That's something that really hasn't been offered before, except by a travel expert who happened to know that Vegas flights were cheap on Tuesday. But with 50 million airfares in the system today, it's pretty hard for anybody to know that.

There are two things that happen when you use this product. One is that you'll find that the lowest fare is offered when you want it, but if it isn't, and you decide to pay a little more to get a ticket, you won't feel so bad about not getting the lowest price because you'll know it wasn't for you. Then when the guy next to you on the plane says he paid $300 for his ticket, you'll realize that he either bought the ticket six months ago or started his trip on a different day. People get very frustrated by someone paying less for the same flight.

The fare information changes five times a day and, of course, the seat availability changes every second as seats are bought and sold. It's exactly the same back-end system that we use for Sabre.

Just Looking?

■ **Terrell Jones** Less than 10 percent of the people who come to our site actually buy anything, but we know that 75 to 80 percent of those people actually do fly. So there are a lot of people coming here for information and then going to their regular channel and saying, "How much is it to Vegas?" and if the guy says $600, they say, "No, no, Travelocity said it was $400." But if they're told the price is $200, they don't say anything, they just buy it.

Generally, what happens with those people is that they'll come back to us two, three, four times, and if they see we're consistently providing them with a great answer, then they'll say, "Why am I shopping? I may as well just buy from these guys."

To convert shoppers to buyers we'll send them a lot of messages, such as, "Did you know it's really safe to use your credit card online? If you're concerned about it you can call this 800 number or mail in your credit card number."

Getting to Know You . . . Too Well?

■ **Terrell Jones** Personalization is going to be quite important online. We already personalize our e-mails. For example, you can sign up to watch the Boston/L.A. market because you're going there in a month, and we'll send you personalized e-mails that give you pricing advice. We also customize e-mails to people based on where they live so they learn about fare sales out of Chicago, if they leave from Chicago. They also get news about Chicago, if they live there. Eventually we'll do more of that kind of personalization as we learn more about people.

On the Internet you can combine the personal service of a small store with the economies of the mass market. The Internet gives us the ability to create this bazaar where there is personal service, but at the same time where there's exceptionally low price and fast service.

> *"On the Internet you can combine the personal service of a small store with the economies of the mass market."*

■ **Kathy Misunas** There are many ways a site can offer customized services to a consumer. For instance, if someone bought a new lawn mower—could that mean he or she moved to a new house and might need some other home-related products? Now, a person could be leery of this approach and think: Is big brother watching my shopping? Obviously, on-line sites must be careful about how they customize this type of service and should ask a customer's permission before doing this type of "shopping" on his or her behalf.

Comparing Notes

■ **Kathy Misunas** We think it's important for consumers to interact with one another and exchange information about their product experiences, both good and bad.

A great example is purchases such as infant furniture, since new parents are very concerned about safety. Our focus groups indicate they want to understand the product differences between cribs and playpens and car seats, but they also want to go online with other first-time parents and find out what they liked about a particular product or what they didn't like.

■ **Terrell Jones** We tried chats when we first started but they failed. The best travel chats I've seen, that are still around, are on Compuserve. Having a good chat is like having a good dinner party. You have to have some good conversationalists who help lead it, and the problem with most travel chats is that there are a heck of a lot of questions and not very many answers.

It's kind of weird that people seem to trust people they've never met because they chat with them on the Internet. Some guy says, "I really liked Antarc-

> *"Having a good chat is like having a good dinner party. You have to have some good conversationalists who help lead it."*

tica," and the next guy says, "Maybe I should go there." Well, if you met that guy in a bar, you would look at him and say, "I don't trust that guy. I'm not going to Antarctica." But over the Web it seems more credible.

■ **George Bell** What makes Internet media different from all other media is that the audience is the content. If you go into the automobile channel on Excite, we think we do as good a job as anybody in allowing you to comparison shop, get features, specs, pictures, and magazine reviews on any particular car you want. The real value of the Internet is in allowing you, in real time or on a message board, to talk to people who have purchased that car or are contemplating purchasing that car.

The Lemon Theory

■ **Alvin Toffler** I have what I call the lemon theory about consumers. It works like this: If I buy a car that has something wrong with it, I take it back to the dealer, the dealer monkeys with it, returns it to me, and it still doesn't work. We do that three or four times and, finally, the dealer gets tired of doing this, and he says, "This is the way it is, and there's nothing I can do about it." Until the Internet.

Now I go online and I say, "I have just bought a 2000 whiz bang number forty-three. Anybody else out there having trouble with the gizmo?" Within half an hour you've got litigation, instant class action. This is consumer power, but it's also neo-Nazi power or right-wing or left-wing power, it's everybody's power. It's available to anybody to organize instantaneously.

Personal Buying Clubs

■ **David Bohnett** A whole new e-commerce model is emerging, which gives you the opportunity to link to various merchants from your personal home page. On GeoCities we call it our "Pages That Pay" program. This will be a very important way of transacting business in the future.

Here's how it works: You create your own little buying club, where you, your friends, and your family all belong; you get discounts based on the volume of purchases made through the merchants you are linked to.

Not every merchant will be involved, but if you're going to buy a book, you can go to Amazon.com and buy it or you could join our "Pages That Pay" affiliate program and get a discount on every purchase you make and get a commission every time you refer a customer. Sometimes the level of discount is based on volume, but basically it works even if you're going to use it just for yourself.

■ **George Bell** The ability of communities to create cartels and organize buying groups is largely untapped. If I had 200,000 people who frequent the television communities on Excite and who wanted to buy television sets, I could pick up the phone and call Sony and say, "Circuit City buys 100,000 television sets from you in a given quarter. I'm willing to buy 200,000 television sets from you right now on behalf of my buying cartel [my consumers in my communities]. What's the price?"

Right now, we use the value of consumer cartels through targeted advertising. For example, if we go into a community and see that its members are really interested in music and they're all discussing the same type of music, we show that log file to an advertiser who publishes that music genre and we say, "Your chances of selling a lot of CDs in this community seem to us to be very high. So we're going to charge you excessively high advertising rates to put your advertising there, but we think it will be more than justified."

Could consumers organize themselves and take advantage of their combined economic clout? Well it's not very far from where we are now to that next step.

Identifying the Dinosaurs

■ **Terrell Jones** There are tens of thousands of travel agencies around the world with very successful entrepreneurs who add a lot of value. Whether they add value because they know all about a destination or they give superior customer service or they package price or they move groups or they handle inbound travel, there are a lot of ways for them to make money.

> "If an agent's statement of value is, 'I write tickets and deliver them promptly,' he's in trouble because tickets are going away."

What isn't going to work going forward is simply writing airline tickets. If an agent's statement of value is, "I write tickets and deliver them promptly," he's in trouble because tickets are going away. Sixty-five percent of the tickets we issue are electronic; there is no delivery and consumers can do it themselves. Those kinds of jobs will go the way of the gas station attendant who pumped your gas, but people still need mechanics to work on their cars. Someone who really adds value will be here a long, long time.

■ **Halsey Minor** There are very few instances where existing physical retailers are simply not needed anymore. They have one advantage—speed. A fully stocked local retailer can always sell you something faster than you can order it.

The best way to explain it is to look at what happened with network TV. The networks haven't gone away, although their ratings have gone down, but they are used a lot less. Now you're beginning to see network TV programming change. It's changing because they have to have really big budget, superexpensive movies to draw a large audience. When they can't afford big-budget stuff, then they tend to do programs that are much cheaper to produce than sitcoms, such as news, magazines, and documentaries. The economics are changing because cable has eroded their audience base and the Internet has reduced TV viewing. You're going to see stores go through the same thing—an erosion in their customer base, which will lead to changes in the way the stores operate.

It may be that the notion of a superstore is a lot less valuable; as big a selection as many superstores have, it's only a fraction of the selection that you can provide online. The notion of completeness as a retail concept may not be as important because of the Web, whereas concepts that are built around convenience may be more important.

If the one advantage that you really have by selling locally is convenience or speed, maybe the next retail concepts that succeed will be those catering to people who want something really quickly. They want to get in and get out. They have to have it today.

How important is "Everything Toys" going to be to somebody who can go online to a larger database of toy products on the Web? If I'm buying for my children's birthday or for Christmas, I don't really care whether I get it today. I'm probably going to buy it a week in advance.

Revolutionary Warranties?

■ **Kathy Misunas** The Internet provides new ways to benefit consumers. For example, a site can offer consumers a place to store their warranty and service manuals. Many people do not fill in the warranty form, and most of us throw the manuals in a drawer—and then don't remember which drawer when we need them. We subsequently never know who to contact when we have a problem! You call the 800 operator and get, "No, manufacturer X doesn't have an 800 number anymore." Consumers we talked to really liked the idea of having a personal electronic file cabinet with information relevant to the products they buy.

Shopping, Broadband-Style

■ **George Bell** Online shopping will greatly increase in convenience in the future. If you look at what the shopping experience is like on @Home, in a high-speed broadband environment, as opposed to what it's like using a 28.8K or a 56K dial-up modem, there's just no comparison. With broadband you have the richness of images and you're able to do many things quickly. I presume it will also be voice enabled.

Moreover, it's going to be driven by many defined preferences that will be governed by personalization. A site will know my waist size, my inseam, my jacket size, my neck size, and I'm probably going to say, "When you find these things at the right sizes at the right prices, please notify me." Shopping will be more controlled by the consumer's preference and will improve as a consumer experience as bandwidth increases and enables people to view rich pictures of things when they shop. In addition, it's going to be more deeply focused on a "market of me," just as content is right now.

What's in Store (for the Future)?

■ **Terrell Jones** I think the biggest change is that you'll shop for travel by looking at real-time video of the destination and you'll talk to the counselor, if one is needed, about the trip through a video connection.

Another innovation will be voice. Most of our computer commands will be made through voice; we won't be using keyboards very much. Last will be the ubiquitousness of the devices. You'll have travel information on personal digital systems, telephones, cell phone screens, and over the television. It's really going to be everywhere. I don't think we'll be talking about Internet travel companies anymore. I think we'll just be travel companies, and those who don't combine this new technology with their offerings won't be around.

Something of this kind is already happening. The new wireless Palm VII [handheld digital organizer] gives you up-to-date flight information on eighteen different airlines. You can't make a booking—yet. And you can get the same flight information on an AT&T or a Nokia Web phone. Today you can get up-to-date flight information on Travelocity, in case your flight is delayed or canceled. In fact, we have something called flight paging, which allows you to be paged if your flight is late. So an hour out, we'll say, "Hey, you better slow down, you don't need to be there" or "You better get out and meet your mother-in-law, she's early."

■ **Kathy Misunas** At the end of the day, empowerment of the consumer will change the way manufacturers develop and sell products. I also believe that although retailers will remain in the distribution chain, manufacturers will sell direct to the consumer and they'll end up having a closer relationship with the consumers who are actually buying and using their product.

Most things go around 360 degrees over time, but I think empowerment of the consumer is going to change many existing business models. Today's middlemen will establish other roles and value-added services. It's not that they're going out of business tomorrow, it's that they might not be doing things as they have historically been done.

Consumers always want alternatives. Therefore, the choice to go to a store or shop via catalogues or online will all be available. In the future there will be an amazing number of options to satisfy how consumers want to shop and buy. The Internet and other upcoming technologies will make the choices almost limitless.

Most Popular Web Sweepstake/Coupon Sites

(Source: Nielsen//NetRatings)

alladvantage.com	iwon.com	treeloot.com
coolsavings.com	mypoints.com	valupage.com
freelotto.com	pch.com	webstakes.com
freeshop.com		

Most Popular Web Travel Sites

(Source: Nielsen//NetRatings)

aa.com	lowestfare.com	travelfileaol.com
cheaptickets.com	mapblast.com	travelnow.com
continental.com	mapquest.com	travelocity.com
cooltravelassistant.com	maps.com	travelscape.com
delta-air.com	mapsonus.com	travelweb.com
expedia.com	nwa.com	trip.com
hoteldiscounts.com	previewtravel.com	ual.com
iflyswa.com	southwest.com	usairways.com
itn.net	thetrip.com	

Most Popular Web Shopping Sites

(Source: Nielsen//NetRatings)

amazon.com	drugstore.com	qvc.com
barnesandnoble.com	ebay.com	reel.com
bestbuy.com	egghead.com	shopnow.com
beyond.com	etoys.com	sony.com
bluelight.com	gap.com	toysrus.com
bmgmusicservice.com	hallmark.com	ubid.com
buy.com	iprint.com	victoriassecret.com
cdnow.com	jcpenney.com	walmart.com
columbiahouse.com	petsmart.com	

EIGHT

THE WORLD IS YOUR STAGE

I was born during the Great Depression (1931) and reading the comics in the newspaper was a highlight of daily life. My devotion to comic strips has continued to this day, but my local newspaper doesn't carry some of my favorites, such as "Tank McNamara" or "Apartment 3-G." Long ago, I resigned myself to giving up this simple pleasure, but once I got a computer and learned of the almost infinite amount of material on the Internet, I found several Web sites that carry almost any comic strip you care to read. It's not rocket science or high finance, but it does enhance the enjoyment of life in my later years.

—**C. William Rogers, Tennessee**

I was at my favorite message board [momsrefuge.com] and found a post from an agent casting "real" working moms (who cook and use the Internet) for a national TV commercial. I responded and we met for a very public, safe lunch. I checked the credentials of the casting agent and the advertising agency before I committed to it, but in the end, she cast our entire family! It was so much fun, plus we got a big tickle out of seeing ourselves on TV.

—**Bree Adams-Coleman, North Carolina**

For decades computers have proven their value as stodgy but dependable workhorses—crunching numbers, analyzing data, and searching for information. More recently, as multimedia technology has enabled new forms of communication on the Web, the computer has added "sexier" functions to its long list of attributes, like video, audio, and voice-enabled chat. Increasingly, the computer is also an entertainment center and is beginning to give television a run for its money.

Over the years television was used as a bargaining chip between parents and their kids. "You have to finish your homework before you can watch television," was a common admonishment. Psychologists debated the effects of passively sitting and staring at the "boob tube" on a generation of kids. Today the dumb box has competition from smart computers tuned into the Web, and parents have something new to use as leverage with their children. In many households watching a monitor trumps watching a TV.

What is the lure behind this bland, beige, monitor networked to hundreds of millions of other monitors? Largely it's the ability it provides to reach out and interact with people you would never meet in the real world. Karaoke online? Goose hunting calls online? Practice your French pronunciation with someone from France over the Internet? Listen to your hometown baseball game, even though you live thousands of miles away? Play word games with someone you've never met? And on top of that, voice-enabled chat is all the rage, enabling new forms of entertainment and fresh ways to indulge your passions online.

Traditional entertainment is not in danger of becoming extinct, but in some cases the way that it is distributed will change dramatically. Take music, for instance. MP3 is an audio compression format that permits listeners to download music tracks from the Internet for free and save them on a PC hard drive or a portable MP3 player that costs about $200. Record companies, record stores, and local radio stations, not surprisingly, are worried that artists will use this technology to bypass their control of the distribution channels.

Likewise, set-top boxes that sit passively on top of your television are facing competition from smart computers that will resemble a VCR or DVD player, connect to a monitor that fits comfortably in your living room, and bring you digital programming from around the world, while also offering computerlike functions such as e-mail, Web surfing, and program guides.

And you won't have to be tethered to your television to follow your favorite shows. Columbia Tristar Interactive, for example, started a *Soap City Daily Dose* newsletter that automatically downloads the latest development on your favorite soap opera to a handheld, digital assistant, such as the Palm Pilot or a Windows CE device.

Computerized competition is not a fantasy either. In February 1999, OKBridge, the online network for bridge aficionados, announced the first Internet World Team Championship. Interested players could register to play against opponents they would never meet in person.

Perhaps the greatest entertainment of all, talking to others, is keeping a new generation of moguls busy as they look for new ways to facilitate a basic human need to comment on the world around them. Never before has it been possible to meet so many people without leaving your home.

We interviewed several prominent executives to get their perspectives on how Web amusements differ from real-world pastimes. We also invited many of our interviewees to share their thoughts on the future of television, books, stereos, journalism, gambling, and more. What they have to say may surprise you.

Peter Friedman, president and CEO of Talk City Inc. [talk city.com], one of the Internet's leading online communities, related a conversation he'd had with his son that demonstrates how the Web is changing the way people meet. "Daddy, I met a new friend today," Peter's son said to him. And as fathers before him have done, Friedman responded, "That's nice." "I met him on Talk City," his son continued. "That's great," Friedman answered, without missing a beat. "He's from Alaska," added his son.

Paul Matteucci, CEO and president of HearMe—a company dedicated to creating live communities on the Internet, where people can meet, chat, and play—finds that when he is far from home his preferred leisure activity is communicating with his wife in a chat room. "We're not doing anything weird or kinky in there," he was quick to add, explaining, "we've been married a couple of years!"

Mark Cuban, vice president of Broadcast Services, Yahoo!, and co-founder of broadcast.com—the leading broadcaster of audio and video programming on the Internet—sees his company's broadcasting services benefiting people wherever they are, at home or in the office, even when catastrophe strikes. "I remember when the space shuttle *Challenger* crashed, everybody crowded into the cafeteria to get information. I remember when the Gulf War started, everyone at the gym crowded into a room around the sole television. No more. Now I'll go to the Internet first. The Internet brings activities to me where I want them, instead of my having to get up and go somewhere to find out what's happening."

While the Web is making it easier to find out what's going on, it's also adding to the pressures on journalists to make news entertaining, as noted author and *New Yorker* columnist Ken Auletta explains in the pages that follow.

Many of the changes envisioned by these experts, as well as Alvin Toffler and Halsey Minor, won't happen for the majority of homes until broadband technologies improve the quality of the video you can receive on your viewing screen. But just as entertainment in the last 100 years was revolutionized by television, entertainment in the twenty-first century will be turned upside down by the capabilities of interactive digital broadcasting over high-speed lines.

It *Is* a Small World After All

■ **Paul Matteucci** What the Internet enables that no other medium can is the ability for people to interact together in a rich media environment, in real time. Years ago we had to be in the same room to play a game together. Now there are people from all over the world playing together in real time every night.

We have people singing karaoke together, playing guitar recitals, performing live concerts [hearme.com]—all sorts of things that just aren't possible in the real world.

People interact in "live communities" in much the same way they would interact in the real world. We have games at Mplayer.com where many people play a game, and people can even drop in and out to see what's going on. It's similar to the experience of being at a football game: you're not interacting with the 60,000 people in the stadium, you're engaging with 5 or 6 people who are immediately around you and you're observing everybody else.

Our karaoke rooms are packed every night with people who log on and listen to one another perform. We didn't invent the first karaoke room on the Internet, we just gave people all these tools and they created their own experiences, such as foreign language practice, where English is not permitted, and teen party line calls.

Some people enjoy creating programming for their own radio stations. Obviously, they're not real radio stations but, like real radio, people come in and listen to the music and the talk. Cyber-radio allows people to interact with one another at the same time the deejay is interacting with them.

Other online tools allow people to share a white board and draw interactively with one another or map out game strategies and surf the Web as a group.

Something for Everyone

■ **Mark Cuban** Everybody goes to the Internet for the things they are passionate about: news, information, education, and beyond that, entertainment. Traditional entertainment is limited by the physical nature of the medium (a disk, a tape) or by the spectrum (a station, a channel). When you're physically bound, there are the limits of time, distribution, and shelf space. After all, there are only so many tapes that Blockbuster can hold.

If you add up all of the radio stations, television stations, the Blockbusters, and the movie theaters, you might have 30,000 choices of entertainment or information from traditional media nationwide. Compare that to the Internet.

You can go to broadcast.com where, in less than four years, we have compiled hundreds of thousands of programs so you can find the ones that suit your fancy—and this is just the beginning. If you're into bridge or collecting tadpoles or basketball, the only place that you can be sure to find something is the Internet.

Talk, Talk, Talk

■ **Paul Matteucci** Voice chat appeals to people because it enables them to do things that can't be done by typing. We have a yodeling group online and people who practice duck hunting or goose hunting calls. They can't type that. You can't type karaoke, you can't type guitar recitals, you can't type hearing your grandchild's voice from 3,000 miles away and seeing her picture on the Web at the same time.

> "Voice chat will change virtually everything online."

Voice chat will change virtually everything online. Live audio, for example, will be added to auction sites over the next year, and will enable live bidding. Sports talk shows, like ESPN, will become much more interactive. Think about what it would be like to watch an event like the Super Bowl or the

State of the Union message on television and, at the same time, address questions to John Madden or Dan Rather.

■ **Peter Friedman** We have a full program of chats and community activities tied to television shows on NBC. People will talk about *Friends* online while they're watching it on TV. When there are award shows, like the Oscars or the Grammys, people like to comment on the clothes the celebrities are wearing.

We also did the chats for *ER*'s live show. Some people would talk about the show and others would talk about their medical problems. Some chats attract thousands and thousands of people. Right now we're the official chat site of *Star Wars: The Phantom Menace*. We've got three months of activities planned around it, including chats and appearances by the different celebrities.

Celebrities are a draw: You'll get anywhere from 50 to 300 people coming to see a B-level celebrity. For a big star, you'll get anywhere from 800 people to 10,000 people. Rosie O'Donnell was a huge draw on AOL, and we had 70,000 people come through for all the *ER* events over the course of several days.

Kids' Stuff

■ **Mark Cuban** Kids' entertainment isn't being changed by the Internet. Well, at least from a kid's perspective it's not changing, it's just the way it is. At broadcast.com we have audiobooks on tape and we have CDs that are available on demand. If you want to listen to a kid's book you can pick a story, like *Hansel and Gretel*, and listen to it from your computer. We have parents sending us e-mail saying they let their kids fall asleep listening to books-on-tape on the PC in their room. We have kids who come to us and say, "Hey, I watched this video about Shakespeare before my test and it really helped me a lot. My next test is on Chaucer, do you have something on that subject?"

■ **Peter Friedman** There are a lot of community activities for teens online. In our teen area, for instance, we have three anchor communities, including a very specific set of moderated chats, discussion boards, user content, home pages, and sometimes professional editorials with a particular style and personality, like a TV show. We have fifty of these themed communities, each with their own brand. We have about 500,000 teens coming to the area, spending 1 million to 1.2 million total hours there a month.

One of the anchor communities is called Youth Online, which is for ten- to fifteen-year-olds. There are a lot of creative workshops, and often parents and kids do them together, including activities done both online and offline. We had a summer camp that was oversubscribed and a holiday camp.

Then we have Insight, aimed at fifteen- to twenty-year-olds, that is more about relationships, growing up, and social and environmental issues. There's even a teenage Ann Landers, called Terra; her real name is Annie Fox. It's so popular that we're actually publishing a book from Annie called *Can You Relate: Real World Advice for Teens on Guys, Girls, Growing Up, and Getting Along.*

The third anchor community is Teen NBC, which is a series of TV shows that are usually on Saturday morning on NBC. We provide the community for it.

Masters of Their Domains

■ **Paul Matteucci** We're seeing microcelebrities develop online, such as the guy who runs the country and western karaoke rooms, Hillbilly John, or the guy who created the Bar Grillers room, Tristinn. These people develop their own followings, not mass market followings, but there are hundreds, and sometimes thousands, of people who log on to find out what they're up to.

■ **Peter Friedman** We have 2,000 trained moderators that operate over 75,000 supervised chats for us a month. You could say there are 2,000 talk show hosts on our site. What they're good at is drawing an audience out and managing a show with audience participation, which can range from something very structured, like a game or a class in HTML design, to a very loose, coffee shop discussion.

The Changing Face of Fame

■ **Alvin Toffler** In the next century, I think there will be fewer mass celebrities, but they will be bigger, if that's even possible to imagine. What we're doing by creating more niches in this society, and more diversity, is creating more niche celebrities.

Being a celebrity is going to be harder, if for no other reason than that your privacy is more invadable. Moreover, the kinds of celebrities are going to change. I think we're moving toward the end of the age of the Schwarzenegger/Willis celebrity. I say that because of the way they're going to work in the future, given the application of these new technologies to Hollywood. So instead of saying, "Arnold, we're going to shoot a movie and it's going to take six months, and we want you to go to lower Slobovia and do the following things," they're going to say, "Arnold, come in on Saturday morning, and we're going to need about three hours of your time. We want you to sit in the chair, stand up, extend a leg, make a smile, raise your fist, and go home." The computer will interpolate all the other motions, and it will look exactly like Schwarzenegger.

We'll also have virtual celebrities. Remember our old friend Max Headroom? I think Max Headroom was a primitive incipient version of characters who will, in fact, be crafted by computer but will look like people and will take on the role that actors and actresses do in soap operas and in other dramatic forms. They will not look jerky and cartoonlike as Max Headroom did. They'll look terrific. In fact, they'll look so terrific that their faces will be exactly what *you* think is beautiful and not necessarily what your neighbor thinks, because they'll be customized for each home.

The other thing about them is they will be sponsored by Nike, or somebody like that. Given the full potential of broadband, why can't you do that? Why can't you create a face or a character? I think the leading soap operas will be made up of casts of virtual actors and actresses. I suggest there will be a lot of jobs for people who design.

Hear Ye, Hear *Me*

■ **Peter Friedman** The Internet is a great storytelling medium. People have been communicating through written words for hundreds of years, but for thousands of years people all over the world have communicated through telling stories. We're now seeing a resurgence of storytelling online, only this time it's through written words. When news happens, people get online, they talk about it. You get different perspectives from people all over the globe. Instead of a one-way, professionally controlled, editorial medium, the audience is telling the story. That's very powerful.

Games: The Play's the Thing

■ **Paul Matteucci** There are two basic groups of game players, we call them avid players, or "gamers," and casual game players. In the gamer category, Mplayer.com has a variety of games like action games and simulations, such as U.S. Navy Fighters, and strategy games, which are not very action oriented, such as Risk or Panzer General. Sports is a huge category for online games; games like basketball, hockey, and golf are the most popular sports games because they're the easiest to play online.

Then there are the classic games for the more casual game player. Mplayer.com offers games like free poker, spades, bingo, checkers, chess; board games like Scrabble and Battleship; and crossword puzzles and triva. Other sites offer game shows like *Jeopardy!* and *Wheel of Fortune*. Some of the most popular games in our service are the classic games, primarily poker, spades, checkers.

There are many more casual game players on the Internet than gamers, and about 43 percent of that audience is female. On some sites, like Gamesville, where bingo's the biggest game, there is an even higher percentage of women. This audience is generally older than the gamer audience, averaging in their upper forties to early fifties. The sweet spot for the gamer audience is really twenty- to thirty-five-year old males, but the market's getting older all the time.

■ **Peter Friedman** People go nuts for word games with text chat. We have one called Silly Sentences where the moderator, who has special technology tools, will type a word like *lazy* and you have to make a sentence out of it. Everybody in the room, which could be twenty or thirty people, very quickly type out a sentence with the word, and whoever makes the funniest one wins. The audience does the scoring and people can win prizes.

How many people like to do that? Well, thousands of people play at a time. We've had to hold game marathon weekends to satisfy the demand. It's a substitute for parlor games like Trivial Pursuit.

Pay Before You Play

■ **Paul Matteucci** For Mplayer.com, the action games require software that players can get from a retail or Internet store or via an Internet download. Most choose to buy the CD because it's faster than downloading it. Frequently a company will allow one level of a game to be downloaded so people can try the game and decide whether they like it; to get the other levels you have to buy it. Action games really aren't free; basically you buy the games at retail then play them for free over the Internet.

All the Hits, All The Time

■ **Ken Auletta** It's wonderfully liberating to suddenly have a distribution system that makes it easy for consumers to get good music. You get to do what I used to do when I was a boy. We had listening booths and you could listen to music before you decided to buy a record.

> "I don't have to go to a store, I don't have to get in a car, I don't have to move. God, that's heaven."

Now you can go on the Web and listen to cuts from a CD before you decide to buy it. Music has changed; broadcast.com's got 400 radio stations that you can access.

Partly what's happening is the middleman is being eradicated. I can sample music on my computer, then click and order. I don't have to go to a store, I don't have to get in a car, I don't have to move. God, that's heaven. I can have friends over, we can sample music together. That's a mall experience without going to the mall, and it's close to your refrigerator.

■ **Mark Cuban** The conventional wisdom says people are just going to download the music they want from the Internet. I don't think that's going to be the preferred model because there will be too many choices. When you've got a million songs, and you can download any one of them, it's too much work. I think we'll have packagers and products that are made available to download—for example, the Barry Manilow collection.

In a digital world music doesn't need to be separated from video, so I believe the more likely scenario is that they'll be packaged together and offered like a subscription. So I could order the lifestyle package that appeals to me with the Billboard Top Ten for Baltimore delivered over my cable modem each night, along with my favorite TV shows that I've subscribed to, all coming over my HDTV signal and the DTV card in my PC for $29.99 a month. That subscription could also travel with me.

There will be different devices that are plugged into your PC that you can unplug and take with you, along with your subscription package that you download onto a 3.5-inch, 20-gig hard drive in your car radio that can show video, play music, or provide information. That's how all things digital are going to be distributed; you'll start to see it happening in the next two to three years.

What's On? Everything

■ **Mark Cuban** Broadcast.com enables people to receive traditional media that they don't normally have access to, anywhere there is a computer. For example, if you want to see all the latest fashions from France twenty-four hours a day you can get them. If you're from Baltimore living in Dallas and you want to listen to WBAL, your hometown station, you can hear it. Previously, if the game wasn't on national TV, you were out of luck. You had to wait for the newspaper to come out in the morning or you could go to a Web page and get the latest scores.

I grew up in Pittsburgh, I live in California, but now I can listen to my favorite announcer call the Pirates' games and, when I close my eyes, it's no different from sitting in Pittsburgh in 1970 listening to the Pirates. The only thing that's changed are the names of the players. That's an experience you couldn't have five years ago.

> "We're really creating the history of the world; we want to archive everything that we possibly can."

If you want to go back and watch the first episode of *I Love Lucy* or the first episode of *Dragnet* or if you want to see crazy drag-racing accidents or see the rivers of Russia or learn about Shakespeare or watch the Alfred Hitchcock movie *39 Steps,* it's all available, and more. We're really creating the history of the world; we want to archive everything that we possibly can.

In the future, anybody and everybody are broadcasters, the only difference is whether it's a business or a labor of love. If it's a labor of love, little Johnny's first soccer game goes on the Internet so Grandma can watch. If she's got a cable modem and little Johnny or one of his buddies records the game with a digital videocamera, then it can be plugged into the PC, posted to the family Web site, and sent to Grandma as an e-mail with a link to the video. Grandma clicks and watches little Johnny's soccer. When you have all these choices, what do you think Grandma's going to watch? *ER* or little Johnny for the fifteenth time? Grandma's going to watch little Johnny.

The Wedding of the Century: TV and the Web

■ **Peter Friedman** We know both anecdotally and from research that a lot of people watch TV while they're chatting online and many, especially teens, are chatting instead of watching TV. We've seen teens move from television and from video games to online. The reason is partly because it's interactive, but mostly because it's a social venue; they want to meet and talk with other kids. The same can be said for adults. People like to engage one another; it's a fundamental human need that's become harder and harder to do in the physical world.

■ **Paul Matteucci** Fundamentally, I believe the Internet is threatening TV. This notion is still reasonably controversial because all the data's not in, but when I look at how people are using our site, a typical guy will use

> *"Fundamentally, I believe the Internet is threatening TV."*

it over 100 minutes in a day; he's not doing something else when he's actively playing games. We also know that people who use voice chat spend more than 300 minutes a month doing it. I know that when I'm using voice chat at home, I may have a TV on in the background, but I'm not paying much attention to it.

■ **Mark Cuban** If we go back twenty years to 1979 and I said, let's talk about all the things that are going to change our lives over the next twenty years, we wouldn't say *USA Today* or MTV. We wouldn't say ESPN or PCs. We wouldn't say microwaves or cellular phones. Yet these are all things that have radically changed our lives in a short period of time. We got rid of turntables, we're getting rid of our tape players.

Is that pace of change going to stop, slow, or accelerate? Well, in a digital world it's going to accelerate because things happen so much more quickly. It wouldn't surprise me if a hundred years from now the word *television* was out of the vernacular, or if we didn't even use the television. Instead there would be things you watch, things you listen to, as well as new forms of entertainment.

■ **Halsey Minor** Eventually television programming moves over to the Internet; either it happens at the network level, where literally the television programming is distributed over the Internet or it's distributed over the same cable infrastructure, but you overlay the Internet on top of it.

What ends up happening is television will remain a very developed art form, movies will remain the number one way that we entertain ourselves, and the Internet will allow us to supplement them with other kinds of interactive features, including additional information that the user can access or overlay. Other than the Internet becoming the new transport for television programming, I don't see it radically altering the TV experience because people have already voted that they like the TV experience the way it is. The Internet is not going to significantly change television, no more than the VCR really changed movies.

In the future there may be a more seamless blending between what the Web gives you and what TV gives you, but there's a role for both. There's a role for sitting down for a half hour and having somebody program the news for you. There will be a new role for TV producers to allow you to come in and get the news and information you want on demand; some of the very same content that was prepackaged in a half-hour show. I think those two kinds of things will coexist side-by-side, not necessarily forever, but for a very long time.

■ **Ken Auletta** I hated *Seinfeld*'s last episode. If I could, I might want to change that, but will Larry David and Jerry Seinfeld's copyright allow me to change their ending? I don't think so.

Ultimately, what's more likely is that I could watch an episode of *Seinfeld* and also search for information about Jerry or the other performers. If Jerry mentions the Nazi soup kitchen, I could do a search and call up previous episodes that mention the soup Nazi and watch them.

It's not what the programmers intended me to do, but they won't care. They're still selling the advertising or keeping me on their site, except I've gone in a totally unanticipated direction, one I didn't think about before I started, but one that really excites me.

R.I.P. Paper?

■ **Halsey Minor** Right now reading on a monitor is very hard, but I wouldn't want to bet on that continuing ten years from now. Display technology is moving very, very rapidly. It's just possible that somebody's going to get it right five, seven, or ten years from now and we're going to find out that it's actually easier to carry around a little pad with text on it and, with improved resolution, it's become the preferred form of reading.

It sounds very sci-fi but there's so much content now available electronically—and the technology is happening fast enough—that I think, for the first time, print would come under a fairly ubiquitous challenge.

Now people are a lot less likely to consume the type of content they get from a *Vanity Fair* or longer-form magazine over the Internet, but I'm not dismissive of that taking place. I think that if somebody can build a tablet that has the right feel, the right size, and the right display resolution, you would see a huge amount of what is typically read in print moved over to an electronic format. I actually believe that within ten years there will be some sort of device that provides a substantive challenge to print-based publishing in terms of resolution display and convenience.

■ **Alvin Toffler** I do believe we're going to have electronic reading devices, not the klutzy kind that we have today, with a very limited number of titles, but customized for the reader. I want mine to have the same weight as a book, to be covered in buckram, and to smell like a book.

I can slip the card in or download the content and have any book I want from a vast library of choices. I can increase and decrease the size of the type according to what I like. If I like to read it in blue print instead of black print, I can have that. I can search to find the first appearance of this Russian character, whose name I can't pronounce, so I can find out where that character came from. I can, of course, do all the matching and research and studying that I wish in the book, but it will not look like a book. It will be electronic paper that has the equivalent of pixels in it and which will go dark for some print characters or light for other print characters, as the case may be.

I do believe we are going to have those kinds of readers that we can carry around with us. Everything that you're seeing while sitting there glued in your chair looking up at a monitor, you will be able to have in the palm of your hand or your back pocket. Eventually, they'll probably be cheap enough to pitch.

■ **Ken Auletta** New technology is coming that will make portable books a reality. ClearType, from Microsoft, looks the same as the printed page, the resolution is extraordinary. It means you can have a portable reading device that you can hold in your hand, with a screen that'll look no different from the printed page of a book. It will have a little clicker that you click to turn the page. If I could take a six-ounce device on vacation with me that includes five or six books downloaded to little disks half the size of a credit card, I would die for that.

Microsoft, like other companies, is working with manufacturers to create electronic books using this software and doing market research to find out what is the most comfortable form for a portable device.

Internet Video: The Picture Sharpens

■ **Mark Cuban** The Victoria's Secret fashion show was a great event. Here's a company that had a Cadillac brand name and a lot of stores, but couldn't get men to walk into them. In addition, they had no traffic on their Web site and they weren't doing any electronic commerce.

Within the span of six weeks, they created the concept for the fashion event on their Web site, they decided to advertise on the Super Bowl, and we created the event for them. Say what you will about what the video looked like, how people could or could not get onto the site, but when all was said and done, the store had gone from having nobody walk in the front door to having 1.5 million people come through its virtual doors in a single day, and hundreds of thousands of people every day afterward. It was the ultimate coup and launched a new form of commerce: entertainment-enabled commerce.

■ **Ken Auletta** Right now I do not want to watch entertainment like the Victoria's Secret fashion show, the pictures are jerky and slow. I might watch it out of novelty, but if you do shows like that every night they would fail because it's not entertainment, it's a form of work. It's entertainment the first time you see it, but after that you have to work hard to view it.

■ **Mark Cuban** The video quality online is as good as what you're willing to pay for your connection. If you're on a T1 connection you can get video quality that's better than your TV. Of course, most people don't have a T1 connection at home, but AT&T is doing everything possible to enable 70 percent of households in the United States to get it, and the regional Bell operating companies are doing almost everything possible to deliver high-quality lines to homes.

We haven't completely gotten to the point where we've learned how to sell people on spending the extra money to get better quality video, but I think the time is coming very soon. The good news is that this is the worst it's ever going to get. We're not going to look back and say, "Ah, those were the good old days of Internet video." We know without any doubt that

Internet video looks better today than it did a year ago, which looks better than it did a year before that, and before that, it didn't even exist.

Journalism: News You Can Use?

■ **Ken Auletta** One of the problems journalism has is that form dictates content. I see this in the Microsoft trial I'm covering now. The daily reporter who has to squeeze a story into 500 to 700 words (maybe 300 words if it's television), acts more and more like a theater critic. The pressure is on him to focus on the most exciting thing to happen in court, not on the most important thing.

> "The pressure is on the journalist to be more entertaining. The subtle message is, Can you top this?"

As a result, the video screw-ups in the Microsoft presentation—which were genuine screw-ups and worth writing about but may not have been the most important thing to happen that week in the courtroom—get blown out of proportion.

The ability to disseminate information quickly alters the content. If you watch a crisis in real time, as we did with the school shooting in Littleton or we do with wars, inevitably you've got to fill the space. You don't know anything, but you've got to say something. So you fill it with nonsense—you say dumb things.

The pressure for television or Internet journalists is to say something new. Their editors are sitting back in the newsroom with TV monitors on and with constant online access. The reporter in the field calls into his office at noon or one o'clock with the story that interests him. Meanwhile, his editor's already seen it on CNN or on the Web or AP wire. The editor says, "No, no, I already know that." So you need something else and the pressure is on the journalist to be more entertaining. The subtle message is, Can you top this?

Cyber Betting: Pretty Dicey

■ **Mark Cuban** It's crazy to try to legislate against gambling online. When old-line companies try to protect something, they legislate against it, but this is an international medium. It's hypocritical to think that you can control things domestically when you can't. The cost of the links from around the world is dropping like a rock. Cuba can drop one big cable and build a whole economy around just Internet gambling. How easy will that be? I'm sure it'll happen. Canada, Mexico, the same thing.

■ **Ken Auletta** Earlier in my life I was executive director of the New York City Off-Track Betting Corp. that started in 1970. Mayor Lindsay appointed Howard Samuels, a businessman and a Democrat, to be the first to set up off-track betting.

One of the things I learned from that experience is that all the protestations that you make—and the government makes—about not wanting to encourage people to gamble is crap. When you're in the gaming business you're trying to maximize the number of customers you get. Inevitably, you are, and you know you are, roping in people who shouldn't be betting.

Does the government want to move that business online? If they do, it would increase their market because gambling is easier to do online and video makes it much more pleasurable. There's no question that when you ask people who envision this pay-per-view world how to make a business of the Internet, they will tell you that there are probably three things that are guaranteed to make money. First, and foremost, is pornography, the same as was true with video stores, followed by movies, and then gaming. Now the government knows that, but this is one of those issues where government, representing the public, has to weigh how much of this do we really want to do?

It's 2005: Entertain Me

■ **Mark Cuban** In the future there will be optical cables that come into our homes to deliver gigabits of information. When you have a lot of bandwidth, your whole sensory environment can be controlled and become part of your entertainment experience. You might say, "Okay, entertainment-enable my house," and all of a sudden you're watching a movie, you're hearing Surround Sound, and the temperature starts to drop because your thermostat's plugged into the show that's on. You'll hear the blinds flutter and the lights will dim.

> "Five years from now no one will even buy a stereo."

For kids today, their PC is their stereo. They listen to CDs on their computer because it has a CD player in it. Five years from now no one will even buy a stereo. They'll go the way of eight-track players. Gone, except for the random turntable. The stereo will be just part of your PC; it'll be a feature.

■ **Paul Matteucci** We've seen the Internet move from an information-based medium to more of a transaction-based medium. Five years from now it'll be a communications medium. It'll be where you go to do everything.

It will be "always on," unlike now where you have to turn on your system, boot it up, and wait for Windows to open your browser. It will function just like a television set; you'll click on it and it will immediately have everything you want: your television schedule, stock quotes, sports scores, whatever. You will replay part of the game if it's already happened, or if not, use your connection to tune it in. You might follow the America's Cup on Quokka Sports [quokka.com]. You'll climb to the top of Everest with the expedition. You'll chose between passive things, like watching *Star Trek* or doing something interactive. You'll be watching TV and see a little envelope appear in the corner of your screen. You'll click on it and your maid-of-honor from your wedding fifteen years ago will be standing there with her three kids saying, "Hey, we're coming to New York for a visit this summer. Can we get together?"

It won't take long for this to happen. The integration of all these things for the major metropolitan areas is possible within the next five years. I would wager that five years from now probably a third of the time we'll chose to do something interactive.

Most Popular Web Sports Sites

(Source: Nielsen//NetRatings)

cnnsi.com
foxsports.com
nascar.com
nba.com
nfl.com

rivals.com
sportingnews.com
sportsline.com
superbowl.com
wwf.com

Most Popular Web Entertainment Sites

(Source: Nielsen//NetRatings)

americangreetings.com
bluemountain.com
boxerjam.com
broadcast.com
discovery.com
egreetings.com
eonline.com
funone.com
gamecenter.com

gamesville.com
ign.com
imdb.com
iwin.com
justsaywow.com
moviefone.com
mp3.com
mtv.com

nbc.com
nick.com
ticketmaster.com
tunes.com
tvguide.com
uproar.com
webshots.com
zone.com

NINE

PRIVACY, SECURITY, POWER, AND CONTROL

You have to understand that on the Internet you're creating records.

—Esther Dyson, EDventure Holdings

Every day we walk around and, if we make a purchase with a credit card, generate information about ourselves.

—Halsey Minor, CNET

If you compared the Internet with the present system, I think the Internet is more secure.

—Dr. C. Everett Koop, drkoop.com

I consider almost no information on the Internet secure.

—Dr. George Lundberg, Medscape

I spend a lot of time explaining to people, "Unless you tell a Web site your phone number, it has no way of knowing it."

—Ellen Pack, Women.com

If you use the Web you have probably been asked to register at a site and provide information such as your name, e-mail address, and zip code. Some sites will ask for more, and if it's a commerce site, they will need your address and credit card information to process an order.

Some of us blithely type in the data, unconcerned with where it is going, who will see it, how long it will exist electronically, and whether or not any of your personal data and buying patterns will be sold to marketers. Others, deterred by stories of online hackers, junk e-mail, unsolicited pornography promotions, technology that tracks you as you move around the Web, and security holes at some sites, avoid going online at all.

Still others fall somewhere in the middle, choosing not to register at sites or giving false information when it is required. Alvin Toffler, for example, noted author and Information Age futurist, who provides his insights on where the Internet is taking us in another chapter, admits he has a pseudo-identity online that he uses when personal data is requested. Of course, when you're buying something online you have no choice, you have to provide your name and address and payment instructions.

On the other hand, Esther Dyson, author of *Release 2.1: A Design for Living in the Digital Age* and chairman of EDventure Holdings (edventure.com), a company focused on emerging information technology worldwide, isn't concerned about providing personal information in exchange for the convenience of being able to shop online or get information she needs. She's more bothered by the time it takes to register at a site and the inconvenience of forgetting her password and calling an 800 number to recover it.

In the future online transactions will get easier to execute. Instead of typing in your name, address, billing information, and shipping address, a large group of leading credit card companies, Web merchants, and developers of online payment technologies are working on creating a standard for transactions (called electronic commerce modeling language). The goal is to make it possible for consumers to buy from different sites without reentering their personal data; that information would be stored on a secure computer and accessed by the stores you want to have it.

Moreover, Privada (privada.net) has a service called Web Incognito that lets users conduct their Internet activities completely anonymously. For a monthly fee of $5, customers can do all their Net activities—e-mail, chats, Web browsing, and even purchasing—without fear of being tracked; Web Incognito hides the source of the data before sending it on its way. Of course, you have to trust Web Incognito with your data.

Protecting privacy takes on additional meaning for Dyson. While she prefers e-mail to the phone at work and uses it to stay in touch when she's on one of her frequent trips, at home it's a different story. She chooses not to have either a phone or computer in her personal space. "If I want to communicate at home," she says, "I go out. But I don't do that. The point of going home is to be alone at home."

For Dyson, life is all about making choices, which extends to all behavior, whether online or not. For instance, Dyson doesn't know how to drive but compensates by taking taxis. The important thing, she says, is "I know what I'm doing and I know the trade-offs." The same is true of the Web.

The more information you provide to sites, the better able they are to give you, in turn, the information that is specific to your needs. But that doesn't mean people are comfortable with that scenario. According to a telephone survey conducted by researcher Cyber Dialogue, one-third of online users say the Internet is a serious threat to their privacy; interestingly, the figure climbs to 50 percent for respondents ages eighteen to twenty-nine.

Many sites now carry seals that indicate they are adhering to policy standards set up by nonprofit agencies, such as TRUSTe (founded by the Electronic Frontier Foundation, the Boston Consulting Group, and a trade association called Commercenet), BBB Online (established by the Better Business Bureau), or the CPA Web Trust (developed by the American Institute of Certified Public Accountants and the Canadian Institute of Chartered Accountants).

Not all sites adhere to these standards, but many do. According to a Georgetown University report to the Federal Trade Commission (FTC) in the spring of 1999, a random sampling of dot-com sites showed that 66 percent posted a privacy policy or an information practice statement. A similar study of the top 100 most-visited sites showed 94 percent of those sites had some kind of policy, up from 71 percent a year earlier.

There are no fast and simple rules about protecting privacy. What one person sees as annoying, another feels is a total invasion of his or her personal life. Ultimately, the choice is up to you—you can frequent the sites that you are comfortable with and avoid the others—but to make an informed choice, you need to understand the issues.

Dyson has spent a lot of time pondering security and privacy concerns, although she prefers to talk about "control over personal data" rather than privacy, since the definition of privacy is so personal. She co-chaired the National Information Infrastructure Advisory Council Information Privacy and Intellectual Property subcommittee and is sought after for her ideas by companies, governments, and organizations in the United States and abroad.

Dyson shares her views on security, privacy, power, control, and other timely and controversial subjects below. Also airing their concerns and advice about the critical issues of security and privacy are Dr. C. Everett Koop of drkoop.com; Dr. George Lundberg, editor in chief of Medscape; Terrell Jones of Travelocity; Halsey Minor of CNET; Ellen Pack of Women.com; David Bohnett, founder of GeoCities; and Kathy Misunas of brandwise.

Defining Security and Privacy

■ **Esther Dyson** Security refers to the integrity of the data, whether people can hack into it or not. Security is a technical term that means, one, you can send something without other people seeing it; and, two, what you send or what you receive is actually what was sent or what was received, the actual data isn't messed with.

Privacy, by contrast, is very hard to define. What is privacy to one person may be completely uninteresting to someone else. For instance, I don't like being phoned at home, whether it's a friend or a telemarketer; other people welcome calls from their friends. Some people don't mind phone calls till midnight, but don't try and call them before 10 A.M. Some people see junk mail as an annoyance; others see it as an invasion of privacy.

The word *privacy* is stretched way too far to cover a wide variety of things—everything from not being bothered to having your personal sense of self invaded. What I prefer to do is talk about control over personal data and control over personal space.

Privacy means more than being left alone; it also means keeping information about someone unavailable. There's a difference between being called at home and being called at home by someone who says, "We understand you have three children and we want to sell you sweaters for them." In some sense, the more information they have about you, the less likely they are to bother you with things you don't want, but the more likely they are to bother you with things you might consider too personal for someone to know.

For my part, I'd like British Airways to know how much I fly on American, because then maybe British Airways would treat me better or they'd give me some special deal or solicit me for upgrades. So each person has his or her own set of what he wants and what she doesn't want. Control over personal data gives the power to individuals to decide for themselves how they want the data used. That control is something that can be delivered, whereas a vague promise of privacy really can't.

Protecting Your Privacy

■ **Esther Dyson** There are a couple of seal programs, such as TRUSTe and BBB Online, and the U.S. government is pushing very hard to have sites disclose what they do with your data. Now depending on who's counting, something like 80 percent of the sites actually have a privacy policy under some name, and frequently they use the terms "privacy policy."

If they have a TRUSTe or BBB Online seal, you can rest assured that they have to follow that policy; if they don't, they're liable to be sued, investigated,

> "Consumers have to understand they have the power. They can go to another site."

and fined and to have the seal revoked. Sites with those seals are audited and regulated, not by the government but by the non-profit organizations that grant the seals. They don't guarantee certain kinds of behavior; they guarantee that what this site says it will do, it will do. What each site says it will do may vary, but it has to keep its promises.

If a site has a privacy policy with no seal, then you hope you can believe it. If it's a reputable brand name you probably can, but if it's a concern you've never heard of, and it has a privacy policy but no seal, you're taking your chances.

Consumers have to understand they have the power. They can go to another site. They don't need to deal with these people if they don't like the way the business treats them . . . whether it's too familiar, or whether the service people don't remember enough about them and they have to do too much work each time they go to the site.

Anonymity, Security, and Sweepstakes

■ **Ellen Pack** I think security and privacy are very important for women and therefore they are conscious and careful about giving out information. It's not just a concern for shopping and credit card fraud—it's about giving out their name, their address, any information about themselves. They're very concerned with where that information might go—more so than men.

What's interesting, however, is that some people will express concern, and then three minutes later they'll be signing up for something because there's a free gift offer or a sweepstakes. So while women say privacy and security are very big concerns, it doesn't necessarily mean that they'll always act on their expressed beliefs.

Should women be concerned about their privacy? Sure, but they should not live in fear—they should manage it. Ultimately their privacy is in their control. I spend a lot of time explaining to people, "Unless you tell a Web site your phone number, it has no way of knowing it." You might be persuaded by a site to give your phone number because of a special offer, but then you should know exactly what they're going to do with that information; a good-quality site will always tell you—they'll have a privacy policy.

At Women.com we're a member of a group called TRUSTe, and we have a policy to never sell our data to a third party. We have rules on our home page about what we will and won't do with the information we collect. And if an advertiser is giving away something free and a member agrees to enter a sweepstakes, we'll tell her up front that we're going to share this information with the advertiser.

You should treat giving out personal information online as carefully and judiciously as you would offline.

■ **David Bohnett** It's important to have a heightened awareness of security and privacy when you're online. There's a lot of worthwhile effort under way with watchdog groups and nonprofit organizations like TRUSTe. I'm hoping people will look for privacy certification when they go to a site, kind of like the Good Housekeeping Seal of Approval.

As for security, the browser itself, whether you're using Netscape or Microsoft, lets you know whether or not you're in a secure environment. I would only put my credit card information in when I know I'm in a secure transaction environment.

One of the things that's fascinated me is the user feedback mechanism on eBay [ebay.com]. People can look for credible feedback from other users who've used this auction service. One of the reasons that eBay has been so successful is because they've tapped into the strengths of the Internet and they set up this user feedback mechanism.

The hosting service also needs to take some responsibility for dealing with complaints. If Yahoo! or GeoCities get repeated complaints about a particular merchant, it's their responsibility to follow up on them.

It's like driving down the street and looking for the kind of store or neighborhood where you feel that you won't be taken advantage of and where you feel safe. You do the same thing online that you do in the real world.

■ **Halsey Minor** People are already used to invasions of their privacy. In fact, they give out more information than they're even required to when they use a credit card; they fill out their names and addresses, which oftentimes aren't even needed. Every day they walk around and, if they make a purchase with a credit card, generate information about themselves. They do it at hotels, they do it at grocery stores, they do it at gas stations, and some of that information is used to market products and services to them.

The Internet is just another place where you give information about yourself, and some of what happens with that information you find annoying and some of it you find helpful. What I hope happens, and I don't know if it will, is that users will not frequent places that misuse information, while places that do use information responsibly will do very well. That way, the market becomes the determinant for regulating the usage of information.

■ **Kathy Misunas** Regarding privacy, our site asserts in very specific language that the information associated with individuals' interactions with brandwise will never be provided to others without their permission. For instance, the use of any behavioral information is compiled in the aggregate and never exposed as individual behavior.

As for security, as the former CEO of Sabre, I come from a *very* strict background. We had literally hundreds of billions of pieces of data in our various databases. To protect it, I have found it is the tone you set with your employees from the beginning—from the documents they sign when they apply to work at your company, to the quality control and measurements that are in place. These aspects let employees know that security is not something ever to be compromised. All the people who work with brandwise know that if they breach that confidence, they are probably not just going to be fired, but executed as well [laugh].

■ **Terrell Jones** We have a straightforward privacy policy on our home page. It says that we simply don't disclose your information to anyone except, of course, those who are participating in your reservation. We have to tell the hotel who you are, just as you would if you called them. But we don't sell our information to third parties, and we pledge that we won't give that information out to anybody.

Skeletons in the Cybercloset

■ **Esther Dyson** You can get overly paranoid about this, but if you want to go to a site and start poking around at things that, for whatever reason, you don't want people to know about, take a careful look at the site's privacy policy. Understand, people can collect a lot of information that, in pieces, doesn't seem to be that interesting . . . but after a year or two, do you want people to know all the things you ever did? That's what these policies are about, controlling what information people can retain about you and what they can do with it.

"Remember that ten years from now if you're looking for a job, somebody can find out the stupid things you said today."

If you go into a chat room or you start posting stuff in newsgroups [Internet discussion groups], understand that the forums are public and there's going to be a record of your visit. You can use a fake name and, unless you do something illegal and you get subpoenaed, it's probably not going to be associated with you. But remember that ten years from now if you're looking for a job, somebody can find out the stupid things you said today. However, the fact is that ten years from now there are going to be so many different people who said so many stupid things it probably doesn't matter. On the other hand, if someone wants to pick on you or you're running for office, they'll be able to find this stuff.

My personal rule is don't do something you'd be ashamed to have people know about because that's the real protection, but nonetheless—people have different behavior; they have different publics they need to communicate with; they have private lives. And so you have to understand that on the Internet you're creating records.

E-mail was supposed to be private, but if you send or receive it on your employer's machine, your employer has access to it. If you send it to someone, you don't know what they're going to do with it. They may forward it to a third friend and say, "Boy, Juan just sent me the dumbest message," or, "Look what Juan said about Alice," or, "This guy really doesn't know how to spell." You have to trust your friends, and they may not all be trustworthy. It's just like saying something at a party that may, or may not, be repeated by someone who may, or may not, have your best interests at heart.

> *"E-mail was supposed to be private, but if you send or receive it on your employer's machine, your employer has access to it."*

A Story About Real-World Privacy

■ **Esther Dyson** I can tell you an incredible story about privacy in the real world. I was getting some health insurance, and they said I should get tested for AIDS privately first, so a doctor came to the office to give me an AIDS test. She walked in and said, "I'm so excited to meet you. I told my boyfriend (who works in computers) I was coming to see you, and he knows all about you." I couldn't believe it. Does she tell everybody whom she tests for AIDS? Now I tested negative, but if I had tested positive I would have felt that my privacy was severely compromised. It was quite extraordinary.

Are Medical Records Safe on the Web?

■ **Dr. Koop** Everybody's concerned about security on the Internet. People talk about the lack of security on the Internet as though we had 100 percent security now. We don't. We have terrible security; your medical record is not the least bit secure.

I know nothing about you or what hospital you've been in, but if you've ever been in the hospital, there are people in that hospital who have access to your record. They can know about things that you'd rather not have them know. They can talk about them to people you know or do not know, but they also can sell your name and your diagnosis to pharmaceutical houses for $10 a name. So if you're an employee in a hospital (and they're caught all the time), you can go through some doctor's stuff in the file, pick out ten names with the same diagnosis, and send them to a pharmaceutical house.

So don't think that you have security now, and therefore that you have to compare the Internet to a very secure system. If you compared the Internet with the present system, I think the Internet is more secure.

■ **Dr. Lundberg** Real hackers can cut through almost any security. I consider almost no information on the Internet secure. For practical purposes there are pretty good security measures, but supersleuths can get through anytime. If you don't mind people knowing about your medical information, go ahead and put it there. If you mind somebody else knowing about your medical information, then you better not put it there.

Could information about buying drugs online get out? Almost certainly. You can pretty much assume that enterprising pharmaceutical companies will find out about online purchases because there are companies that gather that information, sell it to pharmaceutical companies, who then market to you directly based upon the information they get from prior prescription sales.

The fact of security being a problem in hospitals is true. It's a problem everywhere. I learned that when I was a medical student—there are no secrets in hospitals.

When Elvis Presley used to be hospitalized he would enter

than just your credit card. If your credit card is stolen, by and large you're liable for a $50 maximum, and it's a problem for the credit card company but not a big one for you. It can be inconvenient, and it can be worse than inconvenient, but the risks have very little to do with your credit card being intercepted—which, as everybody points out many times, could happen in a gas station or a restaurant.

The risk is much more fundamental: there are bad guys out there, and there's a lot of information available to them. Security is like public health: it's not something you can control by yourself. It gets handled through laws and through business standards. When you go into a restaurant, you assume that the people working in the restaurant wash their hands after they use the rest room, they don't sneeze into the salad plate, and the cook doesn't stick his finger in the soup to taste it. You never know, but you assume that public health workers are tested and follow procedures.

Claim Dropping?

■ **Esther Dyson** We have the same social vulnerabilities with information, and we're probably not as good at protecting information as we are at public health. We need insurance companies to look at a firm's data security practices just as they inspect for oily rags in the stairwells.

What did the most to solve fire problems wasn't fire codes but insurance companies that wouldn't insure bad risks. They come in and they look around. Is there sawdust all over the place? Are there oily rags? Where do you store the kerosene? Insurance companies aren't doing that enough yet with data and information processing practices, but you're seeing the beginnings of it with the SEC-required Y2K disclosures.

the Baptist Hospital in Memphis under the name of Aaron Sivle. Aaron was his middle name and Sivle is Elvis spelled backward. All his medical records were Aaron Sivle; that was a bit lame, but it was relatively successful method of keeping that information from people.

The difference between security on the Internet and in hospitals is that in hospitals you get a piece of paper. How many people can look at a piece of paper? If you have something on the Internet and somebody gloms onto it electronically, the person can spread it out to the world just like that. How many photocopies would you have to make of your notes in order for the world to see your notes? A lot. It's the physical difference.

In Cards We Trust

■ **Terrell Jones** People are very fearful of security breaches, even though last year, according to MasterCard and Visa, there was no in-transit credit card theft on the Web. If you use the security systems provided by Microsoft and Netscape, you are probably safe because they haven't been cracked. So using a credit card isn't something that people should be afraid of at all. We even have a guarantee on our site saying if you have a problem, we'll take care of it. I haven't had to pay anybody.

The number one reason that people don't shop online is fear of using their credit card, and that's too bad because it's not something to worry about.

■ **Esther Dyson** Basically you don't need to worry about using your credit card online. There's another security issue, identity theft, which usually doesn't come from somebody intercepting your credit card online. It's more likely they'll do a methodical search of a database and get a lot more information

We're still at an early stage, but what you want is for insurance companies to say, "Last time that happened, we paid for it. This time we're going to inspect how they run their computer system so that we're not liable." It will take some time. It's like fires. They needed (unfortunately) a few fires before they started passing fire codes.

Right now we're at a point in the insurance cycle where rates are pretty low and they're competing on rates, and they don't want to turn down the business. But as we go through a cycle, they will probably get much more active, and not just insuring against these risks but doing loss prevention and risk management.

Fed or Foe?

■ **Esther Dyson** You need regulations vis-à-vis children and vis-à-vis medical information, where the individual may not know enough or can't bargain. If you need a new kidney, for example, you've got to tell them all this stuff. But in general I think the industry's actions will suffice. Now would industry have taken those actions if government hadn't threatened to regulate? Probably not.

There's a dynamic tension here. The government's saying, "You guys do it yourselves or we'll come in and regulate." So the industry players are now doing a lot more than they were a year ago precisely because they don't want regulation. Certainly the government's playing an important role there, but I think threatening is going to be more useful than actually regulating it, because then the rules would be too rigid.

If there is a move to government regulation, I hope it's for disclosure rather than for specific practices. In Europe, you have much more rigid rules and they don't give much choice to consumers or to businesses. In Europe, British Airways probably couldn't keep the information about how much I fly on American Airlines, even if I gave it to them.

I do not think this benefits the consumer. Personal data control is about individual choice. It's not about the government making the same choice for everybody.

■ **Halsey Minor** What I really worry about is if the government comes in and tries to regulate privacy, they won't get it quite right; and they may, in fact, inhibit electronic commerce or they may create rules that, while it helps one group of users, would make the Web unusable for another group of users. For instance, cookies (which track your progress across the Web) can be incredibly invasive from a privacy standpoint because people can look at what you're doing, but they're also the foundation for personalization.

I hope it evolves into a market-driven approach, where people become much more cautious about who they give their information to. Brands that distinguish themselves will do so through the conservative use of people's information.

I know we live in terror about doing anything with the information people provide that would give us a bad reputation. We are incredibly cautious about it; and in fact, never give our information to any of our advertisers and never allow our database of names to be used by advertisers to solicit for sales. My guess is that if we misused it, we'd have a lot of people who wouldn't want to use us anymore. Especially since word spreads so quickly on the Internet.

Taking Charge of Your Info

■ **Esther Dyson** If you don't want to give out your address to an online store there are services that will have it sent to another address and then forward it to you. Of course, then you have to trust the forwarding service.

There are also new services coming out, like Obongo, which I've invested in; and a service Novell has called Digital Me, which will automate some of the process for you, but again, you need to trust those services.

The way Obongo and similar systems work is they'll store whatever you want them to—passwords, mailing addresses, credit cards—whatever you want to give them, and they'll give it out as you instruct. In the long run, the privacy seals will also be electronically readable, and you can say, "Give my home address only to the sites that make such-and-such agreements about what they'll do with the information and that have such-and-such a seal to guarantee their promises."

The system would follow your instructions about what to give out and you could obviously change it at will, but it would save you the trouble of dealing with registering each time. For example, if you went to Amazon.com, the service would be in the background and would understand what Amazon was asking for and fill it in automatically. It might say to you, "Do you trust this site with your credit card number?" and you would say, "Yes," or you'd say, "No, I want to give my credit card number each time I visit." It gives you as much control as you'd want, but it automates what you don't want to deal with each time.

Spammer Jammers

■ **Esther Dyson** There are services that screen junk mail for you. As a consumer you don't deal with most of them directly because if you're on AOL, for instance, they screen a lot of mail for you. People don't know that because they never get the mail that gets screened, but there would be just awesome amounts of junk mail otherwise.

Critical Path does screening for various Internet Service Providers and Bright Light (which, in the interest of disclosure, I'm an investor in) has software to do that. There are a lot of good market-based mechanisms to deal with this rather than having the government try to regulate it. But, again, one person's spam is a welcome message to another. "Gee, I really wanted to buy a Caribbean island; thank you for the information!"

A Fee for All

■ **Esther Dyson** Should consumers be paid for their own data? Actually, consumers more often will get a discount or other consideration rather than straight cash. You may get a fee for sharing information about what rock music you like so that other consumers can benefit from that information, but the

> "There's a very fine line between good customer service and stalking."

notion of marketers paying fees to have you read an ad doesn't cut it over time, because people who want to be paid for reading ads are probably not very good prospects for the products. I think advertisers are going to discover that it really is not a benefit to them if you read their ad, but it is a benefit if you buy their product. We'll see a lot of companies giving discounts, but I don't think you're going to see that much cash passing hands.

Personalized marketing can lead to better service, but as someone said, "There's a very fine line between good customer service and stalking." And that's why privacy is very hard to define. If you love the guy, it's great; if you don't, it's stalking. If you want the service, it's great, but if your baby died and they come trying to sell you diapers, it's horrible.

Where Truth and Lies Collide

■ **Esther Dyson** It used to be, to be heard at all, you had to stand on a street corner, or go buy a newspaper or tune in a television station. The Internet is a platform for many more people. It's much harder to control, of course, because it's less centralized.

Anyone can put up a Web site, and he or she can tell either the truth or lies. This doesn't mean that journalistic standards will change, but the practices might. What concerns me is that truth and fiction are hard to distinguish, that advertising and editorial are hard to distinguish, and so it's more incumbent upon people to be well-educated and skeptical. But there's a lot of truth that deserves to be heard.

Right now, for example, we're getting a lot of reports coming out of Yugoslavia. Some of them are accurate; some may not be. It's hard to tell. I assume most of what's coming out of Yugoslavia's probably true, but in some sense it's no more reliable than interviewing somebody in a refugee camp.

Now the Internet makes it much easier to write to your legislator, and that's good. Is it going to change humanity? No. But it's going to change the balance of power, and that, to me, is much more important. The legislator may or may not listen to you, but if he does real estate on the side, it's going to be much harder for him to keep it secret.

The balance of power is basically moving in favor of individuals and employees against large corporations, large governments, and large countries. The Internet gives people the communication channel to bypass the authorities.

Will the Good Guys Win?

■ **Esther Dyson** What concerns me most about the Internet is the people on it, and whether they will rise to all these challenges. Will they, in fact, understand these issues, take the trouble to get the control they can have? Will they take good advantage of the medium?

I'm fundamentally optimistic. I think that if you give more power to people, on average they'll use it wisely. But there are also a good many bad and irresponsible people out there, and they'll do bad and irresponsible things with the Internet.

But it's not going to be 90 percent better, it's more like 60 percent of the people will take advantage and do good things. It's worth writing about this to help people understand the good use they can make of it because if the good people don't do it, the bad uses will outnumber the good ones. You need to help tilt the balance toward using the Internet responsibly, understanding the power and exercising it well.

Suggested Web Sites

eff.org
icsa.org
netnanny.com
surfwatch.com

Nevertheless, some visionaries have had an uncanny ability to piece together unrelated events to paint a picture of tomorrow. Since computers and the Web have the power to alter our lives profoundly, we have turned to one of this century's most prominent social thinkers and futurists, Alvin Toffler, and asked him to contemplate the impact the Internet is having on our culture, as well as on other nations. While all of the voices of *Fast Forward* have talked about what's coming, it seemed only right that Alvin Toffler's visionary mind and voice should cap this book.

Toffler is best known as the author of three groundbreaking books: *Future Shock*, *The Third Wave*, and *PowerShift*. Toffler and his wife, Heidi, work as intellectual partners, analyzing seemingly disparate global events and figuring out what they mean for society. Toffler believes a lot of the forecasting taking place today is inadequately global—not in the geographic sense, but in the human sense. It's not easy to comprehend the big picture because our social systems are closely linked and, he says, "We've reached a point of complexity, filled with interacting feedback systems going through a nonlinear upheaval, which makes it even more difficult to predict the outcome." Of course, that didn't stop us from asking him to make some twenty-first-century predictions.

The Tofflers are not technologists, they are "liberal arts products," as Toffler notes, but they have been using a computer since 1976. Their first machine was custom-built, had 16K of memory, walnut sides, a beautiful blue metal case, two floppy drives, a Panasonic television set for a monitor, filled a room, and cost $3,000.

Shortly after getting that system, he and Heidi went online through Arpanet, which was the network system used by scientists and government researchers, but even then, he says, e-mail could be crushing. "We went away one weekend leaving the system on and came back so avalanched and overloaded with material we turned the damn thing off."

RIDING INTO THE FUTURE

Of all the sources of power, knowledge is the one that is most democratic. It's also probably the most dangerous.

—Alvin Toffler, author and futurist

The winners won't come from anybody we know today . . . It's going to come from the kids out there who don't have preconceived notions, who don't come in asking questions based on what we already know.

—Mark Cuban, broadcast.com

My greatest concern about the Internet is that in this country the distance between the haves and the have-nots seems to get greater all the time instead of less.

—Dr. C. Everett Koop, drkoop.com

A s kids, my friends and I were fascinated by futuristic movies that foretold a time when aliens landed on Earth or cities turned into rubble or a demonic Big Brother watched and controlled your every move. No matter how implausible some of these events seemed, we felt compelled to watch and imagine what the future might hold in store.

Predicting the future is risky business. Says Ken Auletta, author and communications columnist for *The New Yorker*, "One of the things you learn as you follow this world is there are no oracles. Just look at how dumb some of the smartest oracles have been—Bill Gates missing the Internet, Larry Ellison talking about the dumb computer."

However, from his earliest experiences online, Toffler knew it was an extraordinary phenomenon that would spread to a much wider audience. The takeoff came when the media discovered the Web in the nineties, he explains, and suddenly Internet mania was born. "I would have expected it to have developed sooner than when it did," says Toffler. "I also underestimated how long it would take to clone a mammal."

Like millions of users, Toffler knows how frustrating technology can be. On the day we met he had decided that he needed one more Internet service provider as a backup. "So you get a different set of lies when it doesn't go right," he joked.

But despite the technical hassles, more and more people are getting online. Their presence will dramatically alter how our society receives and responds to world events. Politicians, for example, are suddenly recognizing the power of the Web to raise funds for campaigns. Helped by a Federal Election Commission vote in June 1999, presidential candidates can now count money collected over the Web in funds that the federal government matches. Consumer advocate Ralph Nader has numerous online sites, including nader.org, where you can read his columns and speeches and citizen.org, where you can access Public Citizen, the organization founded by Nader in 1971 to be the consumer's eyes and ears in Washington. For their part, technology companies are in the early stages of building systems that will enable voters to cast ballots over the Internet, although no states allow Internet voting now.

Even wars are being influenced by a wired world. During the war in Yugoslavia, a trade embargo against Slobodan Milosevic's government led to a controversy over cutting satellite transmission services into the country. Ultimately the Clinton administration reaffirmed that it had no desire to cut off the flow of independent, objective information to Serbia. Those fighting the war were also the beneficiaries of the Web.

Cmdr. Sam Richardson aboard the U.S.S. *Theodore Roosevelt*, off the coast of Yugoslavia, told a *Today* show audience that he and his wife exchange regular e-mail, making it easier than it used to be to stay in touch when on missions. Now, he joked, he knows immediately when the dishwasher at home breaks.

While data and video still move relatively slowly through the wires, plans are under way to build a superfast, extremely reliable, data pipeline (the Abilene Network) that can move data 1,600 times faster than the T1 lines that businesses and universities use today. A test of the network, in February 1999, included a demonstration of remote surgery that allowed surgeons to collaborate over the network while they were hundreds of miles apart.

The Web is a global experience, bringing people from distant locations together to chat, learn from one another, and buy and sell goods. According to StatMarket, a company that tracks Web traffic, surfers from international addresses account for 44 percent of the Net traffic. The Internet is shrinking distances among us, which could lead to a greater understanding among people of different cultures, could speed up the homogenization of those cultures, or could be used as a tool to aggregate those who would divide. The jury's still out on which of these patterns achieves greater velocity.

In addition to Toffler, we've asked most of our other leading technology thinkers quoted throughout this book to ponder where the Internet is leading us, so that you can get a glimpse of the world your children will inherit.

Village Power

■ **Alvin Toffler** There's a village of fifty families in Peru called Chincheros. Since they started selling vegetables to New York through the Internet the income of the village has tripled.

We're going to see a lot of that around the world. I also believe many big companies are going to be pecked to death by microcompanies. The mix between large-scale enterprises and small-scale enterprises is going to change. The cost of production of many, many things is going to go down.

The price of goods will also drop if there's competition; where there's protection, the prices will not go down. Prices going down is like wages going up, as far as the individual is concerned.

We're seeing pockets of this kind of development springing up all over the world. For example, I went to a conference of thousands of teachers in Guanajuato Province in Mexico and talked about all of this stuff. They immediately said, "Yes, but poor people can't afford computers." I said, "What's the percentage of television ownership in this country?" Well, depending on where you are when you ask the question, the response is from 70 to 95 percent. I said, "What if your computer was a television set and cost less than a television set? Wouldn't everyone who wants one have one?" Indeed, I believe that's what's going to happen.

We all know examples of places that are beginning to develop programming and material for that kind of world. Therefore, I've changed, I've become more optimistic than I used to be about the issue of the information-rich and the information-poor.

■ **Ken Auletta** There are two models for success in the future that are at war. One model is increasing concentration of ownership, which you see if you look at what is happening in the television station market. Big companies like Time Warner, Disney, CBS, Fox, and the Tribune Company are gaining a larger and larger share of ownership. The traditional Ma-and-Pa-ownership has been decreasing for many years.

At the same time, you have the growth of upstart competitors fueled primarily by technology. In the past you might look at CNN and think Marshall McLuhan was right: we're going to have a global village. But now, if you look at how cheap it is to put an uplink to a satellite, you start thinking, Wait a second, we're not going to have one global village. We're going to have hundreds of local villages, connected in some way. Instead of watching an American international news service, it's more likely I'll watch cricket scores from India and my local anchor and local weather, and not have Ted Turner impose football scores on me when I'm not interested in football.

Asian Ted Turners and Muslim Murdochs

■ **Alvin Toffler** I travel a lot in parts of the world that are poor. We're always asked, Isn't it terrible that communications is dominated by Murdoch and Turner and is it going to get worse? My answer is, first of all, the sky is going to be for the satellites. You're going to turn on your television set, and the program you're watching could very well come from Nigeria or from Fiji, translated into your own language, and probably with adequate special-effects software to change the ethnic look of the actor, talking in your language with lips moving exactly the right way they should move.

The other question we're always asked is: Can we become third wave and stay Chinese or can we become third wave and remain Mexican? Our answer is with all the stuff coming down from the heavens, from every part of the world, there will be Ayatollahs preaching, there will be Asian Ted Turners, there will be Muslim Murdochs. Everything you can think of will be out there and that will have an impact on your culture.

Now out of that great enormous selection, your people may choose only certain parts and create a unique Mexican culture, but it won't be the Mexican culture of the past. It'll be the Mexican culture of the future.

Internet U.S.A.?

■ **Halsey Minor** Will American culture dominate the Internet? Well, there are two ways of looking at it. One option is it could be Americanized, but I don't really know what Americanization is because we're actually an amalgamation of a lot of other cultures. Basically I've always looked at the Internet as an entirely different country—a country without rulers, a country without borders, and a country that's very, very difficult, if not impossible, to regulate. And slowly but surely we're all getting co-opted in this country and spending more and more of our time there. It's probably a pretty good bet that the primary language of this country is going to be English; if there's anything that's going to push the English language out to most of the world, it'll be the Internet.

The other possibility is American businesses—because the United States is larger, it's adopted the Internet more rapidly and its infrastructure and business are much better developed—will end up being the leading companies in their category in many regions outside the United States.

I think you will see a projection of commerce around the world as a result of the Internet, maybe in a way that's far greater than ever before; from companies like Amazon in books, CNET in computing, and Yahoo! in search, navigation, and media. We just have so many more resources now, so much more money, and so many more people that the language translation problems and cultural problems, while an issue, are far less of a problem than the core issue of understanding and building Internet services that people want to use.

I really think that the United States is going to end up playing a major role in this whole new economy, and maybe to the degree that we've never seen before (even following World War II) because it's inevitable that the Internet spreads to lots of other countries. There's another inevitability, despite these countries best efforts to try to stop it or to shape it in their own vision or in ways that helps their own society and their own culture, the Internet just doesn't lend itself to that. It's going to be very hard to create laws and regulations which make it difficult for American companies to compete.

The Great Leveler

■ **Bob Pittman** I think the Internet is going to have a leveling effect on society. There's not going to be the advantage of being in New York over living in Brookhaven, Mississippi, because we're going to get access to the same information, the same communications network in Brookhaven, as we can in New York City. I think it's going to be somewhat of a leveler in terms of income disparity among certain groups in America because if you're online, you can have access to the highest quality communication and people. You no longer have the physical barriers or economic barriers that you might have offline. I believe it's going to bring about more understanding among people.

I was talking to somebody the other day from Israel about the peace process. He said one of the best things that's helping bring the Israelis together with the Arabs is the Internet. He said when you're talking to people online, you don't know who they are, you meet them first on a basis of what they're talking about, what they're interested in, and what kind of person they are, and later they may reveal who they are. Whereas in real life, you see the person first; any biases you have crop up immediately and color your relationship.

I expect the Internet will break down a lot of global barriers among nations. I think it will facilitate commerce and make us more productive. It will allow smaller merchants to make money and reduce the barriers to being in business, allowing people who really do want to have their own businesses and participate in the economy to participate online.

■ **Alvin Toffler** I was invited to Buenos Aires recently for the world's biggest book fair. I sat on the stage, was interviewed by some journalists, and then I went to sign books. Suddenly eight people materialized in front of me, waiting patiently for me to be finished. Then they announced, "We are your family." And, indeed, they are. My wife and I didn't even know they existed. I went out to dinner with them afterward and discussed our genealogy. What really struck me is when we exchanged addresses, they said, "Here's my e-mail address. What's yours?" That's a story I won't forget. It blew me away.

Truth, Deception, and Nihilism

■ **Alvin Toffler** A lot of the information that's out there is, in fact, misinformation. Some of it is disinformation, which is deliberately designed to delude, not just in personal terms, but in political or other terms. One of the things that the generation to come will need to learn is what I call media sophistication.

First of all, you need to understand that what you see on television or what you get off Web TV or the computer is not necessarily true. You've got to ask, que bono, who is served by this information? If you're really sophisticated you'll ask: How is it created? How is it produced? What are the distortions that the media put into it? No information comes to you that has not been massaged by somebody, with the possible exception of certain kinds of scientific data. But we do run the risk of creating a generation that, correctly, learns to be skeptical of what it hears and reads, but who may go from skepticism to nihilism, which says, therefore, nothing matters.

It's very interesting that at the very time we're talking about the uncertainty of knowing whether what you're getting across the Internet is, or is not, "true," we have a whole movement of Postmodernist philosophers who argue there is no truth. These are two separate phenomena, but it's not accidental that they're coming at the same time. And, indeed, if my friend could create a movie with Clint Eastwood in which Eastwood looks as though he's riding on John F. Kennedy's limousine as his Secret Service protector, and I can't tell that Eastwood was not there, how do I know what happened?

Scientific American, talking about the kind of digital imaging manipulation that is possible, did a story a number of years ago with photographs that showed President Bush and Margaret Thatcher walking in what appeared to be the Rose Garden of the White House. In the first picture Thatcher is walking about five steps behind Bush. In the next photo, they are walking side by side, and in the third photo they're holding hands and he's whispering in her ear. Now that was digitally manipulated.

I've said many times that the technologies of deception are outrunning the technologies of verification, which is really the dark side of what's happening.

De-Nerding the Web

■ **Alvin Toffler** The Internet is no longer the province of teenage nerds. It is for everybody. It was inconceivable when the telephone arrived that the day would come when anybody but a handful of people would ever use the telephone. In England the superrich were the first to have telephones, and if the telephone rang, you did not answer it. You sent the butler to answer it because it was regarded as a doorway into the home. The butler opened the front door; therefore, the butler answered the telephone. It was inconceivable that the day would come when everybody had a telephone, and I think that's where we are today with the Internet.

> *"The Internet is no longer the province of teenage nerds. It is for everybody."*

■ **Bob Pittman** The first people who used AOL were people who had a computer and were looking for something to do with it. The computer was their hobby. That's very different behavior from the mass market consumers who actually have lives and other interests. The computer is not their hobby. Their only interest in the computer is whether it can do something for them. It's a means to an end, it's not the end itself.

We have a mass market today; 30 percent of U.S. households are online. The subscribers who are coming onto AOL now are real human beings with real lives. The kind of activities they are doing are normal ones, in terms of what the general population does every day.

Welcome to the High-Tech Stone Age

■ **Alvin Toffler** All the stuff we're monkeying with today, all the wonderful stuff we read about the Internet or find on the Internet, is a Stone Age version of what we're likely to have within a decade or two. It's primitive; that's why your machine doesn't work when you want it to. That's why you download one thing and it screws up another thing. I believe that it is either going to become radically simplified, which I think is going to happen, or it's going to go away. There's too much hassle at present.

■ **Bob Pittman** I think the best way to predict future innovations is to stop looking at technology and start looking at people and what they want, and if they want it badly enough, someone will figure out how to give it to them. I think the possibilities are limited only by our analysis, not so much by technology. As our technologists say, it's easy to invent stuff, it's just hard to figure out what to invent.

■ **Halsey Minor** Computer usage has already reached a mass market audience, and I don't know whether it's going to take the Internet a while to get into the 90+ percentile range, but I think that what will really drive it up there is not new technology, it's utility. Let me explain what I mean.

Cars are the prevalent means of transportation for Americans, yet they are very hard to learn to use. In fact, they're so hard to learn to use that you have to actually take courses and get certified to use them. And when you use them incorrectly, they can kill you. So there's a lot of learning that has to go into using a car. Then, when you're finally able to drive one, you have to spend some 10 to 50 percent of your disposable income to acquire one and use it.

The question is, you have this device that's hard to learn to use, dangerous, and also expensive, so why are cars so successful? Well, they're successful because to participate in our culture, you have to have one.

Computers have never been like that, but increasingly they are becoming like that because they're beginning to be the way we shop, communicate, and do a lot of ordinary, everyday things that we need to do to be functioning members of society. While computers seem fairly expensive, they're actually a lot less expensive than cars; while they seem fairly complicated, they're a lot less complicated than cars; and they're certainly less dangerous.

The difference between where computers are today, in

terms of the number of households using them, and where they can be, is a direct function of their utility—how useful are they and how much do we really need them? What I believe we're seeing is an explosion in the utility of computers, which means that at a certain point it becomes worth buying a computer because it's the only way you can stay in touch with somebody or it's a way to buy goods and services more cheaply. Then the only threshold for increased use becomes literacy, and that, I think, is the single biggest hurdle: some people simply cannot read and write and, as a result, they cannot use technology.

The 24/7 Web Connection

■ **Ellen Pack** Eventually Web access is going to become a ubiquitous utility. The big difference will be when we can all get it through our cable connection. Right now it is very much like, "I'm going in to work on the computer," and you'll disappear into a black hole for a couple of hours. The big breakthrough will be when your computer is "always on," which basically means that the Internet can be connected at all times and from all rooms of the house for a flat fee. It will be a much more fluid state where there may be a computer in the kitchen and you check the weather in the morning and then walk away from the machine while the Internet is still on.

■ **David Bohnett** Two things are going to have a big impact in the future. One, the faster the connection gets, the easier and more fun it is to go online. And, number two, when people have a persistent connection in the house, it will change the way you use the Internet. Just imagine if you wanted to make a phone call and you had to put the phone on the desk, attach the dial, plug it in the back, and then wait a couple of minutes before you could pick up the phone and dial it. You wouldn't use the phone too often.

When the computer is always on you use it differently, you can just walk over to it and check out who's online or check on the latest sports scores. The Internet becomes a part of your daily life, more like the telephone. I expect that by the end of the year 2000, 15 to 20 percent of connected households will have high bandwidth, always-on connections.

The Network of Networks

■ **Halsey Minor** Fifteen years from now your cable is not going to be delivered, basically it is going to be an Internet service. Even your television programming is going to be digital and packet-switched, and virtually everything will go over the same network; it really will be a true network of networks. It's just that the Internet will co-opt all other networks, from the cable network to the telephone infrastructure.

In that regard you've got convergence, all networks will converge into one network, but then you've also got divergence in the kinds of devices to connect to it. Right now the primary device for information distribution is the computer, with television programming going over the TV, but ultimately content will be repackaged for any kind of device that a user has.

We're already seeing an explosion of devices from Palm Pilots, which are Web-connected, to cell phones that are going to be Web-connected, to set-top boxes that are going to be Web-connected, to even the new VCRs, which record programming on a hard drive, but also use the Internet to build a programming guide and then can suggest shows to you. I think we're going to see an explosion of appliances that all use the Internet to talk to one another. At one point, we may get

90 percent Internet penetration in the home because every toaster or washing machine uses the Internet to communicate with the manufacturer if it breaks.

■ **Mark Cuban** There's no such thing as convergence; either you're analog or you're digital. Convergence assumes that there's going to be something digital in that TV or in that radio. There's no point in doing that. Set-top boxes aren't going to be the wave of the future. Set-top boxes may do okay next year, but after that they'll disappear.

> *"What is a set-top box? It's just a stupid computer with no upgradabilty, manufactured by companies who don't improve them very often, with very limited functionality."*

What is a set-top box? It's just a stupid computer with no upgradabilty, manufactured by companies who don't improve them very often, with very limited functionality. It doesn't enable user creativity or interactivity. Just think about it, it requires the cable guy to come out and install it, versus just plugging in your PC.

Yet manufacturers are creating standards for them because they want people to be able to go and buy them off the shelf in a store. Well, those standards are going to go into the computer, which is going to look like a DVD player or a VCR and move into your living room. It will have complete flexibility, and when a better version comes out that you can afford, you'll just take the old PC and move it to a different room.

Have Your Device Call My Device

■ **Alvin Toffler** In the future there will be a lot of appliances. The danger for the development of various industries, as well as for users, is you get a thousand different devices: your microwave, your car, your everything, and specialized gadgets that do all kinds of wonderful things for you, except when every one of them needs a manual.

Here's what I think is going to happen. In the first wave of these specialized intelligent devices, they will not talk very well to one another, they will not be smart enough. Then they will improve and there will be a great mania for them, followed by a bust. There will be people disillusioned with the damn things taking too much time and people will say, "Maybe I'll just have this one and not all the rest." Down the line—probably a couple of decades from now—there will be another wave of development, which solves the problems and has them talking smoothly to one another so that you don't have to worry about it.

We're Not All Connected—Yet

■ **David Bohnett** There are five electronic things on my desk right now: my laptop, my telephone, my Palm Pilot, my pager, and my cell phone. There's also my date book and my checkbook. Now all these things ought to talk to one another. My cell phone ought to talk to my Pilot so I can download an address and speed dial it, and my checkbook ought to talk to my laptop.

I don't need any more gadgets, I just need all of them to talk to one another. That's why the Pilot is so neat, it already talks to the laptop. The more you connect these discreet devices, the more useful they are and the less need you have for other ones. At some point, one device may do it all.

■ **Esther Dyson** There will be more ways to connect to the Internet. It's not just about having different Internet devices, but more about your devices connecting to the Internet. Your school bus, for example, so you know when it's time to send your kids out to catch it. Your suitcases will probably have a chip on them so even though they get misrouted and end up in the wrong place, they won't be "lost." You'll know exactly where they are. They're just not where you want them. The physical world will become much more visible virtually.

■ **Ellen Pack** Time savings will come in the future when I can save personal information about myself and not have to reenter it each time I go to a different site. I look forward to the day when I can walk into Starbuck's and, because I e-mailed my order from the car before I got there, the drink is made and I don't have to wait.

Video will also make a big difference in the future, not just for entertainment but for group communications. If I can sit here and dial up my mother and have her come up on the screen, then we can have more than a phone conversation, we can have breakfast together.

A Challenge for Newspapers

■ **Halsey Minor** Every day we're given more and more choices for how to get information. First, it was newspapers, then there was radio, and then there was television. Now we've got the Internet, and I think there's got to be some degree of cannibalization from all of these things every time there's a new medium, or at least it takes the growth away from some of them.

The Web has a huge advantage over most other media in that it's more timely. It's pretty clear that some publications are going to have to evolve to respond to the advantages that the Internet brings. It's a real challenge for local newspapers, but they have an advantage in local coverage that no other Internet source can afford to provide today, and that gives them some protection.

■ **Ken Auletta** I moderated a panel about five years ago for the American Society of Newspaper Editors in Dallas, and Andy Grove, chairman of Intel Corp., was on the panel. I asked Grove, "What do you think the value of newspapers will be in an online world?" And Grove, in part to be provocative, said, "Zero value. In fact, I don't know why we need any of the people in this room in the future."

Well, all the people there start looking at themselves, hating this guy up there, and also thinking: Maybe I should go see my shrink or look at my contract.

Three years later, in Davos at the World Economic Forum, I moderated a panel with Andy Grove again, and I said, "Mr.Grove, here you are talking about a major shift in the Internet world, where people like [Bill] Gates and you, who disparaged the networks and the notion of brand name as old thinking, have come to value the importance of brand and of things like authority."

Then I said, "Mr. Grove, let me remind you of something you said on a panel to newspaper editors about three years ago. I asked you what the value of editors would be in the future, and you said, 'Zero.' Do you still believe that? And if you do, how do you square that with what you just said about authority and branding?"

He looked at me kind of startled, and said, "I was trying to be provocative, but I really believed that. I don't believe that anymore because one of the things I've learned is there's such a sea of information that the consumer needs help. I need help sorting it out. One of the things I need to know is, of these thousands of people who are offering us something, whom can I trust? I see CNN or *The New York Times*, I trust that. The brand means something to me, and that's important."

The Write Stuff

■ **Esther Dyson** Before the talkies, if you were beautiful and you couldn't speak English, you could still become a movie star. When the talkies came in, it mattered how you spoke. On the Internet nobody knows if you're a dog, but they know if you can spell. So different qualities come to the fore, and there are people who are better at communicating on the Internet. Inevitably it will have an influence, but it's not terribly clear-cut.

Long ago if you were strong and healthy, that was probably the best thing; then it was whether you were handy with machines.

> "On the Internet nobody knows if you're a dog, but they know if you can spell."

Well, we're getting to where intelligence matters more because the world is more complicated. But a winning personality still matters a whole lot.

You can also use video and sound to express yourself but, in the end, words become more and more important. Even with broadband technology, the Internet is still also a writing medium. Of course, some people are never going to write: they're going to telephone, send voice mail, do online videos. There are other people who won't do anything but write. The more you allow richer media, the more people will use them, but fundamentally they're not as efficient at communicating ideas. It takes longer to listen to a video than to read one. It's easier to edit and forward an e-mail. So the balance is still toward written communications, but it'll become easier to do the other forms.

Making Our Lives Easier

■ **Alvin Toffler** People worry about the disappearance of the middleman, but I believe it's time to start thinking about reintermediation, not about disintermediation.

I think what's going to happen is that new intermediaries are going to arise. For example, the breakup of AT&T, which means that one outfit puts in the wires and somebody else does the house from inside the wall and somebody else manufactures and sells you the phone, has led to companies that put all these things together for you. You do not have to, if you don't want to, deal individually with the Bell operating company and all these players. You can call a local intermediary who puts all these things back together for you. I think we're going to see that in industry after industry after industry.

We're also going to see another layer of people working at home. The growth of work at home has been very rapid, but would have been more rapid, and will be more rapid, once we develop facilitating intermediaries that make it possible for groups of home workers to work together. I don't mean geographically together but in a virtual way with a common health plan, for example, or common facilities or common services that you once got from the corporation you worked for.

You could have a small company, call it a facilitator, spring up and say, "I'm going to hire ten freelance programmers, and we're going to have a temporary organization, a project team to create the following product." You could look upon that person as, on the one hand, an investor, an entrepreneur, or a facilitator of a certain kind of production.

While we are going to wipe out a lot of intermediaries, I also think we're going to find other niches and configurations that are required to make life more convenient for us. That doesn't mean that your insurance broker is going to turn into a tele-phone facilitator, but stranger things have happened I suppose.

A Constant Electronic Voice

■ **Alvin Toffler** The Internet makes it possible to democratize the system by compensating for the disproportionate power of the big lobbies. If you stop and think about the way our democracy works, voters get a chance to throw out the gov-ernment at fixed intervals; two years you get rid of your con-gressman, four years your president, six years your senator.

In engineering terms, that's a batch process, your vote is in-termittent, while the lobby votes 24 hours a day, 365 days a year. It's a continuous-flow process, not a batch process. It is that disparity which gives the lobbies enormous power vis-à-vis the individual voter. The Internet can make possible con-tinuous-flow participation by millions and millions of people in a political process, so that it's not just every two, four, or six years.

Now, on the other hand, you don't want to be voting and being polled all the time, but there are ways to do it. Not every-body has to vote on everything, but we can have a more mean-ingful process by which there is constant participation by segments of a society that may be chosen randomly. On July 13, for example, you can vote on the following issue, and it will be a random panel of Americans, and you're on the Inter-net, it's asynchronous, you can do it at your convenience. When that vote is tallied it will have an effect on the Congress, not necessarily command that Congress do what you said, but it may influence.

That's just one of the many alternate ways that I think the existing political structure can be reconfigured to take account of this incredible tool.

Election 2000 and Beyond

■ **Peter Friedman** I think you'll see a huge number of town meetings between the candidates and people online during the 2000 election. The candidates who don't do it, whether it's national or local, will lose. We've already seen interest from senatorial candidates during the last election in California in doing things online. We'll also create programming for that purpose; so just like candidates go to TV and radio and pay for time to do town meetings, they'll probably do it online.

■ **Halsey Minor** Before I voted in the last election, I spent a lot of time going on the Web and actually looking at what the candidates had to say and learning about their platforms. The way I look at it, every voter is basically a consumer; he or she is making some sort of decision, which they view as an important one, and the more information available, the better.

Just like the process you go through to buy a car or to buy a house or make any other major decision in your life, the Internet provides you a way to do a huge amount of research and to learn a lot more, and the same is true for political candidates. I think this upcoming presidential election will probably be the first time that a significant number of people will actually use the Internet to learn directly about their candidates. It also may be the first time these candidates actually begin to do Web advertising because enough of their constituents are there that it may, in fact, matter.

The Internet does not lend itself to sound bites. It lends itself to more in-depth investigation of information, and that's what people expect from the medium. So to the extent that people adopt the Internet as a medium for learning about candidates or just adopt it as a medium in general, I think it has the ability to make political advertising a lot more substantive.

■ **Alvin Toffler** The interests of the advanced sectors of the economy, of which the Internet is a fundamental piece, are different from the interests of the old-fashioned manufacturing sector, one of whose primary concerns was the cheap labor needed in order to compete. We have a completely different economy beginning to emerge around the Internet and digital technology that is not yet reflected politically.

An enormous mass of regulation favors the more backward, second-wave parts of our economy and disadvantages the third wave, the growing information-based part. A few years ago Congress passed an infrastructure bill. It was somewhere between $100 billion and $120 billion for fixing potholes, bridges, and highways. In that bill there's about $1 billion for electronic smarts. Now that reflects the balance of political power between the old sector and the new sector.

When we talk, therefore, about politics of the emergent third-wave economy, it's not just a question of how do you use the Internet to vote or how do you create the continuous flow process between the citizens and their government, but also how do you organize politically and who organizes.

Congress has been slow to use any of this technology, but by the same token, the information sector of the economy has been very slow to become politicized. But in recent years you do see Silicon Valley organizing.

Toward Universal Online Access

■ **David Bohnett** The challenge that kids growing up today have is how to operate in a world with huge discrepancies between people who are connected and people who aren't. We have such intractable problems as poverty and homelessness. Those problems will continue to be there, but now you have added on top of it people who are online and people who aren't. It's the role of government to address that issue. The government provided and mandated universal telephone access; I believe it needs to do the same with the Internet.

■ **Dr. Koop** My greatest concern about the Internet is that in this country the distance between the haves and the have-nots seems to get greater all the time instead of less. How are we going to bridge that gap? Now the schools will do it to some extent, but I'm sure you know that the poorer schools, the schools in cities like Washington and Philadelphia, are the slowest to do it. And even in a place like Philadelphia, the wealthier suburbs will have a much better computer system than the ones in the center city. I'm worried about these kids.

I've been involved with a couple of programs to try to put a computer into the hallway of a low-cost housing place. It doesn't work. They get vandalized immediately. I think the libraries are a better place to do it.

■ **Dr. Lundberg** The rich get richer, and the poor get poorer, and, unfortunately, in the United States, we're on a major slope in both directions. The Internet is simply an example; it's not a reason for anything, but the people who have education, who have money, will use the Internet all the time. The people who don't have education and don't have money won't have a computer and won't learn how to use a computer. And the public libraries stand a risk of being phased out because of the Internet taking over. So in inner-city areas, people may have even less access to good information, which is a huge threat.

As a responsible society, if we are, we should do our best to keep public libraries of high quality open and to have auto-mated access to information on the Internet in them, espe-cially in the inner city areas where people are less likely to have their own computers.

■ **Steven Swartz** We should all hope that as public policy those who have made so much money on the Internet will help put some of it back. I think that giving money to pro-vide access to computers, just like Andrew Carnegie did with the public libraries, will be a major source of philanthropy. More and more people will have access to the Internet through venues other than simply purchasing a computer for themselves.

The Internet is also driving down the cost of a computer, and competition will drive down the cost of going on the In-ternet. Everything is going in a positive direction, but it's cer-tainly something that policy makers and philanthropists have to look at in terms of helping other people get access.

You Ain't Seen Nothing Yet

■ **Mark Cuban** As bandwidth becomes more plentiful, the best is yet to come. That's my final message, that anybody who thinks he or she is an expert in this business is lying. That's your first rule: They don't have a clue. The second thing is the winners won't come from anybody we know to-day. They won't be coming from me, they won't be coming from Amazon, they won't be coming from Yahoo! They're go-ing to come from the kids out there who don't have precon-ceived notions, who don't come in asking questions based on what we already know. They come in with a wide-open heart, mind, and soul to come up with things we couldn't even imagine.

The ability to create like that has formed a whole new campus. The way we do business will change, the way we live our lives will change, all for the better. You can always find a downside to it, kids getting access to things they shouldn't have access to or the dangers of privacy, but those are just fogeys, people who don't want to change, trying to pick issues that should hold us all back. It's ludicrous.

Finally, There Is No "Internet"

■ **Alvin Toffler** I believe the Internet will be far more pervasive than television because there's practically no aspect of your daily life that it doesn't involve itself in. The Internet will do good things and terrible things; television has done some fantastic things, but a lot of it is simply a huge stupidifier, an addictive stupidifier at that.

> "The Internet will be far more pervasive than television because there's practically no aspect of your daily life that it doesn't involve itself in."

I think the Internet will liberate us in many ways. It will allow us to be ourselves. It will make us wealthier in material terms over time. It'll do wonderful things with respect to our health and provide enormous opportunities for education. Whether we're smart enough to take those opportunities is another matter. Of course, it will also continue to provide the blueprints for how to shoot up a school or how to create a chemical weapon.

To me it's all-inclusive, so many different things are done through it that there isn't a single answer to the question: Will we look back fifty years from now and view the Internet positively or negatively? It depends on your criteria of what's good and bad, your values, how you evaluate it, and you'll find something to illustrate every view.

The Internet is everywhere. It's not like television; it sits in your room, you know where it is, where it comes from, how it works, how to turn it off. You're not going to turn off the Internet and it won't be called the Internet. You won't turn off the "electronic environment" unless you lose your energy system. Your electronic environment will be on 24 hours, 365 days a year.

Most Popular Web Properties (All Categories)

(Source: Nielsen//NetRatings)

About.com	Lycos Network
AltaVista	Macromedia
Amazon	Microsoft
AOL Websites	MSN
Ask Jeeves	NBC Internet
CNET	Real Networks
eBay	SmartBot.NET Inc.
Excite@Home	Time Warner
Fortune City	Viacom International
Go Network	Weather Channel
Go2Net Network	Yahoo!
InfoSpace	ZDNet
LookSmart	

BIOGRAPHIES

POWER PANEL

■ **KEN AULETTA**
Author and communications columnist for *The New Yorker*

Auletta has written the "Annals of Communications" column for *The New Yorker* since October 1992, as well as over fifty articles for the magazine. His profiles have included Barry Diller, Rupert Murdoch, John Malone, Edgar Bronfman Jr., Ted Turner, Gerald Levin, Michael Eisner, Jeffrey Katzenberg, Michael Ovitz, and Microsoft. Prior to his staff position at *The New Yorker*, Auletta was a weekly political columnist for the *New York Daily News*. He has also served as a staff writer and columnist for *The Village Voice*. Auletta is the author of seven books, including two best-sellers: *Greed and Glory on Wall Street: The Fall of the House of Lehman* and *Three Blind Mice: How the TV Networks Lost Their Way*. He has hosted numerous public television programs and served as a weekly political commentator for WNBC-TV and WCBS-TV in New York. Auletta has held several political positions: special assistant to the U.S. Undersecretary of Commerce, aide in Senator Robert F. Kennedy's 1968 Presidential campaign, and state campaign manager for Howard F. Samuels; he was the first executive director of the New York Off-Track Betting Corporation. He received a B.S. in education from the State University College of Oswego and an M.A. in political science from Syracuse University. In 1990, the State University of New York awarded him a Doctor of Letters.

■ **GEORGE BELL**
Chief executive officer, Excite@Home
excite.com

Bell was instrumental in guiding the merger of Excite, Inc., and @Home Network in January 1999. The combined company offers consumers content, interactive services, and high-speed access to the Internet. Bell joined Excite as its first CEO in January 1996 and helped close two rounds of financing before taking the company public in April of that year. Under Bell's direction, Excite has made numerous strategic investments and signed long-term distribution agreements with Netscape, America Online, and Intuit. Previously, Bell was senior vice president of Times Mirror Magazines, where he was instrumental in the launch of the Outdoor Life Network, a special-interest cable channel. Prior to that, he was a producer and writer of conservation and adventure documentaries, winning four Emmy Awards. Bell has produced films in over forty countries and written multipart series for magazines and periodicals. Bell chaired former governor Pete Wilson's California Privacy Committee to establish privacy standards on the Internet. He received his B.A. from Harvard University.

■ **DAVID BOHNETT**
Founder of GeoCities
geocities.com

In addition to founding GeoCities in 1994, Bohnett served as chief executive officer and chairman. The company grew to become the largest community on the Internet. GeoCities became publicly traded on NASDAQ in August 1998, and was subsequently acquired by Yahoo! Inc. in May 1999. Bohnett has been recognized as one of *Time Digital*'s Top 50 Cyber Elite, one of *Upside* magazine's Elite 100, and one of *Newsweek*'s "100 People to Watch in the Next Millennium." He was the recipient of the Entrepreneur of the Year award for Southern California in 1999. His current activities include serving as executive director of the David Bohnett Foundation. He also manages a portfolio of investments through his investment company, Baroda Ventures, and sits on the boards of NCR Corporation, Stamps.com, NetZero, and several other privately held Internet ventures. Before founding GeoCities, Bohnett spent six years in the software industry for Legent and Goal Systems. Bohnett began his career as a staff consultant with Arthur Anderson. He holds a B.S. in business administration from the University of Southern California and an M.B.A. in finance from the University of Michigan.

■ **MARK CUBAN**
Co-founder of broadcast.com, vice president of
Yahoo! Broadcast Services
broadcast.com

Cuban co-founded broadcast.com in 1995 with a mission to turn the Internet into a multimedia-rich broadcast medium. In July 1999 the company was acquired by Yahoo! Cuban continues to lead the division as Yahoo! Broadcast Services. Cuban also founded MicroSolutions in 1983 and helped it to become one of the leading systems integration firms in the United States. In 1990 he sold the company to CompuServe and later became president of Radical Computing, a venture capital and investment company specializing in high-tech companies. Prior to the acquisition, Cuban served on the broadcast.com board of directors. He is currently on the board of GreenMountain.com. Cuban has a B.A. in business from Indiana University.

■ **ESTHER DYSON**
Chairman of EDventure Holdings; editor of EDventure's newsletter *Release 1.0*
edventure.com

EDventure Holdings is a small but diversified company focused on emerging information technology worldwide. Dyson is the author of *Release 2.1: A Design for Living in the Digital Age*. She is also interim chairman of ICANN (the Internet Corporation for Assigned Names and Numbers); a member of the President's Export Council Subcommittee on Encryption; and sits on numerous boards, including those of the Electronic Frontier Foundation, Scala Business Solutions, Poland Online, Trustworks (Amsterdam), IBS (Moscow), New World Publishing, WPP Group, Uproar.com, and Medscape. She is also on the advisory boards of Perot Systems and the Internet Capital Group, and a limited partner of the Mayfield Software Fund. Previously, she was a securities analyst at New Court Securities and Oppenheimer & Co. Prior to that she was a reporter for *Forbes* magazine. Dyson holds a B.A. in economics from Harvard University.

■ **PETER FRIEDMAN**
President and chief executive officer, Talk City Inc.
talkcity.com

Talk City was founded by Peter Friedman in 1996 (then vice president and the general manager at Apple Computer's Internet Services Division, including the AppleLink and eWorld online services). Friedman spent twelve years at Apple, where he held various senior executive positions. Before joining Apple, Friedman was a product-line manager at Atari Inc. He's also been a professional magician. Friedman holds a B.A. in American history from Brown University and a M.B.A. from the Harvard Business School.

■ **GEORGE GENDRON**
Editor in chief, *Inc.* magazine
inc.com

Gendron joined *Inc.* in January 1981 and became editor in chief in 1983. Gendron coauthored and narrated *Inc.*'s best-selling video, *How to Really Start Your Own Business,* which won the American Film Institute award for the most outstanding business and economic programming in the country. In addition, he has been instrumental in establishing business units that complement the magazine, including *Inc.*'s book publishing division, video production group, and conference and seminar division. Gendron began his career in publishing as an arts and entertainment editor of *New York* magazine; he also wrote for its sister publication, *The Village Voice.* Subsequently, Gendron was editor in chief of *Boston* magazine, when the magazine won numerous awards and heavily influenced the design of other city magazines. He is also a regular commentator on entrepreneurship and small business on TV, radio, and in print. Recent appearances include *20/20, 48 Hours,* CNN, and National Public Radio, and he has been quoted extensively in *The Wall Street Journal* and other major publications. Gendron is active in several nonprofit organizations, serving on the boards of City Year and Who Cares. Gendron is a graduate of Manhattan College.

■ **RICHARD A. GRASSO**
Chairman and chief executive officer, New York
Stock Exchange

Grasso was named chairman and chief executive officer of the New York Stock Exchange in June 1995. In his thirty years with the Exchange, Grasso has held numerous managerial and executive positions including president, chief operating officer, and executive vice chairman. Grasso is the first member of the NYSE staff to be elected to any of these positions in the exchange's 207-year history. Grasso is on the board of directors of NYSE-listed Computer Associates International, Inc. He also serves on the boards of directors of the National Italian American Foundation (NIAF) and the Tinker Foundation and on the advisory board for the Yale School of Management. He is a member of the International Capital Markets Advisory Committee for the Federal Reserve Bank of New York. He has received Humanitarian of the Year awards from Tomorrows Children's Fund and Variety—The Children's Charity, the Special Achievement Award in Business from the National Italian American Foundation, the Ellis Island Medal of Honor from the National Ethnic Coalition of Organizations, the Good Scout Award from the Greater New York Councils–Boy Scouts of America, the Brotherhood Award and the Charles Evans Hughes Gold Medal from the National Conference, and the title of Cavaliere di Gran Croce from President Oscar Luigia Scalfaro of the Republic of Italy. He was honored as the 1994 Man of the Year by Catholic Big Brothers.

■ **TERRELL B. JONES**
President and chief executive officer, Travelocity
travelocity.com

In October 1999, Travelocity announced plans to merge with Preview Travel and Jones was named president and chief executive officer of the new company. Formerly, Jones was chief information officer and senior vice president of The SABRE Group Holdings, Inc., as well as president of SABRE Interactive. Previously he served as president of SABRE Computer Services for American Airlines. Jones joined American Airlines in 1978 as director of product development when the airline acquired Agency Data Systems. He later became president of the division and then vice president of product development for the SABRE Travel Information Network unit. He also held the title of vice president of SABRE applications and development and president of SABRE Decision Technologies. Jones started in the travel industry in 1971 as a travel agent with Vega Travel and later served as vice president of Travel Advisors. Jones serves on the AT&T and Lotus customer advisory boards and is also a member of The Research Board. He is a graduate of Denison University.

■ **C. EVERETT KOOP, M.D.**
Co-founder and chairman of the board, drkoop.com, Inc.
drkoop.com

The former U.S. Surgeon General (1981–1989) has more than sixty years experience in health care, government, and industry. Some of his previous positions are Deputy Assistant Secretary of Health, U.S. Public Health Service; editor in chief of the *Journal of Pediatric Surgery;* and surgeon in chief of Children's Hospital of Philadelphia. He is presently the Elizabeth DeCamp McInerny Professor at Dartmouth and Senior Scholar of the C. Everett Koop Institute at Dartmouth. He graduated from Dartmouth College and received his M.D. from Cornell Medical College. He received a Doctor of Science (Medicine) degree from the University of Pennsylvania.

 GEORGE D. LUNDBERG, M.D.
Editor in chief, Medscape
medscape.com

Lundberg was named editor in chief of Medscape in February 1999. Prior to that he served as editor of the *Journal of the American Medical Association* for seventeen years and editor in chief of Scientific Information of the American Medical Association with editorial responsibility for its thirty-nine medical journals, its weekly newspaper, and its Internet site. Lundberg is also an adjunct professor of health policy at Harvard University and a professor of clinical pathology at Northwestern University's medical school. Lundberg holds an M.S. from Baylor University and a B.S. and M.D. from the University of Alabama. In addition he holds honorary degrees from four U.S. universities.

PAUL MATTEUCCI
President and chief executive officer, HearMe
mplayer.com and hearme.com

Prior to joining HearMe, Matteucci was vice president and general manager of Adaptec, Inc. During his eight years at the firm, he served in various marketing positions, until being promoted to general manager in 1990. In addition, Matteucci has held positions at Texas Instruments and Tandem. He received an M.B.A. from Stanford University, an M.A. from Johns Hopkins School of Advanced International Studies, and a B.A. from the University of the Pacific.

HALSEY MINOR
Founder, chairman, and chief executive officer, CNET, Inc.
cnet.com

In 1992 Minor founded CNET to provide information and services relating to computers and technology via the Web and TV. Today CNET produces six weekly television series about computers and technology. In 1997 Minor introduced snap.com, a Web supersite providing a variety of technology services. In 1998 Minor sold 60 percent of Snap to NBC. Recently Snap and Xoom merged with a number of Internet properties to form a new company called NBC Interactive. Minor is a member of The Technology Network, a public policy and political service organization; he also serves on the boards of the International Council of the National Academy of Television Arts and Sciences, the National Association of Television Program Executives, and the Net Advisory Board. Minor began his career as an investment banker for Merrill Lynch Capital Markets. He received a B.A. from the University of Virginia.

■ KATHY MISUNAS
President, chairman, and chief executive officer,
brandwise, LLC
brandwise.com

Misunas manages the strategic development of the company as well as runs its day-to-day operations. Previously, Misunas was chief executive officer of Reed Travel Group, formerly part of the Reed Elsevier Plc group. She also served on the Executive Committee of the World Travel & Tourism Council (WTTC), a global coalition of more than 100 CEOs from all segments of the travel and tourism industry. Misunas started her career as a reservations sales agent for American Airlines in Washington, D.C., and within twenty-four months moved into the American Airlines marketing organization, which supported the sale and implementation of the company's SABRE computer system. In 1988 Misunas was named an officer of the company and president of the SABRE Travel Information Network. She also spearheaded the development of Eaasy SABRE, the travel industry's first online consumer reservations product, and SABRE Interactive, which launched Travelocity. She was appointed president and CEO of The SABRE Group and senior vice president of AMR/American Airlines in 1993. In 1992 she was awarded the coveted YWCA "Woman of the Year" title. Misunas attended Moravian College, majoring in French and political science, and studied French at the Alliance Française in Paris. Her academic background also includes advanced business curricula at American University and executive courses at the University of Virginia's Darden School and the University of Pennsylvania's Wharton School.

■ **ELLEN PACK**
Founder, senior vice president, and general manager,
Women.com
women.com

Pack's first forays online in the early 1990s convinced her that there was nothing online that was relevant to her daily life. In 1992 she founded Women.com, to introduce women to the online world in an environment suited to them. Pack is also the author of *The Women's Wire Web Directory*. Prior to founding Women.com, Pack was the chief operating officer of Torque Systems, Inc., a software company. Packs holds an M.B.A. from Columbia Business School and a B.A. in economics from Columbia College.

■ **ROBERT W. PITTMAN**
President and chief operating officer, America Online, Inc.
aol.com and the America Online network

Pittman joined AOL in 1996 and now oversees the day-to-day operations of the company. He is responsible for the company's business support groups and its four product groups: Interactive Services, Interactive Properties, the Netscape Enterprise Group, and the AOL International Group. Pittman is perhaps best known as the programmer who created MTV. He also oversaw the creation of VH-1, Nick at Nite, and the relaunch of Nickelodeon. He has served as chief executive officer of multiple endeavors, including MTV Networks; Quantum Media, Inc., an entertainment company he founded with MCA, Inc.; Time Warner Enterprises; Six Flags Entertainment; and Century 21, the largest residential real estate organization in the world. Pittman started his career at age fifteen as a part-time radio disk jockey in Mississippi. His many honors include: *Cablevision* magazine's "20/20 Vision" award for the twenty people who have had the most impact on the cable industry; *Advertising Age's* "50 Pioneers and Visionaries of TV"; selection as one of *Business Week's* Top 25 Executives of 1998; and inclusion in *Time* magazine's 1984 Man-of-the-Year issue. He also received the President's Award and an honorary doctorate from Bank Street College of Education for his contributions to education. He serves on many boards, including AOL, Cendant Corporation, the New York University School of Medicine, The Robin Hood Foundation, Millsaps College, and the New York Shakespeare Festival.

■ LINDA G. ROBERTS
Director of the Office of Educational Technology
and special adviser to the Secretary of the U.S. Department
of Education

Dr. Roberts coordinates the Department's technology programs and plays a key role in developing the Clinton administration's Educational Technology Initiative. Roberts steered the development of the Technology Innovation Challenge Grants, the Technology Literacy Challenge Fund, the Regional Technology in Education Consortia, the new Technology Teacher Training Program, the new Community-Based Technology Centers Program, and the new Learning Anytime Anywhere Partnerships Program. As senior adviser on technology, Roberts represents the Secretary on interagency committees and is also a member of the White House educational technology working group. Roberts's work has been widely recognized. She was *Electronic Learning* magazine's Technology Educator of the Decade; the recipient of the U.S. Distance Learning Association's Eagle Award for outstanding contributions to public policy; the Federal 100 Award in Information Technology; and the *Computerworld/* Smithsonian Award for Leadership and Excellence in Educational Technology. Roberts also serves as a member of the George Lucas Education Foundation Board and served on the advisory board of the Children's Television Workshop. Roberts's career started in 1962 when she was an elementary teacher and reading specialist in Ithaca, New York, and Brookline, Massachusetts. She later taught elementary, secondary, and adult reading programs in Oak Ridge, Tennessee, and then joined the faculties of the University of Tennessee and Lincoln Memorial University. Prior to joining the Department of Education, Roberts was a project director and senior associate with the Congressional Office of Technology Assessment. She holds a B.S. from Cornell University, an Ed.M. from Harvard University, and an Ed.D. from the University of Tennessee.

■ CHARLES R. SCHWAB
Founder, chairman, and co–chief executive officer of The
Charles Schwab Corporation
schwab.com

Schwab started his firm in 1971 as a traditional brokerage company and in 1974 became a pioneer in the discount brokerage business; he soon became the nation's largest discount broker. Today, the firm serves over 6.2 million active investors through a network of over 310 branch offices. Schwab is currently a member of the board of three public companies: Gap Inc., Vodafone AirTouch Plc, and Siebel Systems, Inc. He's also a member of the board for Stanford University; founder and chairman of the Schwab Foundation for Learning; and chairman of All Minds of Minds Institute, a nonprofit institute dedicated to the understanding of differences in learning. His book, *Charles Schwab's Guide to Financial Independence*, was published in 1998. He also authored *How to Be Your Own Stockbroker* in 1985. Schwab earned a B.A. in economics from Stanford University and a M.B.A. from Stanford Graduate School of Business.

■ **MAN JIT SINGH**
President and chief executive officer of Futurestep
futurestep.com

Prior to joining Futurestep, Singh was a principal at Sibson & Company, a consulting firm specializing in strategic development and executive compensation, where he was responsible for its strategic and marketing practice on the West Coast. Formerly, he was sector director for business services at BET Plc, a conglomerate providing a full range of outsourcing services to corporate customers. He also served as chairman, CEO, and president of Talent Tree Staffing Services, one of several companies under BET's corporate umbrella. Moreover, Singh served as CEO of the Cast Group, an international general management consulting firm specializing in strategic and organizational planning. He has a bachelor's and master's degree in economics from St. Stephen's College of Delhi University, and a post-graduate degree in management from the Indian Institute of Management. He also has an M.B.A. from UCLA's Anderson School of Management.

■ **STEVEN SWARTZ**
President, chief executive officer, and editor in chief of
SmartMoney
smartmoney.com

Swartz was named president and CEO of *SmartMoney* in May 1995, after having served as the magazine's editor from June 1991. Under his leadership, *SmartMoney* was one of the youngest magazines to be named Magazine of the Year by *Advertising Age.* In 1993 the publication received Temple University's Acres of Diamonds Award as the best new magazine. In addition, *SmartMoney* won 1995 and 1996 National Magazine Awards for service journalism. In late 1997, Swartz launched SmartMoney.com. The site received the 1998 and 1999 ICI/American University awards for online personal finance journalism. In April 1999, *SmartMoney* launched a custom publishing and retirement advisory services business and in July established SmartMoney University, an online tool to teach people about personal finance. Swartz started his career in journalism as a reporter in *The Wall Street Journal*'s Philadelphia bureau. He transferred to the New York bureau in 1986, where he covered the securities industry. He had the foresight to write an article the Friday before the stock market crash of 1987 declaring "the end of the '80s." Swartz became a *Journal* page-one editor in 1989. Swartz is a member of the Investment Committee of the Whitney Museum of American Art. He also serves on the board of the Dow Jones employee benefit committee, and is a member of the executive committee of Settlement Housing Fund. Swartz earned his B.A. degree from Harvard College, where he majored in government.

 JEFF TAYLOR
Founder and chief executive officer, Monster.com
monster.com

Monster.com was formed in January 1999 when the Monster Board and Online Career Center joined forces to capture the online career marketplace. Taylor, who founded the Monster Board in 1994, also is CEO of TMP Interactive, a unit of TMP Worldwide, the online recruitment leader and one of the world's largest recruitment advertising agency networks. TMP Worldwide is also the world's largest Yellow Page advertising agency and a provider of direct marketing services. Taylor is responsible for the growth and direction of all TMP Worldwide properties and developments relating to the Internet. Taylor joined TMP Worldwide in 1995, upon the acquisition of his specialized recruitment advertising agency, Adion, Inc. He serves as a member of the board for the Massachusetts Junior Achievement and Computer.com. Taylor attended the University of Massachusetts and received his executive M.B.A./O.P.M. from the Harvard Business School.

DAVID THORNBURG, PH.D.
Director of the Thornburg Center
tcpd.org

As director of the Thornburg Center, Thornburg specializes in the impact of emerging technologies on the workplace and education. He is active in exploring ways that telecommuncations and multimedia will change education at home and in the classroom. Thornburg is a consultant to senior executives of Fortune 500 corporations, schools, community organizations, Congress, and the offices of the vice president and president of the United States. He is a senior fellow of the Congressional Institute for the Future. In addition, he serves on several nonprofit boards; has written numerous books (most recently, *Brainstorms and Lightening Bolts: Thinking Skills for the 21st Century*); and created several CD-ROMs. He was inducted as a pioneer in the field of educational technology by the International Society for Technology in Education. Previously he worked at Xerox Palo Alto Research Center where he helped develop user interfaces for personal computers. He received his B.S. in engineering from Northwestern University and an M.S. and Ph.D from the University of Illinois in Champaign/Urbana.

■ **ALVIN TOFFLER**
Futurist, consultant, and author of numerous books, including *Future Shock, The Third Wave, Powershift, War and Anti-War,* and, most recently, *Creating a New Civilization*

In the early 1960s, Toffler and his wife, Heidi, foretold the explosive rise of the computer. They wrote and lectured about PCs, electronic "agents," virtual reality, and today's electronic networks decades before they appeared in the marketplace. They described the VCR years before it had a name and forecast the coming of cable television when it was still widely assumed that advertisers would never back cable. As a consultant, Alvin Toffler prepared a confidential report for AT&T management forecasting the breakup of that company twelve years before it happened. The Tofflers wrote about the acceleration of change, the shift to work-at-home, and temporary help services in 1970. They also forecast the crack-up of the Soviet Union, the reunification of Germany, and the massive growth of the Asia Pacific economy more than ten years before these events made headlines. Alvin Toffler has served as a Visiting Scholar at the Russell Sage Foundation, a visiting Professor at Cornell University, a faculty member of the New School for Social Research, a White House correspondent, an editor of *Fortune* magazine, and a business consultant. He holds honorary doctorates in letters, law, and science from Keio University in Tokyo, and in management science. In France he has won the prestigious Prix du Meilleur Livre Etranger, and has been named an Officier de L'Ordre des Arts et Lettres. He is a member of the International Institute for Strategic Studies, and has been elected a Fellow of the American Association for the Advancement of Science.

  ROSS WRIGHT

Entrepreneur, independent sales representative,
and musician
ross.adnetsol.com

Wright has been a musician (playing drums and percussion instruments) and an artist since he was ten. He studied film and music at Los Angeles City College and San Francisco City College. Most of his career he's been an independent sales representative for a variety of music companies, often selling guitars, drums, and percussion instruments. He's also held various sales and management positions for several music industry retailers, such as Spitzer Music Corporation; Eddie's Music; Guitar Center, Inc.; and Sound Genesis. Wright has also worked as a field sales rep for Copeland Industries, a printed circuit board fabricator, and for Intermag, Inc., and ID Disk, software duplication companies. Some of these sales relationships continue to the present. In 1995 Wright started selling software duplication services online and then early in 1998 started selling musical instruments on eBay and other online auction venues. He later added books and videotapes to his line of products. He also runs and moderates "The Sellers' Ring Mailing List," a mailing list for other online sellers. Wright has two companies, RW Marketing (music industry sales rep) and King Media (software duplication services). He maintains his own Web site (ross.adnetsol.com), which links to his online auctions and software duplication service.

INDEX

ABOUT THE AUTHORS

Alfred C. Sikes served as chairman of the Federal Communications Commission, where he helped set the stage for the birth of new satellite, mobile, and digital television services. He is currently president of Hearst Interactive Media.

Ellen Pearlman, a veteran new-media journalist and former editior in chief of *HomePC, HealthWeek, Managed Healthcare News,* and *VARBusiness* magazines, is editorial director of tasteforliving.com, a nutrition and health site.